THE BUMBLING COLOSSUS

The Regulatory State vs. the Citizen; How Good Intentions Fail and the Example of Health Care: A New Progressive's Guide

HENRY FIELD

Copyright © 2012 Henry F. Field
All rights reserved.

ISBN: 1466445548
ISBN-13: 9781466445543

Cover Illustration by Nelson Diaz, nelsart.com

Warmest thanks to my wife, Beryl F. Bergen, for her patience and good cheer in putting up with the research and composition of this book, and for her incisive thoughts along the way.

Thanks also to Sally C. Pipes, Christopher T. Muscarella, Carrie Lee Henderson, MSW, James M. Howard, Dr. Spotswood L. Spruance, and Jessie Corum IV Esq. for their encouragement and in making helpful suggestions to earlier versions of the manuscript.

For my grandson, Benjamin J. Jewett, a future graduate of some great institution of higher learning, an independent spirit, and a lover of life.

Table of Contents

Preface. 1

Introduction 7

A. The Health Care Problem and Its Solution

Chapter I: The Bumbling Colossus in Health Care. . 41
   1. The Importance of Getting it Right: The Trade-off of Health Care Costs and Jobs. 41
   2. Europe Envy: Is Europe the Right Model for America? . . 44
   3. The 2010 Act: Getting it Wrong—The Mess We Have Created for Ourselves 50

Chapter II: The Bumbling Colossus Begins 69
   1. The Start of the Health Care Regulatory Fallacy in WWII Tax Policy. 69
   2. The False Conflict Between Morality and Economics. . .75
   3. Applying the Microscope: Why Are We Unable to Control Costs? 79
   4. The Power of Competition to Constrain Costs Without Impairing Service 83

Chapter III: The Single-Payer Mirage: How Government-Controlled Health Care Hurts the Very Public it is Intended to Protect 89
1. The Naked Truth: Unless Changed, the 2010 Act Leads to Government-Controlled Medicine 89
2. Analyzing the Case for Single-Payer Health Financing ... 91
3. An Overview of the International Experience: Characteristic Single-Payer Shortfalls. 98
4. The English NHS—"Beacon of Progress"—Casts a Fading Light. 104
5. The Canadian Single-Payer System's Slow Morph Towards Free Markets 107
6. The Masking of Single-Payer Deficiencies 115

Chapter IV: Getting it Right: Principles to Follow in a Successful Health Care System .. 119
1. So What Is the Proper Role of Government in Health Care Finance? 120

Chapter V: The Solution—Free Up Insurance Markets, Provide Health Savings Accounts for All and Vouchers for the Needy ... 125
1. Health Savings Accounts Put Skin in the Game 125
2. Vouchers Eliminate the Need for Mandates and Controls 131
3. Information on Prices and Costs Must Be Available 133
4. The Special Case of Preexisting Conditions 134
5. The Danger of Universal Coverage: Without Free Markets, It Becomes Another Huge Middle-Class Entitlement 136

6. The Three Cs and Q (Costs, Coverage, Controls, and Quality), and the Beauty of HSAs, Vouchers, and Free Insurance Markets 138
7. An HSA-Based System with Vouchers is Best Suited for America 139

B. The Regulatory Illusion: Why Government-Control and Single-Payer Failures are Predictable

Chapter VI: First, Understanding the Benefits Markets Bring 147
1. People Talking Past One Another: Liberals Versus Conservatives 148
2. Greed is Not the Root of All Evil: It is Profit-Making Given a Bad Name 157
3. Adam Smith's Paradox and the Role of Competition 161
4. Defining Terms: Free Markets Require Government Rules 163
5. It's Competition, Not Competitors, that Merits Our Protection 166
6. Are Free Markets Based on Selfishness at the Expense of Others? 168
7. What is the Importance of Price in Free Markets? .. 178
8. So Where do We Start in Thinking About Health Care? 181

Chapter VII: Experiences with Regulation: How it Ends Up Protecting Select Private Interests at the Expense of the Public 191
1. The Long, Unhappy History of Populist Regulation of Industries 191

ix

  2. The New Deal as a Model 192
  3. Recent Adventures with the Regulatory Illusion:
     The Financial Crisis........................... 201
  4. Regulatory Capture and the Continuance of Failed
     Programs..................................... 212
  5. The Illusion of Benefit from Failed Programs...... 216
  6. How Do You Tell What Regulation to Avoid
     and What to Keep? 218
  7. Restraints on Competition and Prices are Not
     Beneficial.................................... 220

C. Meeting Complaints, Criticisms, and Other Objections

Chapter VIII: Critics of Free Markets Rely on Failed or Unsupported Theories 227
  1. Health Care is Not a Market Failure 227
  2. Does the Existence of Externalities Justify
     Government Intervention?..................... 239
  3. Is the Free Market Model Based on Unrealistic
     Claims about Human Nature? 241
  4. Does Behavioral Economics Invalidate Free Market
     Economics?................................... 244
  5. What Accounts for the Persistence of Anti-Market
     Belief? 248

Chapter IX: The Time is Now to Set Us on the Right Course 259
  1. A Better Mousetrap; Let's Build a Patient-
     Centered System That Puts the Patient in
     the Driver's Seat Again 261
  2. Our Own Cost Factor: Will Health Care Vouchers
     Bust the Budget?............................. 262

3. Representative Ryan's "Roadmap" Alternative..... 264
4. Conclusion: The New Progressive Approach...... 265

Appendix A: Summary of Required Changes for Health Care on the Right Footing... 271

Appendix B: Are Banking and the Environment Special Cases Requiring Extensive Regulation?.. 277

Appendix C: Selected Major Provisions of the 2010 Health Act and Affordable Care Act (and companion Health Care and Education Reconciliation Act) of 2010........ 285

Preface

A Tale of Two Cities

I lived in Chicago until 2000. While there, and being self-employed, I obtained a health insurance policy with a $25,000 deductible, which suited my needs. It cost me $700 to $800 per year. Then I moved to Boston. In Massachusetts, regulations prohibited carriers from offering such coverage. The highest deductible I could get was $1,500. It cost me $4,200 per year, over five times more.

While in Massachusetts but still covered by my Illinois policy, I needed an MRI to check a lower back issue. Since this was on me, I shopped around. My own doctor's office had a machine and offered the service, but when I asked them the cost, they had no idea. After several interviews with the back office over several days, they finally gave me a price: $1,450. I went down the street to a stand-alone MRI outfit. They knew the cost right away: $750, with $75 more for the "read." Naturally, I employed them for the service.

This experience made me realize that somehow in our growing, ever-more-uniform world of private group coverage, something big is getting lost—that something is a market for health services. Because I had a high deductible, I had an incentive to ask for the price and look around for options. Because I was in a state with legal mandates ensuring no one else could have a high deductible policy, no one else bothered to look around: the only provider with a clue of their own price was someone whose only business was MRIs. For everyone else, price and costs were irrelevant; since the patient had no incentive to ask, no one knew. The only relevant question was, "Who's your insurer?" so we can bill it.

Superficially satisfying, this is a formula for an explosion in private insurance costs, which has in fact occurred.

Several years later I went on Medicare. Medicare copied the all-inclusive formula that group employer-based coverage had morphed into. I have no deductible at all. Everything is covered, soup to nuts. I absolutely never shop or care about the cost of anything the doctor orders. Neither does the doctor. Whatever you need (or might need, or in an excess of caution possibly could need), you get. Everyone else in the waiting room is on the same cruise, and we're immensely happy with it. We get the service and someone else picks up the bill; it feels like the ultimate free lunch.

Again, this is a surefire formula for an explosion in public budgets. Graphs in the newspaper and on the Internet show the portion of the federal budget devoted to "entitlements" (Medicare, Medicaid, and Social Security), and it scares the dickens out of us. In 2011, for example, about 52 percent of the entire federal budget was spent for entitlements—the retirement and medical care of those of us in the waiting room.[1] Interest on the national debt is bigger

---

1   Of the entire 2011 $3.7 trillion federal budget, $1.918 trillion (about 52 percent) is "entitlements," principally Medicare, Medicaid,

than defense, and growing, especially after the debt explosion of 2008 through 2010.

With health costs expanding faster than general inflation, it takes no genius to see that this situation is unsustainable. We're beginning to look like Europe, with its seemingly intractable euro-zone sovereign debt crises threatening its standards of living and the world economy.

The dream world (created by Medicare/Medicaid and federal and state law mandates), where we get whatever we want without regard to cost, is driving our country off the cliff. Either we cut benefits drastically or change the system. One thing is clear: there is no room in our state and federal budgets, and in the private (regulated) insurance world, for meaningful reductions without taking on the multiple state and federal insurance mandates and the open checkbook policies of Medicare and Medicaid. Entitlements and mandates are the elephant in the room.[2]

The 2010 health reform act gives lip service to this reality without seriously addressing it. Its biggest such feint is

---

and Social Security. Only 20 percent of the budget goes to "discretionary" items like defense, foreign diplomacy (State), energy, veterans' health, and others. See "Obama's Budget Proposal: How 3.7 Trillion is Spent," *N.Y. Times*, 2/14/2011, based on OMB figures.

2   The European sovereign debt crisis, beginning in 2010, with successive efforts by the northern euro countries to "bail out" the PIIGS—Greece, Portugal, Italy, Spain, Ireland and others, puts up a mirror to our local, state, and federal future if our own fiscal profligacy continues. Gerald P. O'Driscoll, former governor of the Federal Reserve Bank of Dallas, sums up the basic problem: "The [EU's] underlying dilemma is that governments have promised their citizens more social programs than can be financed with the tax revenue generated by the private sector. High tax rates choke off the economic growth needed to finance the promises... If you want to know how the debt crisis will play out here, watch the downward spiral in the EU." Gerald P. O'Driscoll, Jr, "Why We Can't Escape the Eurocrisis," Opinion, 11/2/2011, *Wall St. Journal (WSJ)*.

a proposed $575 billion in cuts to Medicare. But this is pure political posturing, since such gigantic cuts are counterproductive: how are my doctor and hospital going to afford me and my fellow waiting-roomers at a fraction of our cost? The result is all too predictable—pretty soon they would stop taking us or go out of business, and we would be out on the sidewalk. This is why Congress routinely votes down such reductions. So cuts alone won't do the trick.

If cuts are out, what's left? Is there a way to maintain our expected levels of service and quality but without breaking the bank? Can the system be changed so both taxpayers and premium-payers can afford the health care they want? Is there a way out of the invidious trade-off between higher costs and lower services? What can we learn from experience with regulatory regimes in this and other areas that can point us down a more productive path?

These are the questions we address here. What follows in Part A is in effect an extended footnote and response to the issues raised by the tale of two cities. It is clear something has evolved to unpin our system from the incentives needed to contain costs. Our present way of financing health care both in the private economy and the public entitlements (Medicare and Medicaid) looks like a giant free lunch—we get the service and somebody else pays the tab.

But this is a profound illusion; ultimately, it is us reaching into our pockets for the money to pay for lunch through taxes and premiums. It is not free at all; in fact, as taxpayer and private employee alike increasingly realize, it is getting more costly every minute.

PREFACE

What put us there? Misplaced incentives, created by the Regulatory Illusion and promoted by the Free Lunch Fallacy. Experience with a multiplicity of similar regulatory regimes, discussed in Part B, reveals that too often the noble purposes of supporters are perverted and the reality of entrenched, protected interests dominates at the expense of taxpayers, patients, consumers, insureds, and the public. Part C addresses popular and academic critiques thought to justify extensive government controls but which lack substance in theory and experience.

The impulse to regulate for the public good ushers in expanded bureaucracies, overt and hidden costs which grow and grow and relative economic slowdown. In this way the Bumbling Colossus rules our lives and harms us in ways most people are unaware of.

Progressives and liberals seeking a way to accommodate their ideals and impulses with unpleasant realities of cost, stagnation, and decline will find this essay of great help. Their goals—health care to all that does not threaten to destroy our growth economy and the many benefits it brings in work for the unemployed, income gains for the poor and less educated—are reachable if good economics are followed in the means and political biases are put to one side. Conservatives seeking to understand the deeper roots of their cool embrace of Big Government and the Regulatory State will find many points of interest and correction. For both groups, what renowned economist Thomas Sowell calls "the vision of the anointed" (see Ch VIII, *post*)—those who assume they hold a monopoly of good intentions, a view which allows its holders to ram poorly formulated elite views down the throats of the public—must be suspended.³

What follows is a roadmap or guide for progressives of all stripes to navigate through these waters.⁴

---

3   This attitude underlies the unhelpful expansion of government and the Bumbling Colossus. Sowell describes how elites promote crusades (welfare state, socialism, failed Keynesian prescriptions, single-payer health care, etc) wrapped in an aura of high purpose but lacking basic economics and solid evidence. There is a "moral exaltation of the anointed above others, who are to have their very different views nullified and superseded by the views of the anointed, imposed via the powers of government." Thomas Sowell, *The Vision of the Anointed: Self-Congratulation as a Basis for Social Policy*, at 5 (Basic Books 1995).

4   "Progressive" as used here and in the subtitle refers to policies centering analysis on the interests of ordinary people, and the broadest-based proxy for this group of stakeholders is taxpayers and consumers. We explicitly adopt this referent as our starting point-of-view here. This avoids the dependencies on government of narrow special interests—both of the right and the left— and results in a new progressive approach with recommendations and analysis that differ from traditional liberal, progressive, and conservative orthodoxy while often pursuing similar goals and outcomes—benefit to the needy and to the whole of the economy based on solid economic principles and analysis.

Introduction

This book is divided into essentially two parts. The first part, Part A, explores our health care system's problems and dilemmas, its history, commonly advocated alternatives, and how to improve and shift to a better system that solves our cost problems while maintaining quality and patient satisfaction. The second part, Parts B and C, explores major pro-government, anti-market assumptions underlying many popular alternatives, and sketches both the history of regulated industries and the foundational work in political economy that bears on that experience and guides proper analysis from here on out. The tension between government regulation and markets, and the proper role and limits of each, is central to the discussion.

*

The Economics of Health Care and the Importance of Incentives

Steven Landsburg, in *The Armchair Economist*, his wonderful 1993 romp over diverse implications of the economic approach, and Steven Levitt and Stephen Dubner, in their similarly engaging *Freakonomics* (2005) and *Superfreakonomics* (2009), boil down much of modern economics to the phrase, "people respond to incentives [and disincentives], although not necessarily in ways that are predictable or manifest."[5] "Therefore," they add, "one of the most powerful laws of the universe is the law of unintended consequences." These two young economists at the top of their game (Landsburg and Levitt) elaborate on a few of the myriad ways in which well-meaning government policies result in consequences that are harmful, bizarre, counterproductive, and unanticipated to those who proposed and enacted them, if less so to economists who study them.

Although our health care system is not one of the topics included, it surely could have been. We have forgotten the basics in our ever-increasing search for ways to expand the universe of care to all comers. The push for universal coverage—so that all persons have the health care they need—has unmoored the incentives at the core of the system from what enables costs to push downward instead of upward, and what enables quality of service to ascend higher rather than be pressed ever lower by the need to constrain costs.

What accounts for the change? Although many causes have been offered without much headway in solving anything, what we focus on here is something that can be understood and remedied. Careful examination shows that time and again what spins things awry are well-intentioned government policies that have unintended consequences. Often this comes in the form of the Regulatory Illusion. Most Americans, especially after the fall of the Berlin Wall with its revelations of the obvious decrepitude socialism brings, realize that the security socialism promises disap-

---

5   Steven D. Levitt & Stephen J. Dubner, *SuperFreakonomics*, at xiv (William Morrow 2009); Steven E. Landsburg, *The Armchair Economist* (The Free Press 1993); Steven D. Levitt & Stephen J. Dubner, *Freakonomics* (William Morrow 2005).

points, indeed brings forth a nightmare. On the other hand, some feel threatened by what they see as a world of free-market uncertainty, especially of the pre-New Deal era, which in the popular mind left many people short and brought on calamitous cycles including the Great Depression. A Third Way, which appears to offer solace from this Manichean contrast of market risk versus socialist decay, is the economic regulation of business.

Neither socialist government ownership nor free market government hands-off, the regulatory approach seeks to have government pass laws that hedge and confine business judgment in the public interest, supervised by high-minded agents of the people in agencies with eponymous acronyms like FSLIC or FTC or Freddie Mac. The Third Way seeks to avoid the perceived Scylla and Charybdis with which socialism and capitalism appear to threaten us. It is premised on the belief that monopoly is the tendency of business and the consumer is a tool of producers and advertisers, manipulated and deceived at will, thereby justifying intervention by public agencies to redress a perceived imbalance of power. Regulating the industry appears to be an easy way to achieve apparent public benefits without the visible public cost of government ownership and the moral hazard of direct subsidy.

Apart from justifications based on misperceptions of the strength or endurance of monopolies and manipulative power over the consumer, the political seductiveness of economic regulation as a Third Way is that it appears as a free lunch. Some people receive obvious benefits, and the harms are largely invisible. But we have learned that this Third Way is itself an illusion, that the benefits often accrue to select private interests, not to the public, and the harms to the public are widespread, if hidden from easy view.

Unlike public budgets, the costs of regulation are hidden and often difficult to quantify. Nonetheless, as discussed later, these hidden costs are enormous and create powerful undertows on growth.[6]

Like interest that compounds over time into huge sums, government regulation that distorts markets compounds harms over time until finally some cataclysm brings the situation to public awareness. This has happened both with health care and in the 2008 financial crisis. Then, because the true cause of the cataclysm is unrecognized, the tendency of politicians is to *increase* rather than decrease regulation, thereby making things worse. The Bumbling Colossus. As we shall see, this is a tale oft told.

The Financial Crisis of 2008 and Health Care: Case Studies in the Free Lunch Fallacy

It may seem strange to start off an analysis of government regulation and health care systems by talking about

---

[6] Two types of hidden cost are 1) compliance cost and 2) lost productivity cost – the cost of decline in an industry that is over-regulated so investment stagnates and people are left to less efficient competitive alternatives. An example of the second form of cost, which has not been well quantified, is decline in the railroad industry prior to President Carter's highly successful deregulation in 1979. As for compliance costs, it has been reliably estimated that "in 2008, US federal government regulations cost an estimated $1.75 trillion, an amount equal to 14 percent of US national income. When combined with US federal tax receipts, which equaled 21 percent of national income in 2008, these two costs of federal government programs in 2008 consumed 35 percent of national income. This obviously represents a substantial burden on US citizens and businesses... Had every US household paid an equal share of the federal regulatory burden, each would have owed $15,586 in 2008." *Report* (funded by the federal government's Small Business Administration), "The Impact of Regulatory Costs on Small Firms," by Nicole V. and W. Mark Crain, at pp. iv, 6 (September, 2010, Lafayette College).

the financial crisis of 2008 and ensuing deep recession, but no better or more painful concrete example exists, to which everyone can relate and tell their own stories, of the same folly we are building up and designing in health care. For both the financial crisis and health care, the underlying cause of distress is found not in what is presented in popular media clips and headlines, but in the prosaic legerdemains of government policies, largely invisible to the public, whose long tendrils loose unanticipated consequences that, compounded over time, finally ooze out into public consciousness disguised in the dress of other causes and camouflaged by blinders imposed by political ideologies.

In both finance and health care, the Regulatory Illusion has proved irresistible to public and politician alike, who have sought false shelter by the political free lunch of regulation—intervening into markets trying to improve them by empowering discretion in a public agency to change the rules, especially the way participants assess risk, thereby creating perverse incentives and misdirecting resources to ultimately great harm.

The desire to help others through government regulation of markets causes people to forget what markets are about and what they do best. Markets serve those who want to and do participate. If it is important to bring others into the market who cannot afford it, allow them to do so by direct government support, designed so as not to skew market outcomes or incentives for other market participants or create moral hazard. If you want all persons to have refrigerators, you don't nationalize the manufacturers or require them to lower their prices, you subsidize those without.

Everyone thinks they know what caused the financial crisis, and largely they are wrong. What brought the financial world to its knees was not the popular media bête noirs—corporate greed, deregulation, unregulated actors, complex derivatives, CDOs, MBSs, Wall Street, etc—but a very simple, largely hidden, and well-motivated thing right at hand: government affordable housing (AH) policies, pursued over two decades by both the Democratic and Republican administrations of Bill Clinton and George W. Bush, primarily through HUD. To understand this, one needs do no more than read the Conclusions of the Majority and the Dissent by Peter J. Wallison to the Report of the Financial Crisis Inquiry Commission, appointed by President Obama and published January 2011.

Mr. Wallison summarizes what happened:

> This analysis lays the principal cause of the financial crisis squarely at the feet of the unprecedented number of NTMs [non-traditional mortgages] that were brought into the US financial markets by government housing policy. These weak and high-risk loans helped to build the bubble, and when the bubble deflated they defaulted in unprecedented numbers. This threatened losses in the PMBS [private mortgage-backed securities] that were held by financial institutions in the US and around the world, impairing both their liquidity and their apparent stability.
>
> [T]hese loans and the bubble to which they contributed were the direct consequence of... US government housing policy, which—led by HUD over two administrations—deliberately reduced mortgage underwriting standards so that more people could buy homes. While this process was going on, everyone was pleased... But the result was a financial catastrophe... [7]

---

7   Available online at www.fcic.gov/report. See also Charles W. Calomiris, Professor of Finance, Columbia Business School, "The Mortgage Crisis: Some Inside Views," Opinion, 10/27/2011, *WSJ* ("The decision

INTRODUCTION

In a complaint filed December 16, 2011, against the previous top officers of Fannie Mae and Freddie Mac – a complaint in which Fannie and Freddie admitted the facts – the SEC revealed that its investigation confirms Mr. Wallison's analysis. Not only did government AH policies provide crucial incentives and mandates driving the financial crisis, but systematic deception of the public by top Fannie and Freddie executives about the huge size of their portfolio of subprime, Alt-A, no doc, and similar low-quality mortgages misled the market, banks, regulators, and the investing world about the true extent of the impending catastrophe. All of this was cloaked with the best of intentions.[8]

So what was the most fundamental force that caused the crisis? Political meddling (through government interventions and regulation) in market judgments of risk. Starting in 1992, but really gaining traction in 1999-2000, coercive HUD affordable housing policies, designed to increase home ownership among the poor, forced banks and other mortgage originators to reduce their traditional underwriting standards, and in the process made opaque what was

by Fannie and Freddie to embrace no-doc lending in 2004 opened the floodgates of bad credit. In 2003, for example, total subprime and Alt-A mortgage originations were $395 billion. In 2004, they rose to $715 billion. By 2006, they were more than $1 trillion.")

8   SEC press release and linked complaint filed 12/16/2011, http://www.sec.gov/news/press/2011/2011-267.htm. Freddie Mac and Fannie Mae entered into non-prosecution agreements in which they concurred with the SEC's facts and accepted responsibility for the events. Both entities held over ten times more of the high-risk loans than they acknowledged, a large and growing percentage of their portfolios. "The misleading disclosures were made as Fannie Mae's executives were seeking to increase the Company's market share through increased purchases of subprime and Alt-A loans, and gave false comfort to investors about the extent of Fannie Mae's exposure to high-risk loans," according to the SEC. Huge bonuses were tied to increasing the GSE's high risk portfolio.

really going on and its extent. This included both AH goals for GSEs (Fannie and Freddie) as well as AH scoring for all banks and mortgage lenders under the Community Reinvestment Act and HUD's "Best Practices Initiative."

Fannie Mae led private home lenders into the subprime market by open-ended contracts for low- or no-documentation loans, including a July 1999 agreement with Countrywide Home Loans by which Countrywide agreed to search out no-documentation loans for resale to Fannie Mae. Soon others followed.[9]

In other words, government intruded into the market to improve outcomes, fundamentally altering risks, and sought to do so via a free lunch—costing the taxpayer nothing (in theory) by having private market participants dig deeper into poor credits and create incentives for them to spread those increased risks out among the investing public, including banks themselves. This is a classic example of intrusive government regulation. It was a beautiful scheme in which homeownership climbed from 64 percent to 69 percent, no down payment-no documentation mortgages flourished, and everyone was happy. Until it all crashed and everyone—even those who never heard of CDOs, CMOs, or MBSs, or ever sought a mortgage—was in pain.

Why didn't the politicians avoid the regulatory approach and just expand direct subsidies through FHA? No free lunch that way; the costs would have to show on the federal budget as costs to the taxpayer. The beauty of the HUD scheme was that it was all off-budget. The illusion was, you could have your affordable housing cake and eat it, too. The plusses of direct subsidy through an FHA-type agency

---

9   SEC press release and linked complaint filed 12/16/2011, http://www.sec.gov/news/press/2011/2011-267.htm. Fannie Mae gave one of its "expanded approval" programs the telling name "Say Yes."

are negatives to politicians—subsidies are public, accountability can be reckoned, and benefits and costs can be figured.

On the other hand, with HUD-type intrusive regulation—including pressure on the GSEs to fund increasingly high-risk credits— mortgage industry underwriting standards were quietly degraded, subsidies were masked, benefits and costs were unmeasurable, and no accountability existed. No one even knew the number or size of poor loans out there or who held them. The regulatory free lunch illusion blinded everyone—even the most intimate market participants—to the nature and dimensions of the problem. The Bumbling Colossus grew, like a tsunami, until it finally broke upon the shore.

This kind of market-altering regulation comes as a wolf dressed in sheep's clothing. It appears utterly benign, promising, as President Clinton did, that it would "not cost the taxpayer one red cent," because government is simply regulating private actors (in this case mortgage originators and packagers), forcing them to do all the heavy lifting. Making them lower traditional underwriting standards so that the poor can live in houses they own seems a small thing. These big banks and other outfits can afford it, we tell ourselves, and besides, they peddle the risks off to other investors around the world, who are big boys, through many varieties of collateralized mortgage obligations (CMOs).

But when the crash happened, suddenly all this didn't look quite so free at all. The ruin all around was phenomenal and devastating, not just to taxpayers, but to everyone. All the housing ownership gains, which were the point of the laws and regulations, were lost almost overnight. Banks and mortgage houses had to be bailed out or fail. The mortgage market dried up. People could not get loans, not just for houses but throughout the broader economy. Jobs shrank. The markets dived to half. So much for the "not one red cent" promise and the free lunch.

And the legislative response? Rush through the Dodd-Frank Act, heaping taxes and harmful fee restrictions on banks needing to regain their health and increasing their already pervasive regulation (and doing nothing about the AH policies that brought on the crisis), before even looking at the Report of the Financial Crisis Inquiry Commission set up to understand its cause. Blind to the true causes of distress, politicians needing to report home that they have done something—anything—grow the Bumbling Colossus and its debilitating regulatory apparatus to ever greater size.[10]

If You Liked the Financial Crash, You'll Love Where We're Going With Health Care

What does this have to do with health care? For health care systems, the exact same lesson exists. If you want to

---

10 The FCIC Report had three groups of "explainers," a five-person Democrat majority, a three-person Republican separate statement, and the Wallison dissent. The eight members other than Wallison found fault with virtually everyone involved in the financial provision of mortgages. But asserting that *everyone* involved at all levels— homebuyers, mortgage originators, brokers, insurers, banks, investment bankers, etc—was corrupt, stupid, blind, asleep at the switch, in breach of their duties, and so forth confuses participation in the crisis with *cause*. All of these factors are omnipresent and, if true, are always true and therefore not explanatory of causing a crisis on a date in September 2008. The Wallison dissent cogently points out that none of the multiplicity of factors and actors except one *explains* the novel incentives driving the crisis. It is the only statement providing a persuasive picture, indeed one consistent with the known world of finance. See the trenchant analysis by Professor Raghuram G. Rajan, *Fault Lines: How Hidden Fractures Still Threaten the World Economy*, Ch 1, "Let them Eat Credit" (2010, Princeton University Press).

help people who otherwise can't afford the health care they need or want, the sure road to destruction is to pursue the Regulatory Illusion—by distorting markets through regulating health providers and other market players to force them to service or support people, and take and spread risks they wouldn't otherwise. This skews market outcomes and incentives in the same way the HUD regulations put the financial world on the tracks to disaster. People lose their sense of appropriate costs and benefits, and costs escalate. Unfortunately, this is exactly what we've been doing for some time in health care, and we've gotten so used to it, we think it's the only way to do things. But it's not—it wasn't even the way we did things for hundreds of years until recently. Yet obvious, superior alternatives remain unexplored.

It has not taken long after the enactment of the 2010 health reform act for the harmful unintended consequences to become obvious.[11] The process began, however, some years before, and once again, we look to government distortions of the market—health-related policies with large unintended consequences. The initial error was in a WW II tax ruling that allowed companies to pay their employees' health insurance without that being considered income to the employee but remaining deductible to the company. This small change created an unanticipated incentive; employees and unions began to press for more and more employer-supported coverage. Pretty soon (actually over decades), almost every employer provided low-deductible coverage. When we enacted Medicare and Medicaid, we copied the same system.

---

11   The Patient Protection and Affordable Care Act of 2010, sometimes called ObamaCare, is here referred to as The 2010 Act or the 2010 health reform act.

But this move from individually financed coverage to employer-provided low-deductible coverage and government programs brought its own unforeseen problems, principally sharply rising costs. Added to this was legislation forcing everyone into what is in essence one great big insurance pool. This happened because political pressures to expand coverage beyond what markets deemed acceptable risk resulted in increasing (initially mainly state) mandates and controls requiring policies to cover all kinds of items or conditions and include all kinds of questionable treatment modes that previously one could exclude as worthless, unnecessary, or unduly expensive. The previous market for coverage, which featured many policies offering varying risk profiles and choice, became monolithic—in essence one great pool covering all, albeit segmented by employer.

This was not done because consumers wanted it but because this is what politicians required. Without so intending, these cumulative actions unmoored the system from the principal driver of lower costs and better service—the individual motivated to get the best for self and family at the lowest cost. People no longer cared. What we substituted was a system in which everyone else was thought to be responsible to contain costs—doctor, hospital, insurer, government, each with their own quite different incentives—and therefore no one was actually responsible, and costs started to escalate.

The story is similar for finance and health care. Apparently well-intentioned government policies distort market incentives by forcing politically desired but unnatural risk assessments unto market participants, who go along because that is what is required, not because that is what the market wants. The potential for disaster expands unseen. HUD's AH policies distorted mortgage markets, creating incentives and pressures to create ever-riskier loans, in the same way the IRS tax ruling exempting health services from employee incomes (and later mandates curtailing risk assessment) incentivized the creation of today's no- or low-deductible approach in private and public arenas, which separates patients from cost-awareness and sensitivity.

Recognizing the problem correctly allows us to avoid the noise and static of popular misconceptions and to pursue the best way forward.

Let's Not Let Health Care Become the Next Financial Crisis

Before WW II, each of us was responsible for our own insurance and provision for health care, and costs were not exploding. The problem today is how to re-achieve the old system's advantage of having at its core the incentives for both low cost and high quality, but without going back to a world in which some are left out of the health care coverage universe.

The system that we have evolved since the Second World War, exacerbated by the 2010 Act (ObamaCare), has moved us rapidly toward control of markets by intrusive government regulation and away from individual responsibility. Already people no longer pay for their own care; payment is separated from them by employer-based plans or government programs. This means that at the core of the system the incentives to save costs and obtain quality service are separated from one another and lost in space amid disassociated, non-responsible others. This creates an either/or world where costs spiral upwards without limit or service quality is reduced in a futile or harmful effort to keep the system's financial head above water.

The Better Way: Cut Regulations, Subsidize Directly Where Needed

A better way is to do exactly the opposite—to enhance the power of the individual patient with his own financial resources, abetted by government's purse where and as needed, and eliminate the spider's web of rules, regulations, agencies, bureaus, commissions, and other tentacles of control that increasingly rob us of our incentives, confine and limit us in our choices, and ultimately will strangle us in its costs and wound us in its declines in service. No one cares as much about our health and our pocketbook as each of us, and no one else can reckon our preferences as we do, certainly not bureaucrats who have to operate by general rules.

The system needs to place the incentives for lower costs and high levels of service with each of us. Placing incentives with individuals has remarkable and unmatchable results. When people shop for goods and service, including their health care, they drive down costs *and* maintain or improve service. No system of government control can achieve this. To pretend otherwise is to consign us to a world of uniformity, conformity, and relative impoverishment of outcome.

The lesson of the tale of two cities and shopping for the MRI is that people can be effective shoppers if given the incentive to do so, and the lesson of the financial crisis is don't fall for the Regulatory Illusion. Instead, subsidize directly those you want the market to include, and do so in a transparent fashion that allows everyone to know the true costs and benefits. A system of government-supplied supports or vouchers for those unable to otherwise afford health insurance, scaled to avoid creating disincentives to employment, is a start. More is needed to make the system work properly, as will be discussed. But the key first principle to establish is: avoid the road to ruin paved with regulatory good intentions.

Two starkly contrasting visions of the future exist. The first, exemplified by the 2010 health care act, foretells a future of widespread expansion of public health programs (e.g., Medicaid) and related bureaucracies and agencies, with concomitant squeezing of benefits and deterioration of service caused by the inevitable explosion in public and private costs. This is a future of higher equality at the expense of lowered quality, constantly higher taxes and premiums, and reduced freedom to choose.

The other vision is to reduce dependence on public programs, shift to more direct public support for lower-income individual and family insurance premiums, and cut the red tape preventing insurance companies from offering a widespread, individually tailored menu of coverages. This is a future of freedom of choice, real universal health coverage, enhanced personal responsibility, and lower costs.

With some education into economic thinking and history, it should be obvious which is the better way, the one that truly achieves the goals of progressives and liberals while meeting conservative objections to increased government. What follows is a progressive's guide to understanding why and how this is true.

**

The Revolution of 2008: Apotheosis of the Progressive Era

The inspiration for this work was the takeover of the political landscape in 2008 by a new administration versed in progressive ideas for health care and other matters and full of confidence and enthusiasm that a new order was to begin with their push and energy. So confident were they of the mandate and correctness of their ideas and approach that they felt able to, and with sufficient votes did, govern without need to compromise with an opposition wearied by war and faltering in its own self-image as carriers of the way. Although the war in Iraq had turned a corner with "the surge," at home things had degenerated into quite a mess with the financial implosion of 2007-2008 followed by the economic recession of 2008-2010. Everyone was in shock and experiencing the greatest felt crisis since the Great Depression of 1929-1941.

The upshot was a series of large scale, massive federal enactments led at the top by a president eager for sweeping change but unwilling to bridge political gaps or compromise essential views, who largely turned over the details to leadership in Congress, which also had emerged from the party's left wing. They did not lack for boldness. The size and sweep of the governmental efforts in the financial, economic, and health care fronts were stunning. This embarked them, and the nation, on a bold and risky gamble; if they were on the right track, everyone would be better off and the country would prosper regardless of the reluctant, recalcitrant opposition or silent disapprovers.

If they were not on the right track, all would suffer the consequences. On the macroeconomic front, the country, unstimulated by nearly a trillion dollars of new debt and still suffering unemployment at high levels, would not pull rapidly out of its economic doldrums as promised by supporters and as had happened in similar situations in the past but would labor for years under the debt overhang and uncertainty that ties business to the ground and removes the optimism enabling that sector to invest for the future and create employment. On the financial front, the already highly regulated banks and their customers would labor under burdensome new rules and costs without the country getting the comfort that the problem at the heart of the crisis was addressed and corrected. On the health care front, the creaks and groans of a health care system experiencing unfathomable and painful continuing cost increases would become a cacophony.

All the legislative activity would have been, in the words of Macbeth, "a tale told by an idiot, full of sound and fury, signifying nothing."

One could call this the Revolution of 2008, except the revolution was less one of concept and more one of size. That is, the ideas behind the stimulus, the Dodd-Frank, and the 2010 Act were off the shelf progressive or liberal plums ranging back in most ways to the 1930s. The stimulus was largely driven by pure 1936 Keynes (*The General Theory* was published that year)—pour public money into the channels in any way you want regardless of productivity of potential result. The effect was sure, in this telling, to immediately increase aggregate demand and jobs. The Dodd-Frank was pure 1930s off-the-shelf regulation—target highly unpopular and visible private industry actors (banks, mortgage originators, investment houses) and, after punishing them with taxes and fees, put them under the control of agencies with even more ill-defined powers to investigate, limit, and control what they do. The 2010 Act on health care was an extension of demands to bring more and more people under the government umbrella of public-funded programs, and to control or drive out private insurers, legislation made fiendishly complex by layers of new bureaucracies and rules.

None of these were fresh ideas. Indeed, they were straight from the progressive era 1930 playbook and were supported by some powerful current popular beliefs. One is the belief in government spending to create aggregate demand and create growth, originated by the towering figure of John Maynard Keynes. Another is the belief in government's ability to improve upon market failures and end depressions, supported by the towering figure of Franklin D. Roosevelt and his New Deal.

Many people believe in these today. They are perhaps the most prominent lessons teachers seek to draw from college courses in government and history and impress upon each new crop of students. So the actions of politicians in responding quickly to the financial crisis by Dodd-Frank and in imposing a regulatory approach on health care by the 2010 Act have broad popular roots and support among the educated. They are expressions of what most learned people today think they know.

What follows demonstrates the error of this view and the folly of the enactments that flow from it. The assumption underlying this view is that we have learned nothing, or that there is nothing important to learn, from the time that has passed since 1936. Happily this is not so, as is particularly demonstrated in Parts B and C, which follow.

Imposing a progressive agenda from the 1930s on the American economy of the 2000s suggests what the political perspective behind these enactments really is—that only self-interested, reactionary market players or those blind or insensitive to the obvious have kept us for over seventy years from reaching the Promised Land of health, welfare, and prosperity for all. This view, what economist Thomas Sowell calls "the vision of the anointed" (see Ch VIII, post), lends high moral status and may help explain the rough political tactics undertaken to enact these new laws by the 111th Congress. But true progressive goals, those supported by sound evidence and economics, are left behind in the rubble.

There is another view. That view sees these efforts not as the high tide of enlightened progress, but as its opposite, as a high-water mark for the Free Lunch Fallacy and the Regulatory Illusion. We explain this contrary view here, in depth but without excess detail or complexity, for those who do not already understand it and who find resistance to the popularly expounded progressive agenda perplexing. True progressivism follows the path of reason and evidence, not popular or media stereotypes. Understanding the fallacies underlying the old false progressive agenda, while recognizing the validity of some of its objectives and claims, allows us to redirect its impulses in a more constructive direction, one that truly meets the objectives all share towards a prosperous and secure future.

Japan's "lost two decades" with zombie banks and zero growth and the stagnation of the euro zone's sovereign debt albatross are cautionary tales for the future of America if policy makers fail to grasp the true underlying causes of our slow-motion decline amidst the noise of distractive popular misperceptions of the benefits of regulation and failed theories of the benefits of spending unattached to productivity. An unholy cycle begins. Good times usher in promises and commitments to various politically-favored constituencies made without care to the ravages that excessive debt or taxes can bring in worse times, which in turn, when they arrive, bring on further profligate efforts to spend our way out, creating more debt, more taxes and regulations, slower growth, and a world of stagnation, high unemployment, frustration, and despair. The Bumbling Colossus grows.[12]

Groups benefiting from these regulations and laws at the expense of everyone else form powerful political interest groups resisting needed change. Political leaders responsive to those groups and their media cheerleaders camouflage resistance to their protected status quo in populist rhetoric. Attack the banks, the rich, the other. Leaders lacking the economic perspective and history set out here walk us down false paths.

Liberals and Conservatives at Perpetual Odds

Recognizing the stark conflict of ideas Americans have as to the best way ahead, it became clear to me that there is a critical piece missing from the popular national dialog on goals and means. The left talks to the left and reads publications put out to satisfy their cravings for victims and villains of a preconceived sort, and so too the right reads its publications and talks to its own, but never the twain

---

12 "Across the US and Europe, big government is winning the crisis game, adding taxes, regulatory power, and whole new institutions. Voters want restraint, but there's no mechanism to control government spending, so debt-to-GDP ratios go up rather than down. Even at the state and local level, which is supposed to be closer to the people, governments find ways to grow. In an age-old government shell game, tax increases are projected to cause big revenue gains, which governments rush to spend. When actual revenues fall short, the government blames the economy, borrows the shortfall, and proposes new taxes, creating a debt cycle. This budgeting trick is replayed year after year around the nation… To win elections, politicians have promised practically endless government spending and covered up the cost, leaving generations of taxpayers obligated to pay off the debt." David Malpass, former Deputy Treasury Secretary, *"And the Crisis Winner is? Government,"* 12/16/2011, *WSJ*.

do meet. Like trains passing in the night, Republicans and Democrats, liberals and conservatives, progressives and reactionaries talk past one another, never connecting. Yet there are many things upon which they could agree if only a common ground were uncovered upon which each could stand and see where the other is coming from. Often the differences are not in ultimate goals; most people share a willingness to expand the common weal to include the less fortunate and create opportunities for all regardless of ethnicity, race, religion, class, and the like. The differences lie in the details, the how to. Much of this turns on education, not motivation.

It turns out that we have indeed learned much since 1936, but what we have learned is not commonly understood by the educated public, at least to the depth desirable. The aim here is to change that. We do so by shifting the discussion from politics and media-level reportage to the highest level of economic understanding. The economics of public policy, sometimes called political economy, is the application of economic theory and methods to government and laws. Governments make mistakes, and from those mistakes—well-meaning and conscientious though they may be in motivation—much has been learned. Although much of the modern academic work involves advanced math, much does not and it is not necessary to be learned in such or specialize in esoteric theorems to understand the insights that the economic approach yields, but it does take time, reading, and the motivation to understand.[13]

---

13 Mathematical economics is only as good as the assumptions underlying the equations. Like computer science, garbage in, garbage out. Ultimately economics is built on a few key insights into human behavior in society, reflected over time. These insights can be tested by real-world conditions and results, and math is useful for quantifying and assessing these relationships and maintaining focus with complex variables.

The Advantage of the Economic Approach: Avoid the Superficial and Seductive

The insights the economic approach offers yield much to those thinking about health care systems. To be sure, much debate and disagreement among good economists on some issues goes on and always will. But to seize on the differences without recognizing the large areas where continual research and evidence points in the same direction—especially as it relates to the subjects of regulation, markets, and single-payer systems—is to throw out the baby with the bathwater, and to elevate skepticism and ignorance over better-supported knowledge. Although some reflexively dismiss the economic approach with the game: "I'll pit my Nobel Prize winner against yours"—my Paul Krugman versus your George Stigler—the fact is that with time, testing, and research, better emerges over worse, and the game degenerates into an excuse for ignorance. Even among Nobel Prize winners, the better supported ends up ahead.

For example, at Harvard in the 1950s and 1960s, the lion of the economics department was John Kenneth Galbraith, whose best seller, *The Affluent Society*, scolded Detroit for putting fins on cars and Washington for not prohibiting them. The free market was ridiculed as nonexistent and obviously inadequate, leading to the Great Depression and need for the New Deal. Milton Friedman and the "Chicago Boys" were seen as troglodytes far off the map of sensible economics.[14]

---

14 A decade later, this situation had not changed. Harvard's Paul Warburg Professor of Economics, Robert J. Barro, recounts: "At the Harvard University that I knew as a graduate student in the late 1960s, Milton Friedman was treated as a right-wing midwestern crank. Most of the derision applied to his views on money, including the argument that inflation was always and everywhere a monetary phenomenon.

But by the 1980s and 1990s, the picture was reversed; legions of Nobel Prizes found their way to Chicago, and the best economic departments (gradually including Harvard) were staffed with the Chicago-trained. Today, the contribution of J.K. Galbraith to economics is next to zero, and Milton Friedman is considered a giant of the age. What caused the shift? An extraordinary body of studies probing and confirming the insights of the latter and of the Chicago School. Through the hard work of research and scholarship, the radical and scorned had become the groundwork of the discipline.

The advantage of turning to the better-supported ideas and findings of economics as the ground for analysis—beyond their soundness in reason and evidence—is that in the usual political discussion, everyone's opinion is as good as anyone else's, so no conversation between left, right, or center can get anywhere. When the discussion shifts into the arena of the economic approach to policy, however, everyone's opinion is not as good as everyone else's. The view backed by sound theory and solid empirical work will prevail over the weak, prejudiced, unsupported, or simply asserted—no matter how many prizes the sponsor is awarded or how fervently the view is held.

Thus the economic approach allows reason and evidence to prevail over ignorance, bias, and dogged conviction. It narrows the area of disagreement, enlarges the area of agreement, and allows us an escape from intransigent polarization.

However, even the permanent-income theory of consumption—his scientifically impeccable model in which consumer demand depended on a household's anticipated long-run income—was subjected to poorly reasoned criticism." Barro, *Nothing Is Sacred: Economic Ideas for the New Millennium*, at 1 (MIT 2002).

It also allows the knowledgeable reader to sift out the noise from the truly helpful. Many are led off course by writing that enchants and reportage that impresses but where analysis is weak or unsupported by basic tenets of the economic approach. A case in point is "The Cost Conundrum," a July 1, 2009, article by Atul Gawande in *The New Yorker* on the high degree of doctor-ordered testing in McAllen, Texas. This piece is reputed to have had a profound effect—causing President Obama to tell staff to follow Gawande's lead in shaping the 2010 Act.

Although beautifully written and keenly reported, the knowledge of economics reflected is shallow. The article tendentiously leads the reader into a cure of more and better regulation with no hint of the downsides of that approach or suggestion of how patient-centered or other alternative systems of health care might do the job better. Nowhere is the reader told that Gawande himself as a post-graduate student was one of the architects of the infamous "HillaryCare" proposals that brought the first Clinton administration to its knees. This does the intelligent reader a disservice. It is to help move beyond the impact of the simply enchanting but meretricious, and to arm the reader with a firmer grasp of what is possible, that the material here is presented. The effort is designed to reach the fundamental bases of discord.

***

What Exactly is the Cost Problem and Why?

In this vein, we first examine in Part A, Chapter I what is wrong with our present system of health care, principally its financing, as it has developed over the last decades. We need to understand the nature of the cost issue and locate why it is intractable under present conditions. Part of that is seeing what the 2010 health reform act was about in its broadest dimensions and approach and how it fits into the overall system of health care that we have evolved.

Chapter II unearths the historical roots of our present health care dilemmas, sketches their relation to the Regulatory Illusion, and also discusses certain preliminary issues such as the supposed conflict between morality and economics.

Is Single-Payer the Solution?

Chapter III examines single-payer theory and experience. Because we are so often told to look elsewhere for a better way, it is appropriate to next see how various other countries have attempted to handle the same issues we have by adopting such systems, by which the government takes over the financing of most health needs and spreads coverage to all persons in the country. But shifting costs to the taxpayer does not eliminate them, and the unholy trade-off begins – costs swell, taxpayers feel the pain, and politicians respond by reducing services, their quality and prompt availability. These and related failures of single-payer systems are characteristic and unavoidable.

It appears from this review that attempting to create universal coverage and also contain costs while preserving service via a single-payer type approach involves intractable and painful trade-offs that it would not be advisable to inflict upon the people of this country.

How to Create Universal Coverage While Avoiding the Single-Payer Mirage

Chapters IV and V set forth a positive solution that avoids the Regulatory Illusion, the Free Lunch Fallacy, and returns proper cost/benefit incentives to health care. Moving beyond the single-payer model while trying to achieve its aims of universality and cost-containment—"quality service for all at reasonable cost"—requires returning to the basics of economic thinking and to the traditions of individual responsibility which have generated increasing prosperity for generations of Americans. Chapter IV sets out the basic principles of such a system for health care, and Chapter V, amplified by Appendix A, sets out how to meet the goals of universal coverage, quality service, and lower costs by building on the existing but restricted legal structure of health savings accounts supplemented with scaled vouchers for the needy and a freed-up market for insurance that allows everyone to sort out and obtain high-deductible coverage tailored to their individual needs and wants.

This eliminates the "one size fits all" coverage that single-payer and other government-control approaches seek to foster and better meets the needs of each one of us, with our diverse and variegated situations. It places the incentives for costs and quality where they belong—with the individual. It solves the trade-off dilemma inherent in government-control approaches whereby the only way to reduce costs is to curtail service across the board. Instead, individual preferences balancing cost, quality, and need prevail. The role of government in all this is limited but critical – to create the proper framework, to deal with preexisting conditions, to fund premiums for the needy, and to help ensure information on providers and service is out there.

INTRODUCTION

What Markets Do Best and How the Regulatory Illusion has Hobbled Economic Progress

Part B, Chapter VI addresses what it is about markets that, regardless of politics, should gain our respect and attention. That discussion is needed to advance the conversation between liberals and conservatives, since it is not enough to simply locate and describe the failures of our present system and do the same for the single-payer systems some admire and advocate. For all their imperfections and shortfalls, markets usually work to the advantage of most, not just the participants in transactions, and it is that understanding or lack of it that most divides the various political groups.

So Part B, Chapter VI discusses the essence of markets and what it is about them that is advantageous and why. This includes forthrightly addressing the common complaints about markets, and the antipathies that many hold concerning them—especially the fostering of greed, self-interest, and denigration of charity and concern for others. Adam Smith's paradox is central to this understanding, an idea whose simplicity and power has proven elusive to generations of the most highly educated and elite among us.

Chapter VII follows this discussion of the advantages of markets with discussion of the disadvantages of economic regulation of business, the Third Way between failed socialism and perceived unbridled cowboy capitalism. This chapter explores what our best economists and researchers have learned since 1936 about the nature and pitfalls of efforts to modify and change markets and market outcomes by economic regulation, defined as legislative and administrative commands seeking to restrict and limit the competitive environment – especially entry, pricing, mergers, and similar aspects of normal business behavior of otherwise freely interacting individuals and entities.

The Regulatory Illusion is the dominant approach American politicians have of dealing with felt political needs, in finance, health care, and elsewhere. Health care costs and the 2010 health care reform act, which was supposed to address them, discussed in Part A, exemplify this illusion. So too does the financial crisis and the Dodd-Frank Act, which was Congress' regulatory response. Chapter VII, building on earlier chapters, discusses this response and the previous major such responses—the New Deal programs, the true outcome and legacy of which have been well and extensively analyzed by generations of professional economists.

These recent experiences with the Regulatory Illusion make clear that further steps down the road towards single-payer health care are predictably bound to be costly failures. Yet few recognized or self-proclaimed experts in health care policy are familiar enough with the history of regulatory failures to include this critical understanding in their material. Neglecting these experiences makes analysis hollow and inadequate.

The historical lesson is clear—regulation starts in high hopes and good intentions and ends in harm to the very public it is aimed to protect and whose welfare it is designed to promote. Understanding this experience allows us to predict with great certainty that similar regulatory efforts, which are indeed the heart of the 2010 health care act, will fail to meet the expectations of proponents and will fail to meet the needs of the public.

INTRODUCTION

Additional Anti-Market Criticisms, Fallacies, and Biases

Part C, Chapter VIII, addresses certain academic and popular criticisms of applying the economic approach to health care, criticisms that at bottom are unfounded and that serve to create much of the noise and confusion among health care policy experts. Prime among these is the assumption held by many single-payer and other government-control advocates that health care is a unique area marked by market failure, so that the usual ideas and approaches of economic thinking do not apply. This leaves them free to push for various harmful schemes of government control and neglect the most relevant evidence undermining that approach.

Chapter VIII addresses, among other things, this idea of market failure and reveals it to be either flimsy and unmeritorious or trivial and the occasion for overreaching. The meaning of rationality in economics and the challenge and limitations of behavioral economics are examined as well.

The upshot is that those advocating government-controlled schemes in health care are urging us down a path where not only are the examples they give from abroad leaky and unpersuasive, but the basis for denying our own highly relevant experience with regulated industries is leaky and unpersuasive as well. Thus, that path promotes an extremely high risk of failure and harm.

****

The Third Way Leads Down a Blind Alley

What we call capitalism has grown slowly over the centuries, leaving at any point of time large disparities in income and wealth, which for better or worse have largely proven

35

irresistible to political attempts to ameliorate. The mid-nineteenth century saw the rise of various flavors of socialist theory in intellectual circles, but it took the cataclysmic devastation of the two world wars for these to take wide root in British and European economies. In this country, the Great Depression spurred numerous efforts at regulation of business in the public interest as a third way.

In all of this, the tension is between two psychological parts of the individual and collective personality, the thirst for security on the one hand and on the other the realization that without personal and social risk there comes no reward.

The thirst for security through collective economic arrangements forged by government, resulting in socialism, has achieved enough obvious decay and decrepitude around the world that most everyone realizes its promises of security are illusory, the security of a sinking ship. Yet still the fear of risk—the process of cyclical advantage and disadvantage that economist Joseph Schumpeter called the "creative destruction" of capitalism—makes many people shy away from the idea of untrammeled free markets.

As Parts B and C reveal, however, the Third Way of economic regulation proves to be as illusory as the government ownership model it is supposed to improve on. Under both government regulation and outright ownership, ordinary people usually end up worse off than if nothing had been done at all. So we need to work through just why this is so and what policies actually provide the security and justice people seek without setting society back and harming everyone in the process. That is the task set here.

What the national conversation on health care and the proper role of government regulation lacks is a comprehensive review of what the discipline of economics has revealed since the New Deal. Parts B and C give an overview of the actual effects of economic regulation of industry when viewed under the magnifying glass of our best economists. This amplifies and confirms the analysis in Part A on our health care system itself.

How to Avoid the Bumbling Colossus

Where this leads is to a new progressive thinking, which rejects the vision of the anointed that treats problems of economic and social justice as simply areas for further government regulation to subdue the unworthy impulses of the multitude and correct market failures. That attitude ushers in more harm than good and fails to advance social and economic needs. Maintaining the progressive goals of ever increasing the spread to all of the economic benefits that our economy creates requires a deep appreciation of the benefits of markets and freedom. Only on that foundation can true progress build.

Old progressive thinking and its legislative manifestations has led us to diminish and threaten to choke off the engine of growth in a morass of regulation and poorly conceived government intervention as the cure-all for social and economic ills. This has led us to the Regulatory State and the Bumbling Colossus.

From affordable housing mandates underlying the 2008 financial crisis to the debt-swamping Keynesian stimulus that failed to stimulate to the regulatory octopus of the 2010 health care act to the lending-crushing restrictions in Dodd-Frank, tired and old progressive thinking is alive and flourishing. It does not serve us well.

The times call for a new progressive approach. Maintaining the goals of improving the lot of the underprivileged while freeing the engine of the economy to expand benefits to all requires adopting as a central vision the role of markets and freedom, a strong presumption against regulation, and observing careful limits on what government can do well. Work with the market, not against it. Subsidize individuals and families directly – yet carefully and with great transparency – where needed to allow people to participate in markets without destroying incentives or promoting undue distortion. Promote competition as the great driver of lower cost.

This vision, replacing the vision of the anointed, allows progress instead of ever dragging us downward into a failed and less beneficent past.

A. The Health Care Problem and Its Solution

the most important change which extensive government control produces is a psychological change, an alteration in the character of the people...even a strong tradition of political liberty is no safeguard if the danger is precisely that new institutions and policies will gradually undermine and destroy that spirit.

The guiding principle that a policy of freedom for the individual is the only truly progressive policy remains as true today as it was in the nineteenth century.

FRIEDRICH A. HAYEK[15]

---

15   Friedrich A. Hayek, *The Road to Serfdom*, at xiv, 240 (U. Chicago Press, 1961 ed.)

CHAPTER I:
The Bumbling Colossus in Health Care

1. The Importance of Getting it Right: The Trade-off of Health Care Costs and Jobs

In March 2010, Congress passed, and the president signed, the largest increase in federal control over health care coverage and the largest expansion of costs since the creation of Medicare and Medicaid in the 1960s. The question addressed here is whether that enactment, on top of the rest of the system that has evolved since WW II, is the best system for America going forward.

It is very important to get our health care system right. The right system not only delivers quality health at reasonable cost, it also helps to allocate resources to productive uses. The wrong one fosters declining quality, unnecessary costs, and slower productivity growth. The increasing burden of health care costs prevents employers from investing the capital they must spend on excess benefits, and it is productive investment that creates jobs and expands income.[16] Increasing premiums and taxes mean individuals have less to spend and have to work harder just to stay in place.

In terms of fairness, unnecessary health care costs are a particularly insidious form of reverse wealth transfer—from the relatively less well-off working population of patients to people in the relatively better-off health care sector (doctors, nurses, administrators, medical researchers, etc). As we shall see, the 2010 Act gets it wrong on all these counts and, by disregarding better alternatives, burdens us with unnecessary costs and slower growth.

The Obama Administration and 2008-2010 Congress are responsible for three of the most burdensome programs in American history—the stimulus, the Dodd-Frank Act, and health care reform—arguing they were imperative, respectively, to create jobs, to avoid further financial crises by increasing regulatory oversight, and to create affordable care. None of these goals has proven nor will prove true; the stimulus failed to stimulate and, by creating a huge debt overhang, slowed recovery.[17] The Dodd-Frank Act totally missed

---

16 Economists treat the best measure of costs not by out-of-pocket expenditures, but by "opportunity cost"—the foregone gains of alternative uses, or gains that would have accrued had the same resources been allocated to another use or source. George J. Stigler, *The Organization of Industry,* at 10 (U. Chicago Press, 1968). If you can obtain the same goods or services through another channel or set of arrangements at lower prices, the foregone advantage is a part of your cost, although it doesn't show up in your accounts. Thus the cost of our present health care system includes the foregone costs of the alternative, superior system described here and in other literature on patient-centered care. These foregone costs are true waste, and they deplete the economy of productive capital and labor that otherwise would enhance economic growth and income.

17 The 2009 American Recovery and Reinvestment Act (aka the stimulus), singularly misnamed, sought to increase spending by combining short-term individual tax rebates with block grants for targeted spend-

the real cause of the financial crisis and compounded woes by heaping unneeded regulatory burdens on an already overregulated financial sector.[18] The health care reform will exacerbate an already threatening cost explosion for taxpayers and the insured public.

All three programs were seen as necessary extensions of government influence and control over an economy suffering from its lack, but each represents the least advantageous from among available choices.[19] Their profligacy and misdirection of resources will burden our futures as well as make more difficult growth of the economy and job creation for untold numbers of unemployed Americans. The Regulatory Illusion they embody is alive and well.

Although the folly of the stimulus and Dodd-Frank are discussed here, the principal focus is to understand why the health care reform is a failure, why its failure is predictable, and what to do about it.

---

ing to state and local governments. Neither was effective. Instead of increasing spending, individuals paid down debt, and state and local governments substituted the federal grants for ongoing debt issuance. So even apart from arguments about the size of any multiplier, the net increase in individual and government spending was zero and there was nothing to multiply. John F. Cogan & John B. Taylor, "The Obama Stimulus Impact? Zero," 12/9/2010, *WSJ*. This undercuts those like Paul Krugman, who, recognizing that the first "stimulus" failed, argued for another. How many trillions until substitution stops?

18 See Peter J. Wallison, *Dissent* to the *Report of the Financial Crisis Inquiry Commission*, www.fcic.gov/report.

19 Harvard economics professor Alberto Alesina's study of stimulus type efforts around the world found such spending unproductive as contrasted with tax cuts. Alberto Alesina, "Tax Cuts vs. 'Stimulus': The Evidence is In—A review of over 200 fiscal adjustments in 21 countries shows that spending discipline and tax cuts are the best ways to spur economic growth," 9/15/2010, *WSJ*; see also James K. Glassman, "The Failure of the Liberal Economic Experiment?" *Commentary* (August 2010).

2. Europe Envy: Is Europe the Right Model for America?

Some people believe that the Europeans have it right and we have it wrong, so let's start with the desire to model ourselves on others. In the 2009-2010 run-up to passage of the ironically misnamed "Patient Protection and Affordable Care Act" [the 2010 Act],[20] we were told to look to Britain, Canada, and Europe for inspiration and emulation on health care, where it is said to be open to all without payment and almost universally publicly funded. And the agenda didn't stop there; it was not just the free health care, but also Europe's greater job security, enhanced welfare benefits, low military budgets. A seductive pitch. What's not to like?

But this only looks at part of the picture. In assessing public policies, one must always ask two questions: "Who benefits?" and "Who pays?" If those who benefit also pay, resources are generally maximized; people get what they want. If those who pay are not those who receive the benefit, the chances for erroneous incentives and misallocation are magnified, and questions need to be asked.

The argument that we should emulate Europe provides an example. Low military budgets? Without America's

---

20 The "Patient Protection and Affordable Care Act" (Pub. L. 111-148, 124 Stat. 119, 42 USC. ____), signed into law March 23, 2010, as well as the companion "Health Care and Education Reconciliation Act of 2010," signed March 30, 2010 (referred to herein collectively as "The 2010 Act"), are sometimes referred to as "ObamaCare." The bills were passed by voting along strictly party lines in the Senate, and with only thirty-four Democrats and all Republicans voting against it in the House. The unusual legislative process called reconciliation was used to avoid need for sixty Senate votes and hence any possible filibuster. The specific provisions were crafted behind closed doors by Democrat leaders in Senate and House chambers with White House participation, and even members of Congress were kept in the dark until final passage.

CHAPTER I: THE BUMBLING COLOSSUS IN HEALTH CARE

250,000 or so military and families, and related missiles and hardware—a legacy of WW II—Europe would live in a security partial vacuum.[21] This free ride in defense promotes passivity abroad and welfare extravagance at home. Greater job security? What about those with no job at all? Long-term unemployment in Europe is chronically high—typically over a year (large variations among countries to one side). Ask the long-term unemployed how they feel about laws protecting other people's job security.[22]

Extensive welfare? What about its effects on standards of living and jobs? From 1982 to 2007, France grew at a rate of 2.1 percent per year, as did Germany, with Italy at 1.8 percent, whereas the US grew at 3.3 percent. Thus Americans got a third richer over that quarter century. Michael Boskin and Edward Lazear, former chairmen of the Council of Economic Advisors, point to swollen European governments—including health care—as the principal reason European standards of living are 30 percent lower than ours.[23]

---

21 United States European Command (Eucom), at eucom.mil. US Defense Secretary Robert Gates in a blunt speech to NATO decried military shortfalls in Europe's NATO Afghanistan and Libya efforts due to declining budgets. Whereas US military budgets doubled since 9/11/2001, NATO member budgets declined 15 percent. Only five of twenty-eight NATO members reached the 2 percent GDP goals. Julian Barnes, "Gates Questions NATO's Future," 6/10/2011, *WSJ*.
22 Oliver J Blanchard, "Explaining European Unemployment," *National Bureau of Economic Research Reporter*, (Summer 2004).
23 Michael Boskin, Opinion, 5/6/2010, *WSJ*. Edward P. Lazear, "The Euro Crisis: Doubting the 'Domino' Effect," Opinion, 10/31/2011, *WSJ* ("the fundamental problem facing Europe is one of governments becoming too big to be supported by the economy."). A typical political response to deficits is higher taxes on income—promoted as needed to reduce inequality and fund social programs—which instead slows growth and retards GDP: "Nobel Prize-winning economist Edward Prescott examined international labor market data and showed that changes in tax rates on labor are associated with changes in employ-

Less growth means fewer lift themselves out of poverty, hence more reliance on an extensive welfare net. The ideology of equality is appealing and carries high popular favor, but there is little solace in an equality of relative impotence abroad and lower living standards at home.[24] Slow growth and fewer jobs especially impact the poor. And politicizing economic relationships freezes people in an unsatisfying status quo. The forces arrayed against change—public and private labor unions and protected business, subsidized classes of all sorts—picket and clamor at the least threat to their privileged positions. Bad politics trumps good economics.[25]

---

ment and hours worked. From the 1970s to the 1990s, the effective tax rate on work increased by an average of 28 percent in Germany, France, and Italy. Over that same period, work hours fell by an average of 22 percent in those three countries. When higher taxes reduce the reward for work, you get less of it." "Principles for Economic Revival," by George P. Shultz, Michael J. Boskin, John F. Cogan, Allan Meltzer, John B. Taylor, 9/16/2010, *WSJ*.

24 According to interviews appearing in the N.Y. Times, the cracks in the welfare state have become obvious even to the European "man-in-the-street," who foresees the end of the promised dream. Erlanger, "Payback Time: Crisis Imperils Liberal Benefits Long Expected by Europeans," 5/22/2010, *N.Y. Times*.

25 Note the episodic riots in Europe whenever governments try to reduce existing benefits or alter laws favorable to certain protected groups. The 2011 European sovereign debt crisis, initially focusing on Greece but with Italy, Spain, France, and other countries in the wings, presents political leaders with the choice of maintaining benefit levels and creating default, or riots if benefits and protections are reduced. [The usual option of inflation—the cruelest tax of all—is hedged by the legal mandate of the European Central Bank to focus on price stability.] The crisis developed under the radar and invisibly over time as too much was promised without concern for ability to pay and as tax rates achieved maximum levels of efficiency. "The sad fact is that there is not enough money in the EU to pay off the public debts incurred by the governments. Most countries have long since squeezed as much tax revenue from their citizens as they can." Gerald P. O'Driscoll, Jr.,

CHAPTER I: THE BUMBLING COLOSSUS IN HEALTH CARE

The euro-zone sovereign debt crisis that began in 2010 and continues should be a huge warning light for those seeking to emulate the European model of high promises on health, welfare, job protection, wage control, and the like. Governments ultimately need to meet these promises with either taxes or debt creation. Raising taxes unfortunately runs into the fact that above a certain point this recipe is unproductive; paradoxically, higher taxes can slow growth and reduce, not increase, total revenues. And debt must be sold into markets that, as the world has seen dramatically starting in 2011, can simply say no, or require levels of interest that make default inevitable. The merry-go-round where government promises lead to higher taxes and debt, then leading to budget cuts and political clashes, comes to a spinning, cascading halt.

The political fallout of the corrections needed to meet the economic reality—reduced pension, health and unemployment insurance, lower wages for government workers, cutting of services, and the like—ushers in violence, the fall of governments, and general lowering of GDP and incomes. Far better to avoid this from the beginning and seek a different road. The sovereign debt crisis shows that instead of seeking to emulate Europe, America should seek to understand and avoid Europe's mistakes.

The Health Care Icon Crumbling

Now in addition comes the news on national health care itself. Britain, Canada, and Europe long ago adopted various flavors of socialized or government-controlled medicine, to mostly good press. Britain's health services were nationalized in 1948, along with many other sectors

---

former governor, Federal Reserve Bank of Dallas, "Why We Can't Escape the Eurocrisis," Opinion, 11/2/2011, *WSJ*.

of the economy. Although many of these other sectors were privatized under Margaret Thatcher in the 1980s in order to rid them of grossly noncompetitive conditions and drains on the budget, the National Health Service seemed above criticism and immune to change. Its premise––"free at the point of use and available to all based on need, not ability to pay"—set a standard for idealism for many across the globe as well as at the top of the US government.[26] Indeed, our British and European cousins have long cluck-clucked at us for shying from the lure of free service for all.

But this last redoubt is starting to crumble. In July 2010, thirty years after the Thatcher denationalizations of other industries, the English government issued to Parliament a white paper (discussed in detail later) that, while clinging to the ideal of free care, starkly recognizes the failure of the National Health Service to serve the needs of patients and recommends a "revolution" in all its aspects. Why this and why now? Costs. "The reality," the white paper frankly admits, "is that there is no more money." After sixty-two years of pooh-poohing competition and private initiative, the white paper seeks to "free providers from central or regional control and let them compete."[27] As will be seen, the actual recommendations fall short of what is needed to

---

26 In July 2010, President Obama appointed Dr. Donald Berwick, an unabashed and vocal admirer of the NHS, as principal administrator for The Centers for Medicare and Medicaid Services (CMS), making him the federal government's top health care "czar" and implementer of regulations under the 2010 Act. This appointment symbolized top government's admiration for the NHS model. This appointment was "recess," thereby side-stepping consent by Congress, reflecting the battle this ideology would have engendered. It is telling that this appointment was made the same month the failure of the NHS was announced in the English government's white paper (see discussion).

27 "Equity and Excellence: Liberating the NHS," submitted by the prime minister, deputy prime minister, and secretary of state for health,

CHAPTER I: THE BUMBLING COLOSSUS IN HEALTH CARE

achieve the goals. But recognition of failure is the beginning of improvement.

Why did this take so long? Hayek's observation, quoted at the beginning of this chapter, is more powerful than commonly realized—government control ushers in attitudes of dependency and acquiescence that are very difficult to shake.[28] Whether the government control takes the form of regulation or outright socialism, it causes people to abdicate their own judgment and independent thinking.[29]

One must be careful in looking elsewhere and neglecting our own experiences. Certainly there is much to love and admire in Britain and Europe, especially culture, history, art, ambience, incomparable old world charm, lifestyle, cuisine, and cathedrals, but as we shall see their total taxpayer-funded approach to health care is not among them. Too many promises, too high increases in costs, too much deterioration in service, too much tax and debt burden retarding growth and job creation.

So why, even in the face of a deteriorating NHS, did the administration and 2008-2010 Congress look to Britain and Europe as a model, seeking to force America further down these roads that turn to quicksand?

This question is suitable either for historians or psychoanalysts, but one answer is the seductive lure of the Free Lunch Fallacy, the illusion that benefiting some by spread-

---

July 2010, to the Parliament of England "by Command of Her Majesty" (available on the Internet).
28 In fact, a study of the NHS showed exactly this phenomenon to exist. Goodman, Musgrave, and Herrick, *Lives at Risk; Single-Payer National Health Insurance Around the World,* at 197 (Rowman & Littlefield, 2004).
29 Even the sinking of the Titanic reveals this. Analysis of the records and reports shows those responsible relied on outdated lifeboat regulations instead of thinking for themselves. Chris Berg, "The Real Reason for the Tragedy of the Titanic", 4/12/2012, *WSJ.*

ing costs to all makes the good or service free, disregarding the powerful effects of misplaced incentives. Like an enormous Fata Morgana, free health care rises like a chimera beckoning from across the ocean.

We have a preliminary question to address. As indicated, with the 2010 Act, America has now enacted a major expansion of our own health care structure, by which its proponents explicitly sought to bring us more into line with the European-British-Canadian state-control or state-run models. The preliminary question is, what is the likely impact of the recent enactment on top of our current health care system in the terms most important to all of us—the continuing availability of quality services when needed, at reasonable cost? Has the 2010 Act taken us in the right direction? If things are broken, how do we fix them?

As we shall see, our present system (much like Britain's NHS) delivers ever-increasing costs that can only be addressed by ever-lowering quality—squeezing providers, reducing benefits, cutting options. This unholy trade-off is inherent in present arrangements. But while Britain is seeking ways out of its socialist decline, with the 2010 Act America is rushing headlong into it.

3. The 2010 Act: Getting it Wrong—The Mess We Have Created for Ourselves

To get to where we need to go, first we have to recognize clearly where we are and what are the impacts of the recent enactments. The 2010 Act, complex and multidimensional, is based on significant additional government—primarily federal—interferences into the economy of health care and its financing in a way that reaches all of us, some beneficially, many adversely. These include

CHAPTER I: THE BUMBLING COLOSSUS IN HEALTH CARE

increased *mandates on individuals and carriers banning risk assessment, and penalties for non-compliance* (insurers must not bar preexisting conditions or charge more based upon health status, everyone must buy coverage with penalties for non-compliance on individuals and employers), increased *controls over policies, which limit consumer choices* (policies, premiums, and coverage must fit federal regulations), increased *taxation ultimately on consumers* (higher-income people, insurers, drug and device makers are hit with surtaxes), significant *benefit reductions to the elderly* (a half-trillion dollars of Medicare will be cut), and increased *subsidies based on income without concern for incentives* (Medicaid eligibility and subsidies for coverage and care for individuals and small employers are extended further up the income ladder).

Together these create a huge cost bulge and an increase in demand. Major parts of the 2010 Act are set out in Appendix C.[30]

Certain people benefit, and certain necessary coverage holes are closed. These benefits are phased in from 2011 to 2014. Lower-income people benefit by the Act's expanding eligibility for Medicaid up to 133 percent of the federal poverty level. Persons with preexisting conditions are afforded a separate, subsidized program, although this disappears in 2014 when the mandate requiring insurers to pool these risks with everyone else becomes effective. Persons up to 400 percent of the federal poverty level not part of employer-sponsored plans can get premium

---

30 Also a short summary of the 2010 Act from the proponents' viewpoint can be found at "Responsible Reform for the Middle Class," Democrats.Senate.Gov/Reform (3/31/2010); and in Theodore R. Marmor and Jonathan Oberlander, "The Health Bill Explained At Last," 8/19/2010, *The New York Review of Books*.

subsidies and cost-sharing through "exchanges" in which insurers can offer certain set policies with mandated coverage. Medical underwriting (pricing coverage according to health risks) is virtually eliminated. Persons with health issues that might otherwise result in higher premiums are required to be included in everyone else's pool, causing premium reductions for those with such issues and causing raises for everyone else.

In all, it is expected that these provisions will serve to extend coverage to 34 million of the approximately 57 million previously uninsured, leaving about 24 million without health insurance coverage.

The 2010 Act's Cost Calculus: Public Promises Versus Hard Truth

One could ask why it is necessary to discuss the costs of the 2010 Act at all since its proponents promised that it would be "revenue neutral"—that is, that the taxes, fees, cuts, and other features of the Act counterbalanced rather exactly the expenses it contains—and the CBO blessed this view during passage. This blessing was needed to achieve passage by the controversial tactic of "reconciliation" and to avoid opportunity for legislative derailment or delay. Since the Act was kept secret during its long gestation, contrary views were unable to surface. Nonetheless, it has rapidly become apparent that the sanguine view of its proponents was a contrivance created to achieve political victory, not historical truth. So it is necessary to examine the cost implications of the 2010 Act anew.

Let's start with a memorandum dated April 22, 2010, by the Office of the Actuary of the Center for Medicare and Medicaid Services (CMS), which attempts to calculate the increased coverage, costs, and impacts of the 2010 Act.[31]

The CMS actuary estimates the Act's cost of expanding coverage for the ten years from 2010 to 2019, before offsets, to be $828 billion. Since most of this is phased in starting in 2014, however, this figure is really the cost over five years. Most of this comes from raising Medicaid eligibility to 133 percent of the federal poverty line (FPL) and subsidizing individuals up to 400 percent of that line in the health insurance exchanges set up for individuals and small employers.

All of this cost and more was said by the Congressional Budget Office, in support of passage of the Act, to be offset by revenue and cost reduction provisions, principally 1) the projected $575 billion in reduced Medicare reimbursements, 2) additional taxes on insurers, drug companies, and device providers, 3) penalties for non-compliance with the individual and corporate mandates, and other items. Thus the 2010 Act was presented to the American people by its political supporters, citing the CBO, as a way to actually save future health costs through lower premiums and lower taxes.

But the CBO uses a static analysis under which large cost elements are omitted and politically unrealistic

---

31 The memorandum is entitled "Estimated Financial Effects of the 'Patient Protection and Affordable Care Act,' as amended" by Richard S. Foster, Chief Actuary, CMS, HHS [Chief Actuary Memo]. It is available online. The memo underlines the speculative nature of its findings: "The actual future impacts of the PPACA on health expenditures, insured status, individual decisions, and employer behavior are very uncertain. The legislation would result in numerous changes in the way that health care insurance is provided and paid for in the US, and the scope and magnitude of these changes are such that few precedents exist for use in estimation."

assumptions are taken at face value. By contrast, the CMS can not operate in fantasy-land. A major point of divergence is the effect of the Act's provision cutting Medicare reimbursements to hospitals, doctors, and other medical providers, which amounts to $575 billion of the alleged savings.

The CMS chief actuary points out that squeezing hospitals, skilled nursing facilities, and home health services results in a reduction of the numbers of these that can remain solvent and serving patients (under the Act's formulas, more than 15 percent would fail). As a result, to avoid these reductions in available providers, Congress had overridden similar cost reductions each of the previous seven years (and did so again in 2011-12).

Thus a very large chunk of the purported cost savings disappears because experience shows it to be illusory—making these cuts would counterproductively reduce the supply of health service providers, in addition to directly harming those receiving the cuts in benefits, primarily the elderly, disabled, and poor.[32] Congress and the CBO knew this when they enacted the 2010 Act, but nonetheless included the fictive half-trillion cuts as cost savings.

---

32 The cuts in Medicare hit the elderly and less-well-off particularly hard: "The reality is that the cost of ObamaCare will be quite high for some people. By 2017, thousands of people in Dallas, Houston, and San Antonio will be paying more than $5,000 a year in lost healthcare benefits to make ObamaCare possible... For some New York City dwellers, the figure will exceed $6,000 a year. Unfortunate residents of Ascension, La., will pay more than $9,000 in lost benefits. Who are these people? Are they the rich and the comfortable...? [T]he people getting hit with these very expensive tabs live in predominately low-income households. They are disproportionately minorities... In many areas, Medicare Advantage enrollees will lose about one-third or more of their health-insurance benefits." John C. Goodman, "How Seniors Will Pay For ObamaCare," 9/23/2010, *WSJ*.

CHAPTER I: THE BUMBLING COLOSSUS IN HEALTH CARE

After the Hype, the Truth

So despite the assurances by its political sponsors of "revenue neutrality," the actual cost impact of the Act will be very different than advertised. Independent analysts confirm and flesh out further the CMS chief actuary's view. Former CBO head Douglas Holtz-Eakin estimates that, once its unrealistic accounting is removed, the Act adds over $562 billion to the already swollen federal deficit over its first ten years.[33] Add in the $105 billion that the CBO projects as "implementation costs" and the fact the CBO scoring omits the first four years, and one reasonable estimate of the true ten-year cost from 2014, when the major costly provisions kick in, is $2.7 trillion.[34] This represents an unprecedented non-wartime increase in government health expenses as a proportion of GDP.

Public debt overhangs of the magnitude projected (without corresponding increases in productivity, which the Act does nothing to promote) have severe implications for job creation. One economist estimates that "such astronomical debt crowds out other productive investments and will lead to an estimated 690,000 lost job opportunities per year."[35]

---

33 Douglas Holtz-Eakin, "The Real Arithmetic of Health Care Reform," 3/20/2010, *N.Y. Times* Op-Ed. "Removing the unrealistic annual Medicare savings ($463 billion) and the stolen annual revenues from Social Security and long-term care insurance ($123 billion), and adding in the annual spending that so far is not accounted for ($114 billion) quickly generates additional deficits of $562 billion in the first ten years. And the nation would be on the hook for two more entitlement programs rapidly expanding as far as the eye can see."
34 Michael D. Tanner, "The Real Impact of the Health Care Law," 8, *Cato's Letter* (Fall 2010).
35 Karen Campbell, Ph.D, Nell & Winfree, Opinion, 3/19/2010, *WSJ*.

And that's just the public cost. What about the premiums we pay? The Act's complexity and uncertainty caused CBO to punt on its estimates of premium impact: it said that a "paucity of data" about the impact of the Act's mandates means that there is "tremendous" uncertainty about how much premiums will go up. But go up they will. The CBO put the tentative impact on premiums in the open market for the average family at an increase of $2,100 per year.

The Future is Worse: The 2010 Act Has No Systemic Means to Contain Cost Increases

Even discounting the accuracy of all cost estimates, it is obvious that the Act creates health price escalation on a grand scale. Principally this is because neither it nor any other aspect of our system provides any systemic or natural means to control cost increases, which already outpace significantly the rate of inflation.[36]

Lacking this, premiums and medical costs will continue to increase at super-inflationary rates. The Act feeds

---

36 Surveys show that over time premium costs continue to far outpace wage rates. "On average, the total cost of a family health insurance policy rose just 3 percent last year [2009], to $13,770 in annual premiums, according to a survey of employer health benefits released on Thursday by the Kaiser Family Foundation, a nonprofit research group. Employers chose to keep their costs steady by passing the higher costs onto workers. As a result, the employee contribution toward family coverage rose an average of 14 percent, or almost $500, from what employees paid last year. Workers are now paying nearly $4,000 a year for a family policy, a jump of 47 percent since 2005. Wages have increased by just 18 percent during that time, according to Kaiser. Employees are not only paying higher premiums but also higher deductibles… From a consumer perspective, the cost of health insurance just keeps going up faster than wages, said Drew Altman, Kaiser's chief executive, in a news release." Reed Abelson, "Survey: Employers Pass on More Health Costs to Workers," 9/2/2010, *N.Y Times Online*.

demand for health services and raises costs in at least the following ways: 1) it increases subsidies, which promotes usage, 2) it taxes factors of production like insurance and drug companies, which (as the actuary notes) pass these added costs on to consumers, and 3) it requires people with costly conditions to be included in everyone's insurance pool, raising everyone's premiums.[37]

Not only is the demand side of the health care equation pumped up, but also nothing substantial is done to increase the supply side—the numbers of providers (hospitals, doctors, nurses, home health aides, etc)—to meet the increased demand that comes with greatly increasing the Medicaid eligibility and exchange subsidies. Pumping up demand for health services without corresponding increases in the supply of such services is a formula for juicing up prices and costs and for increasing waiting times for services.[38]

The inevitable conclusion is that the drafters postponed any realistic concern for costs in a rush to enact expanded entitlements designed to bring more citizens under the

---

[37] Paul Howard, director of the Manhattan Institute's Center for Medical Progress, and Stephen Parente, professor of Health Finance at the University of Minnesota, conclude: "In short, ObamaCare aims to treat the symptom (the uninsured) without treating the disease (healthcare costs). Not only will it fail to control these costs, but it will in fact cause them to rise—in turn squeezing patients, doctors, and insurers as regulators inevitably turn to price controls in a desperate attempt to salvage some shred of fiscal solvency." Howard and Parente, "Toward Real Health Care Reform," 4, *National Affairs,* at 105 (Summer 2010).

[38] The CMS actuary artfully couches it this way: "For now, we believe that consideration should be given to the potential consequences of a significant increase in demand for health care meeting a relatively fixed supply of health care providers and services... The additional demand for health services could be difficult to meet initially with existing health provider resources and could lead to price increases, cost-shifting, and/or changes in providers' willingness to treat patients with low-reimbursement health coverage." Chief Actuary Memo, at 20.

government umbrella. The Act makes worse the trade-off by which increasing the scope of coverage causes costs to rise and triggers clamping down on providers and benefits. This trade-off leads to queues and deteriorating quality and availability of service—exactly the opposite of the outcome sought to be achieved.

Efforts to patch up this system with new taxes, reduced services, increased premiums or all three increase the harms and prolong miseries, and are no substitute for systemic, built-in cost containment.

The 2010 Act Multiplies Bureaucracy: A Brave New World Imposed for Our Benefit

> *He has erected a multitude of New Offices, and sent hither swarms of Officers to harass our people, and eat out their substance.*
>
> **DECLARATION OF INDEPENDENCE**

The handmaiden of regulation is bureaucracy, for without public agencies and their employees, who is going to administer the new laws and create and interpret the new rules? And if you like bureaucracy, you'll love the 2010 Act.

First of all, it runs to thousands of pages which few can read. It creates a huge and pervasive regulatory apparatus, including at least (by some counts) 159 new boards, commissions, and agencies, many with powers to establish more.[39] It grants powers to the secretary of HHS and her

---

39 A Congressional Research Service report found it impossible to estimate the number of new boards, commissions, and agencies since so many can create additional ones on their own—"a sort of infinitely expanding federal bureaucracy." Michael D. Tanner, "The Real Impact of the New Health Care Law," 9 *Cato's Letter* (Fall 2010). It is hard to read the 2010 Act without concluding that its authors believed that in-

representatives to regulate every corner of medicine, insurance, and patient life. By one count the words "The Secretary shall" appears 1,563 times, each time empowering and directing rule-making and discretionary actions. The entire domain of health care covered is now subject to federal enactment, regulations, and agents. The end result is the creation of a bureaucratic regime with controls over all ordinary Americans and an elevation of rules, agents, and regulations unique in modern America.

Where Does This Lead? To Further Controls

Statutory and regulatory prolixity is a red flag warning of intellectual confusion. Dodd-Frank makes the same mistake in banking that the 2010 health care act makes for health financing. Whereas the enactments following the crises of the Great Depression and earlier ran to less than 32 pages, the Wall Street Reform and Consumer Protection Act (Dodd-Frank) runs 848 pages, calls for at least 243 rule-making procedures and 67 studies by at least ten separate federal agencies. The statutory and rule prolixity, and the discretion authorized to be exercised by countless bureaucrats implementing these – similar to the approach of the 2010 Act – represent Old Progressivism run riot.

The 2010 health care act appears designed to put us on a trajectory quite at odds with the limited and benign assurances of proponents. The duplicity of its salesmanship on costs, the secrecy of its congressional formulation, the legislative sleight of hand of its passage, and its neglect of the supply side of the health care equation while pumping up demand all suggest an ulterior purpose. What they

surance companies are the major impediment to health and that "the Secretary" can cure whatever ails the system and us by imposing regulations of a seemingly infinite sort.

appear to have wanted was single-payer or other total government takeover of health care financing.[40] Unable to get this outright, they created a reform bill that, while falling short, would create the conditions for a cost crisis such that complete government control becomes a seeming inevitability.[41]

Mandate Madness

There are alternatives to this course, alternatives that build upon individual responsibility and enhance choice rather than restrict it. Looking back to the recent past, it is easy to see that part of the reason for the historical explosion in costs is that government mandates and controls have restricted what the private employer-sponsored coverage universe can offer and what people can and cannot obtain. In a well-meaning effort to ensure more people have insurance, over the last few decades, government (primarily at the state level) has been incrementally imposing limits on

---

[40] Indeed, in a 2003 video interview when he was a relatively unknown Illinois state senator, Obama stated that he favored a single-payer universal health system for America. It is hardly surprising, therefore, that the 2010 Act took the turn towards government control that it did. And had the "public option" for insurance been included as the administration wanted, the slide into single-payer would have been accelerated even more.

[41] An irreverent but useful taxonomy divides the explanations and justifications put forth in support of larger government and greater regulation into three categories: bullshit (things said without concern for truth), horseshit (outright deceptions and lies), and chickenshit (regulations and interpretations to flummox the individual and enhance bureaucratic advantages). James A. Montanye, "Merdecracy," 15 *The Independent Review* at 295 (Fall 2010). Under this taxonomy, much of what was said by proponents of the 2010 Act fits the definition of bullshit, some horseshit. The result of the 2010 Act (as with the Dodd-Frank Act) is a whole lot of chickenshit.

medical underwriting through insurance mandates and controls—requirements that insurers not exclude listed conditions, marginal treatments, or high-risk persons from policies they issue. Forcing unwanted risks into the pool lowers costs for some but raises it for most. These mandates limit choices and force most people to be in pools that include risks (and attendant costs) they do not want to pay to be insured against.

One mandate or two would have minimal overall impact, but what does have enormous impact is the cumulative effect of numerous mandates, many of which simply respond to favored political constituencies and have no substantial medical purpose.

What are mandates, and how do they affect premiums? As defined by the Council for Affordable Health Insurance: "A health-insurance 'mandate' is a legislative requirement that an insurance company or health plan cover (or offer coverage for) common—but sometimes not so common—health care providers, benefits, and patient populations. They include: ...[naturopaths, morbid obesity treatment, wigs, chiropractors, podiatrists, massage therapists, mammograms, drug abuse treatment, dependent students, grandchildren, and so on]."[42] Rare in the 1960s, mandates have rapidly proliferated—more than 1,961 different state mandates were in place as of 2008—and "it's the cumulative effect that drives up the cost of coverage...when people can't afford coverage, they join the ranks of the uninsured."

In Massachusetts alone, instructive because of its adoption in 2006 of a system upon which much of the 2010 Act was patterned, a study "found that the state's most expensive insurance mandates cost patients more than $1 bil-

---

42 Bunce and Wieske, "Mandate Update," 2/8/2008, *WSJ*, at A17.

lion between July 2004 and July 2005."[43] With the 2010 Act extending mandates to every section of the country, this amount multiplies exponentially.

Most states also control insurance premiums and coverage. These controls often have pernicious and counterproductive effects. One example: responding to political pressure, in January 2010, Massachusetts' regulator rejected 235 of 274 requested premium increases in the individual market that the carriers involved (all nonprofits) claimed were needed to cover costs.[44] Victory for the consumer over the carriers? Hardly. Something has to give: either premiums are allowed to rise or soon Massachusetts has no carriers offering policies. (In fact, the next day all but one carrier stopped issuing policies, and the parties went to court, where the battle continued.) Either way, Massachusetts' policyholders are crucified on the cross of health care "reform."

The 2010 Act takes this process of increasing mandates and expanding the risk pool to the extreme: it almost completely eliminates medical underwriting (the pricing of risk) and the freedom people have hitherto enjoyed to choose pools of risk appropriate to their circumstances at prices they can afford.[45]

---

43 Turner, "The Failure of RomneyCare," 3/16/2010, *WSJ*.
44 "Health Insurers Sue to Raise Rates," 4/6/10, *Boston Globe*.
45 As the Democratic Senate summary explains: "Beginning in 2014, more significant insurance reforms will be implemented. Across individual and small group health insurance markets in all states, new rules will end medical underwriting and preexisting condition exclusions. Insurers will be prohibited from denying coverage or setting rates based on health status, medical condition, claims experience, genetic information, evidence of domestic violence, or other health-related factors. Premiums will vary only by family structure, geography, actuarial value, tobacco use, participation in a health promotion program, and age (by not more than three to one)." Democrats.Senate.Gov/Reform, (3/31/2010).

CHAPTER I: THE BUMBLING COLOSSUS IN HEALTH CARE

This process (mandated pool expansion) exemplifies the Regulatory Illusion at work. It rests on the assumption that if pools of insured are sufficiently opaque to the people who have to bear the costs of each successive mandate, they will not protest what they do not understand and can do nothing about, thus achieving the free lunch politicians desire. But as these mandates accumulate, costs explode; people start to notice. The predictable political response is to find the popular villain (the insurers) and force them to eat or reduce premium increases. But if premiums are controlled, insurers caught in the squeeze flee the market. The free lunch starts to be not so free at all, and the lunch gets smaller and smaller.

An example is the requirement that all insurers cover persons regardless of preexisting conditions. Where this has been tried, the results were not those desired. As Angela Braly, CEO of giant health insurer Wellpoint, Inc. recounts:

> In Maine, when guaranteed issue went into effect in 1993, there were eleven carriers in the individual market, now there are two: us and another company that would not be called in any circle an equivalent health insurance company. In Kentucky, forty-five insurers fled the state, with Wellpoint 'the last one standing until the state started in 1998 to repeal most of these regulations.'[46]

So the system of creeping mandates and controls hits a wall as costs escalate and insurers flee. The 2010 Act increases this process exponentially. Since the Regulatory Illusion is unrecognized, people have no idea what to do. The original impulse to benefit those with costly conditions results in increasingly hard times for all others.

---

46 Joe Rago, "A Wasted Opportunity," 2/7/2010, *WSJ*, quoting Angela Braly, CEO of Wellpoint, Inc.

The problem is how to maintain affordable coverage for the few with large and expensive needs while avoiding breaking the bank. The inevitable question is: do we turn to more government—perhaps government insurance as some suggest—on the theory that we are "in for a dime, in for a dollar" and that this response will achieve at last the goals we set out to achieve? Do we attempt to fine-tune what we have? Or do we turn away from mandates and controls and try to achieve these goals by reintroducing market forces? Is this even feasible? How do we begin to think about this issue?[47]

Was It Worth It? To Increase Coverage 10 Percent, We Imposed Costs, Taxes, and Government Controls on 100 Percent

In thinking this through, it is important to start with recognition that (according to the CMS actuary figures) even before the 2010 Act the vast majority (about 83 to 85 percent) of Americans had health insurance, half of those through their employers, about a quarter each from either Medicare or Medicaid and CHIP (children's health), and 10 percent in the individual market. Thus all the complexity, taxes, penalties, cost, regulations, commissions, agencies, and bureaucracies in the 2010 Act was to increase health insurance coverage from 83-85 percent of the population

---

[47] Some believe escalation of our health costs would disappear if only doctors were freed of fear of liability from unwarranted medical malpractice lawsuits. Were it only that easy. Unfortunately, even immediate elimination of all such lawsuits would only provide a one-time benefit to the cost problem, albeit a needed one. The stark imbalance of demand for services and limitations on supply, and the misplacement of incentives at the foundation of our present system, would guarantee ever-escalating costs regardless.

to 93 percent—at most a 10 percent gain—and for all that, falling short of the goal of universal coverage.[48]

To get a feel for how counterproductive is the rationale for this policy, let's look at the uninsured. Contrary to popular opinion, this 7 to 13 percent of the population was not and is not now left without basic health care. Nor is this population primarily poor by any definition. As discussed later, two-thirds choose to be uninsured because their health prospects cause them not to incur the cost of coverage. For those who are poor, there is Medicaid. The poor also have other ways of accessing health care. By federal law, anyone without insurance has access to emergency room treatment whenever they seek it.[49] In addition, state and federal laws require hospitals to provide charity care, and matching funds are available to those serving poor or uninsured populations.[50]

Some argue that these options fail to provide strict equality of access. The rich, better connected, better informed,

---

48 Chief Actuary Memo, at 3.
49 The Hill-Burton Act of 1946 first imposed this requirement in a limited form, but it was made universal and perpetual in the Public Health Service Act of 1975, 42 USC. Section 6A. All recipients of federal funds (virtually the universe of hospitals and clinics) must open their emergency facilities to all regardless of ability to pay. The unintended consequence of this law is that certain young, healthy persons decline coverage, secure that if the worst happens, the emergency room must admit them. This led to the "individual mandate" in the 2010 Act, forcing these potential free riders (if they don't pay their bills) into the insurance pool. The well-intentioned compounds its errors with the obnoxious—and stretches the Constitution to the breaking point in the process.
50 John C. Goodman, Gerald L. Musgrave, Devon M. Herrick, *Lives at Risk: Single-Payer National Health Insurance Around the World*, at 35 (Rowman and Littlefield 2004). This seminal study by three highly regarded economists is a foundational work for understanding single-payer systems.

smarter, find ways to get better doctors or treatments. But this is inevitable under any system (see single-payer discussion, Chapter III, *post*). Moreover, it is clearly true that the fundamental problem we have, before and after the 2010 Act, is not *access* to basic health care for the poor but the *costs* of health care to the non-poor, who bear the burden.[51]

Framing the issue in terms of percent of coverage hides this fact. While it is certainly true that improvements in access are needed, real reform would find a way to both improve access and lower costs while avoiding the trade-off of degeneration in service that inheres in the 2010 Act and, as will be seen, in single-payer systems.

Removing Patient Responsibility is the Common Denominator

Our failure to halt the increasing escalation of premiums and taxes associated with our health care programs is apparent whether one looks at public (Medicare and Medicaid) or private coverage. The common denominator is that *all* of the major means for health insurance coverage, private and public—employer, Medicare, Medicaid, and CHIP—lack significant patient payment responsibility. Without this, demand escalates. There is no systemic, countervailing incentive or means for restraining costs. Instead, we have created an incentive for cost-shifting to others or

---

51   The chief actuary describes the remaining 23 million uninsured as follows: "For the most part, these would be individuals with relatively low health care expenses for whom the individual or family insurance premium would be significantly in excess of any penalty and their anticipated health benefit value. In other instances, as happens currently, some people would not enroll in their employer plans or take advantage of the exchange opportunities even though it would be in their best financial interest to do so." Chief Actuary Memo, at 8.

curtailment of service, both harmful results. We are in a trap of our own devising.

Understanding how to extricate ourselves from the cost trap requires understanding how we got there. Since our cost problems began with the private employer-sponsored universe, which provides over 90 percent of private health insurance today, let's start there. This coverage is obtained from an employer and is no- or low-deductible (or low co-pay). Everything is covered, soup to nuts. The employee pays nothing or next to nothing at the time of service but pays a sum monthly in an amount disassociated from the individual's or family's actual costs or service choices.

This removes from the core of the system the individual's incentive to ferret out the best service at the lowest price; no matter what services we demand, our costs are the same. Nonetheless, we think this is the natural way of things, the way it should be. We think everyone should have this kind of coverage, that this should be the goal of public policy.

Guaranteed Coverage is Not Insurance

But even calling this kind of coverage "insurance" is misleading. Insurance is to protect against the *unexpected* (think home, auto, life)—protection against risk—not provision for the certain, routine, and predictable. Private, low- or no-deductible group employer-based health coverage in America is not really insurance at all, but a kind of guaranteed coverage, far removed from historical notions of what insurance is all about. The public discussion confuses everyone when these two very different concepts are conflated. Insurance allows the insured to balance cost and risk. Guaranteed coverage implies a form of tax and invites the recipient into the Free Lunch Illusion, where services are free and costs are invisible. Is it any wonder people continue to demand it and then are shocked when taxes and premiums inevitably skyrocket?

There is no doubt all this describes quite a mess. It is worth asking, how did we get into it?

CHAPTER II:
The Bumbling Colossus Begins

1. The Start of the Health Care Regulatory Fallacy in WW II Tax Policy

To understand how our present health care dilemma came to pass, we must go back to WW II. To avoid wartime wage/price controls, enterprising employers seeking to attract workers and get around Office of Price Administration maximum wage rules offered to pay for their health insurance directly instead of paying the worker an amount over the wage limit that he could use to buy his own coverage. (The employer was indifferent whether the money went to wages or deductible health cost.) This subterfuge didn't change the economics of wages; it was an accounting ploy, so that the employee wasn't credited with the income directly but got the same benefit without being taxed.

Perhaps buckling to wartime realities, the IRS played along, ruling anomalously that an employer paying his employee's premiums was not income to the employee—although such a ruse would not be tolerated anywhere else in the tax code. After the war, Congress codified the anomaly.[52]

Thus began the Regulatory Illusion in health care. The natural result of this lapse in tax integrity was to create an incentive for employees and their unions to press for more and more tax-free benefits to be shoved under the health insurance umbrella, until gradually we reached today's situation where everyone thinks it perfectly normal to have virtually *all* their health costs paid by the employer-sponsored plan. This tax-favored subsidy to the presently employed creates exactly the wrong incentives—promoting unnecessary tests, treatments, and exams—and exactly the wrong disincentives—promoting ignorance of costs and separating patients from any sense of cost/benefit for the services they need.

It also ushers in a huge misallocation of resources. It drives up demand, denudes patients of power of choice, freezes people into jobs because coverage is not portable should they leave, and the unemployed and self-employed are effectively discriminated against since they lack the tax favoritism and pay higher premiums and costs. Costs continually escalate, forcing cuts in coverage and services. Patients lacking control over costs or power over services feel like they are in "NHS light."

And it is not free. Economists tell us that wages would be higher by a roughly equivalent amount if the employer ceased providing the health insurance benefit.[53] Apart from the tax effect, there is no net benefit to the employee

---

52 "Employee Health Insurance—The History and Economic Theory of Employer-Provided Health Insurance," medicine.jrank.org. See also Bridger Mitchell and Charles E. Phelps, "National Health Insurance: Some Costs & Effects of Mandated Employee Coverage," *Journal of Political Economy*, 84:3 (June 1976).
53 Ibid.

from having the employer provide the coverage. Without the employer-provided coverage, he or she would have more cash wages to spend on equivalent health insurance if that is what is wanted. Moreover, the employee would be in charge of the decision over what kind or coverage and benefits to pay for given his or her needs. If health savings accounts are available, the employer-provided coverage system is a net loss to the employee, since *all* health costs paid from an HSA receive a tax benefit.

So our present system of soup-to-nuts employer-supplied coverage was not the inevitable result of rational policy choices or untrammeled free market forces. Rather, it was the inadvertent side effect of government responses to temporary WW II labor shortages.

Compounding the error, when Medicare and Medicaid were passed in the mid-1960s, Congress modeled them on the same all-expense-covered soup-to-nuts approach that the private employer-based system had morphed into. The minimal hospital deductible and service/physician deductible were added later to contain costs [54] but are at best only partial solutions. Similar efforts to control costs by price reductions on providers [55] have been counterproductive, reducing their desire to service government-supported patients and shifting costs to others, particularly those in the individual market.[56]

The 2010 Act continues this train of costly, wrong-footed legislation, expanding Medicare eligibility far up the income levels and regulating providers in all aspects,

---

54 42 USC. 1395e.
55 42 USC. 1395f & g.
56 See, e.g., Daniel P. Kessler, "Cost Shifting in California Hospitals: What is the Effect on Private Payers?" California Foundation for Commerce and Education, (Stanford GBS, June 6, 2007) ("Cost shifting from Medicare and MediCal is substantial").

including, most dramatically, pricing and coverage. With the 2010 Act, the Regulatory Illusion and its free lunch corollary have reached a new high-water mark. Today the entire health insurance universe, government and private—excepting only the 10 percent in the individual market who buy their own—is an open-ended, largely cost-shifted regime in which almost no one pays substantially or directly for the health care they receive and everyone expects someone else to do so.

The Regulatory Illusion Seduces Proponents With the Promise of a Free Lunch

To recap, the Regulatory Illusion this history reveals started with the WW II tax ruling declaring employer payments for their employees' health care not to be income to the employee. This appeared to unions and employees as a free lunch, where they got health benefits but were not taxed for receiving them. This seductive impression caused our entire system to shift from individual and family-based policies to employer-provided coverage.

Of course the free lunch was an illusion. Not only, in time, did the employee receive lower pay commensurate with the cost of the untaxed benefit, but the shift tied employees to their employers and, by encouraging no-deductible, soup-to-nuts policies, unmoored incentives for cost containment. The resulting cost explosion then seemed inexplicable, and people looked all around for demons to vilify.

The obvious demons are the nearest at hand—insurers. Easy political targets since they are already heavily regulated for solvency, politicians and media jump on the bandwagon. But insurers' profit margins don't allow them to meet the demands without either exiting the market or declaring bankruptcy. This dead-end approach ultimately fails its objective, and costs continue to escalate.

We Kissed the Market Good-Bye Without Even Knowing It

These developments—principally tax favoritism for the employed resulting in widespread low-deductible coverage, and politically imposed mandates limiting choice—have brought about an enormous unintended consequence. In essence, there is no longer a real health care market. Someone other than the patient who consumes the service or product actually pays for it—either government (i.e., the taxpayer), or insurance companies (i.e., other premium payers).

Nowhere in our present system is there a built-in cost corrective such as markets provide. There is no information on relative pricing and costs, no effective competition among providers for patients' services, nothing resembling a normal market in health care. The covered person goes to the doctor or hospital and gets the service, and the bill goes elsewhere. Without adequate skin in the game, the patient/consumer lacks the ability to act like a normal consumer, maximizing personal cost/benefit and social gain. Our health care system therefore provides an illusion of security and protection but rests on an ever-deteriorating bed of sand as skyrocketing costs threaten the system's ability to survive.

The 2010 Act not only failed to address this problem, it increased it and upped the ante. Expanding Medicaid to cover ever more up the income ladder, as the 2010 Act does, reduces the number of uninsured but disregards the basic fallacy of the system: patients lack incentives to match costs with benefits, and no one else (doctors, hospitals, government, etc) does either.

Instead of creating a system where all are better off, the 2010 Act purports to shift serious burdens from one group, those uninsured whose personal cost-benefit causes them to prefer not to pay for insurance, most often younger workers, to seniors, who are no longer in a position to alter their circumstances to improve them.[57] Added to this, younger workers stand to be hit not only with the larger costs of an aging population today but the likelihood of large future debt burdens to deal with as the cost of the system continually escalates.

This "rob Peter to pay Paul" approach raises serious moral questions. Imposing the Siamese twins of costs and regulation on everyone to provide enhanced benefits mainly for a population the bulk of which chooses not to insure, and harming seniors to get there, lacks clear or persuasive morality. It is based on a fallacious premise to begin with—that our economy is a pie that can simply be rearranged with bigger slices for one group at the expense of another without harm to the whole, ignoring the critical role of incentives and disincentives.

Rather than enact a policy based upon a fallacious economic model promising failure that harms a large group of the relatively impotent among us in order to benefit others with often questionable claims upon our sense of social justice, how much better would it be to create a health care system in which *all* are better off based upon an economic

---

[57] See, e.g., John C. Goodman, "How Seniors Will Pay for ObamaCare" ("In many areas, Medicare Advantage enrollees will lose about one-third of their health insurance benefits. The cuts will finance new subsidies for younger people."), 9/23/2010, *WSJ*.

model that is proven over time and geography to actually work?

The existence of a system that allows *both* Peter and Paul to prosper and be health-secure brings into sharp relief why many see the recent enactment as reckless and immoral. What follows describes just such a better way, explains why it is better, and explains why the recently enacted alternative takes us down a path littered with failures.

But first let's deal with some issues that obscure the view.

2. The False Conflict Between Morality and Economics

Some politicians and academics (as well as ordinary citizens) see the absence of a real market in health care as a good thing; they hold a moral vision of health care as beyond economics, where everyone deserves the best in health treatment regardless of ability to pay. They believe the view that health care is a market to be understood in economic terms to be fundamentally wrong—leading to a world in which someone without resources struck by a bus is left to die. They rely upon a simple morality—everyone should get health care when needed regardless—and money is deemed irrelevant to the matter. Costs, in this view, can be managed by taxes and controls.

Usually they justify this deviation from sound economics by relying upon the weak and long-discredited view that health care is a "market failure" (discussed later) where the rules of the game have to be reinvented, allowing a kind of free play time for the health care dreamer. Hobbled by anti-market bias or belief, they can imagine only various forms of nationalization—government control of the market and taxpayer funding of services—and look outside the US for models to draw on.

But the division between morality and economics is a false dilemma. Not only are there far fewer in a market economy who lack resources and might have to lie abandoned, but it is that economy which provides the income and capital to provide for those in need so that they never have to. There is a moral illusion fostered by those critics who focus on the person in distress without recognition that the market system has enabled many to lift themselves *out of* distress. The question to be asked is whether the imposition of government regulation and controls that socialists and many progressives insist upon in the name of morality has the unanticipated consequence of reducing the ability of the market to benefit the many, undermining the very goals for which the government intervention is undertaken. To borrow Marx's phrase, there is no morality in the equality of universal "immiserization."

Fundamentally, we cannot avoid the need to understand and deal with the realities of economics. Avik Roy points out that even if we treated health care as a universal government-supported right:

> Modern health care is an expensive commodity. So even if we agree that it is unjust to deny some citizens access to it, we must still recognize that money is limited—and figure out the best way to allocate care. The moral conviction, therefore, leads back to inherently economic questions, because the problem of allocating a scarce resource is by definition an economic problem—indeed, *the* economic problem.[58]

---

58   Avik Roy, "Health Care and the Profit Motive," 3 *National Affairs*, at 47 (Spring 2010).

CHAPTER II: THE BUMBLING COLOSSUS BEGINS

There are basically only two ways to constrain costs in health care, as in any other industry. One is government control of prices or the other factors of production such as hospital charges, doctor fees, drug prices, testing and laboratory work, treatment facilities. The other is some form of market arrangement based upon the disciplining power of competition. Both approaches carry unpleasant shortcomings or trade-offs that have to be addressed; which system best suits the needs of the public depends upon which delivers the best outcome. Most countries have some mixed form, where government tells some or all the players what they can charge and for what service, and competition is allowed within those parameters.

The problem all face is how to reconcile the desire for universality—that all persons have available to them some level of care—with the trade-off such expansion brings in terms of higher costs or declining levels of service, or both. Idealism is unlimited, but resources are limited, and no one has yet figured out how to achieve universality with cost discipline and flourishing service levels. As will be seen, this can be achieved, but the system we now have will have to be modified.

The Price Control Option Leads to Rationing, Queues, and Lower Quality Service

Price controls and other forms of government intrusion are designed to achieve such benefits but have proven not to deliver and to have predictable negative effects. Government can tell doctors that they can't charge more than X for procedure Y, but if these rules are not circumvented services will be curtailed, existing doctors will leave (or form "concierge" practices), and fewer qualified persons will undertake the burdensome and expensive training needed to enter the profession.

The 2010 Act already shows this effect: according to an Athena Health poll, 66 percent of doctors are considering dropping out of Medicare and Medicaid (under which they already receive on average 81 percent and 56 percent of private fees). As government squeezes more, consolidation among providers increases in self-defense, bureaucracy grows, queues form, investment lags, the wealthy and powerful find ways to get to the front of the line, and if they can, people cross borders for service elsewhere.[59]

Popular focus on the number of uninsured deflects attention from the real issue of how to realign the system's incentives so costs are normalized and contained and people can afford reasonable, decent care. One uninsured is one too many, so whether there are 41 million or 52 million as the 2010 Census tabulated is less important than forging a structure of coverage that allows everyone to have access at reasonable cost.

We know many among the uninsured are there by choice to avoid the high cost of coverage,[60] and that by federal law everyone without coverage nonetheless has access to emergency care. So while one can cavil about the quality of emergency rooms and the desire for preventive care, the big issue is not really the bus victim without means (Medicaid pays his bills) but the pressure that the premium- and taxpaying public feels making coverage increasingly unaf-

---

59 As noted later, exactly this outcome is occurring under Canada's budget/price control regime.
60 Goodman, Musgrave, and Herrick, *Lives at Risk; Single-Payer National Health Insurance Around the World,* at 35 (Rowman and Littlefield, 2004)

fordable and crowding out other necessities and public and private priorities.

Fundamentally, to avoid excess taxation or rationing and its concomitant harms, any remedy for our present system including the 2010 Act must deal with the underlying problem creating the cost explosion; the patient lacks information and incentive to shop for products and services and be the target of competitive forces on providers.

3. Applying the Microscope: Why Are We Unable to Control Costs?

In a nutshell, our problem is that the person responsible for *deciding and ordering* the good or service (the patient) is not the same as the person or entity *paying* for the good or service (government in the case of Medicare and Medicaid, and for others employer-sponsored, all-inclusive, low-deductible group health insurance). This divorce causes the patient to cede authority and responsibility to the doctors, most of whom act unaware of and unconstrained by cost—indeed are often driven by fear of malpractice awards to recommend additional treatment and tests or the *more expensive* alternative regardless of lack of demonstrated cost/benefit advantage.

Delegating responsibility for the economics of care to doctors asks them to do something they are untrained to do. Their training is in science and medicine; they are not economists and can't play that role. The insurance carriers and the government, which do the actual disbursing (on behalf of taxpayers and premium-payers), are constrained by politics and lack of desire to create waiting lines. Their efforts to limit costs are ineffective, especially given the interest groups created around present arrangements.[61]

Thus we have destroyed the one thing that promotes cost/benefit consideration—the incentive the patient/purchaser has to shop for service and product. What we need is a system that creates this incentive while affording universal coverage and without disrupting the strengths of the system we have.[62] To do this, we need to reimagine a system of universal coverage based upon a true insurance model with substantial individual responsibility and not the "guaranteed coverage" where others pay and choose for us, which we have fallen prey to.

Don't Separate Decision-Making from Financial Responsibility

Where else in life other than health care does *someone else* directly pay for something you want? When I go to the grocery and buy food, I decide and I pay. Same for gasoline,

---

[61] For an interesting review of the politics of health care reform through the last century, see Theodore R. Marmor, *Understanding Health Care Reform* (Yale, 1994)

[62] Incentives and disincentives are key to understanding and creating effective policy, in health care as in other areas of the economy. For example, marginal tax reductions have been shown to directly add to economic growth (and tax increases to subtract) because of the extra incentive effect of consumer optimism. Harvard economics professor Robert J. Barro has run the numbers: "Reagan cut the average marginal income tax rate to 21.8 percent in 1988 from 29.4 percent in 1981. The GDP growth rate between 1982 and 1989 was a strong 4.3 percent per year, and I estimate that 0.6 percent per year of that seven-year growth came from the tax cuts. Similarly, George W. Bush cut the average marginal rate to 21.1 percent in 2003 from 24.7 percent in 2000. The GDP growth rate between 2001 and 2005 (including negative effects from the 2001 recession) was a respectable 2.7 percent per year, and I estimate that 0.5 percent per year of that four-year growth reflected the tax cuts." Barro, "Obamanomics Meets Incentives," 9/14/2010, *WSJ*.

housing, communication and Internet services, entertainment, sports, transportation—the list is endless. The only areas that come readily to mind for which this is not the case are 1) public education and 2) health. As for the first, Milton Friedman introduced the idea of school vouchers many years ago in *Capitalism and Freedom*, published in 1962. His simple observation was that tax-based school funding could be routed through parents, not bureaucrats. Believing people prosper better under conditions of freedom, he advocated school vouchers as a way to introduce competition among schools while providing universal access.

The same principle applies to health care. Public funding in the form of vouchers for those needing it can be routed through individuals, not government bureaucrats, given a legal structure such as health savings accounts to do so: unlike with public school vouchers, only those in the lower income brackets would be eligible for public funding. All others fund their own accounts with tax-free dollars. A simple incentive change with great positive effects.

This much is a fairly obvious answer—returning patients to their historic role of deciding their own care and costs. So why is this simple idea so hard for some to accept? One is tempted to look at the self-interest of entrenched groups and the blinders of anti-market skeptics. It is also hard to resist the suspicion that taking responsibility away from people, as the 2010 Act's expansion of complete subsidized benefits up the income scale does, reflects a belief by proponents that people are not competent or smart enough to deal with their own health care financing. But for generations, people did so, guided by the recommendations and thinking of doctors and professionals they trusted and applying the financial resources they wished to meet their overall needs and priorities. Since the bulk of health care costs arise in the earliest and latest stages of life, individual decision responsibility is particularly appropriate.

Certainly putting corporate and government agents in charge treats people like children. This assumption of incompetence is reinforced by current laws and practice—particularly open-ended low- or no-deductible government programs for the poor and elderly, and tax laws favoring the spread of low- or no-deductible employer-supplied coverage—that conceal costs and information from patients and doctors and turns them into stupid purchasers.

Are We Up To It?

Advocates of government control look at the mass of stupid purchasers and say, "See, it's too complex. People are incapable of figuring out their own advantage." Others look at it and say, "This assumption that people are incompetent is arrogant. People are able to shop everywhere else in life, including equally complex services and products (think computers, cars, cell phones, lawyers), so why not here, where they themselves are the subject? What they need are information sources, like a Consumer Reports for medicine. Let's change things so they have them."

A system that turns people into stupid consumers is self-defeating. Like any other simple or complex buying decision, the customer/patient is the *only* person who can weigh his or her own preferences against costs. Should you pay $100,000 for a difficult operation with serious side effects that promises perhaps an additional 10 percent benefit—and is more likely to fail? Should you have a new treatment with 20 percent greater chance of benefit but at 800 percent the cost? At your age, do you really want the latest high-tech innovation? Do you want to raise a child with total permanent incapacity, which an expensive operation affords a 30 percent chance of allowing?

Delegating this responsibility of weighing costs and benefits to anonymous others robs the system of the main force for controlling costs and achieving the best outcomes. This poses a dramatic challenge to those who advocate government control and underscores the potential in a "patient-centered" approach by which tax and subsidy policies are aimed at providing the individual with the means to purchase his or her own care. The example of shopping for an MRI with which we began this inquiry illuminates the path.

4. The Power of Competition to Constrain Costs Without Impairing Service

Assuming we are up to it, will the market do the rest? A pure market system based upon individual responsibility alone leaves some people who are unable to meet the financial needs of adequate health care outside the market. This has proven to be an unacceptable outcome in all Western developed nations. In response, most have undertaken to nationalize in some form or other the arena of health care, including price controls.

But this is an unwarranted and unnecessary overreaction; no need exists to go to extremes where limited interventions do the trick. Why rob the entire population of benefits just to help a few? Both in theory and in practice, price controls harm everyone – they lead to declining levels of service, in the usual form of waiting lists or underfunding of facilities and other negative effects. Yet without price controls, nationalized systems swiftly and ineluctably veer towards bankruptcy as costs overwhelm and taxes slow growth.

Two Everyday Examples: Transportation and Communication

So what does constrain costs without price control's damaging side effects? The facts show, time and again, that allowing competitive freedom of choice and the elimination of intrusive regulation and government control does just that. Imagine an American health insurance market free of the existing prolix mandates where companies are free (under conventional state insurance department supervision of solvency and actuary soundness) to create coverage and policies, and people are free to choose among them according to their best judgment of needs and resources. Under this (deregulated) world, would average premium costs decline without loss of service quality? In other words, how does deregulation fare?

We can look to our own experience for answers, and the results are striking. We have right at hand several clear everyday examples of successful de-control, in the Carter-era deregulation of transportation – railroads, airlines and trucking – and in the Reagan-era breakup of the AT&T monopoly.

With airlines prior to 1978, the CAB controlled routes, entry, and prices. Flying was a luxury. Today, after deregulation, and despite fears of slipshod practices and mayhem in the skies, ticket prices are similar in absolute terms to what they were then, after thirty years of inflation. What was transportation for the few who could afford it has become transport for everyone, without loss of timeliness or safety. Average cost per flight mile in 1969 (adjusted for inflation) was $0.34; in 2009 it was $0.14. Fatal accidents per 100,000 departures were 1.3 in 1969; in 2009 they were 0.098—in other words, far better on both counts.⁶³

With telecom, statistics are unnecessary to describe the extraordinary benefits that the breakup of the government-sponsored monopoly held by AT&T brought, since we enjoy them every day. In 1982, AT&T chose to settle two antitrust suits brought against it by MCI Communications Inc. and the Department of Justice by divesting itself of its government-sponsored monopoly over phone lines and service (the "Baby Bells"). This opened up telecom to competition and led to a revolution in communication, Internet business and shopping, mobile phone/connectivity devices, etc—a revolution in which every child revels and many adults find of never-ending perplexity. Long distance rates, formidable barriers for earlier generations, dropped to near zero. Today it is hard to imagine the horse and buggy world in which telecom would have remained had AT&T chosen to keep its government-supported monopoly.

These familiar examples—telecom and air travel—reveal the power of competition in free markets to drive costs lower while maintaining essential service, safety, and quality. It is hard to look at these examples and argue that deregulation and competitive free markets aren't powerful forces advancing benefits to ordinary people.⁶⁴

---

63 Scott McCartney, "The Golden Age of Flight," 7/22/2010, *WSJ*, citing ATA figures. The story for the other deregulated modes - rail, truck, bus, barge, etc - is the same. See, e.g., Berndt et al, "Mergers, Deregulation and Cost Savings in the U.S. Rail Industry", nber.org/papers/w3749 (Nat. Bureau Econ. Research 1991).
64 The financial crisis of 2008 brought forth numerous media and academic views to the effect that deregulation and free markets brought on the problems and are dinosaurs whose usefulness is limited and whose time has run. As explained in more detail later, the exact

Considering Single-Payer Systems and Their Market Failure Hypothesis

Some question the relevance to health care of experience drawn from elsewhere in the economy, arguing health care is inherently different and requires a separate analysis. These people usually rest upon claims that health care is not a market subject to the usual demand and supply constraints but is one where information is asymmetrical and unavailable, so patients cannot act as people do in other areas of the economy. Their views usually fall under the rubric of market failure, and it is so pervasive among health care experts advocating forms of national health care financing that one can read through entire tracts without finding other than a fleeting reference to the subject and hardly ever any reference to highly pertinent experience with previous efforts to nationalize or control by government agency or rules the operation of markets in these other areas.[65]

As we shall see in Part B, this failure puts blinders on their analysis and weighing of options and leads them ten-

---

opposite is the truth for the financial crisis. In fact, contrary to popular wisdom, we have few areas of actual deregulation. Except in several notable areas of pronounced success, including airlines, trucking, railroads, oil, and natural gas, the period from 1970 to 2008 saw an *increase* in the regulatory state, not its diminution. How do we know? For starters, look at the volume of new regulations in the pages of the Federal Register (the bible of the Regulatory State), and the number of new regulatory hires by the federal government over that period. They increased under all administrations except the Reagan period. For all the shouting, there has been steady regulatory creep since the 1960s. See, e.g., David R. Henderson, "Against Regulations," 2 *Hoover Digest* at 48 (Spring 2009). The need for deregulation at all levels of government is as acute today as ever.

65 See, e.g., Theodore R. Marmor, *Understanding Health Care Reform*, (Yale, 1994).

CHAPTER II: THE BUMBLING COLOSSUS BEGINS

dentiously to overlook or minimize failures or shortcomings in the nationalized or government-controlled systems they admire. Treating economics as just one of a number of approaches to health care systems is like treating Darwinian natural selection as just one of many approaches to evolution; yes, there are other approaches, but disregarding the power of natural selection puts one's analysis and recommendations at sea and outside the most fruitful area of inquiry.

Before getting to the best solution to the problems of cost escalation and service decline—unleashing the power of markets and individual responsibility in a voucher regime—it is useful to take a look at the solution most often offered as the best alternative to our present hodgepodge of government control and competition, the various forms of single-payer or other nationalized systems. It is this comparison that most health care policy analysts make in recommending that America adopt such changes, so it behooves us to look first at that alternative.

The question is, are there approaches to single-payer systems that can achieve the goals of quality care for all at reasonable cost?

The following is a brief look at this question. It does not purport to be exhaustive but is focused on bottom-line realities in countries most often touted as models for America that have adopted some form of national health long enough to allow conclusions to be drawn. The answer appears clear: all single-payer or other nationalized systems share similar defects along similar lines.

If you think health care is expensive now, just wait until it's free.

P. J. O'ROURKE

CHAPTER III:
The Single-Payer Mirage: How Government-Controlled Health Care Hurts the Very Public it is Intended to Protect

1. **The Naked Truth: Unless Changed, the 2010 Act Leads to Government-Controlled Medicine**

   The first question to address, before getting to the international experience, is whether the 2010 Act represents the natural stopping point for government intervention—the *end* of the process of intervention, falling well short of nationalization—or merely a way station along the way to more complete government control. We have touched on this before, concluding that the designers of the Act probably saw their creation as a point along the trajectory towards a single-payer system. There are additional reasons to see it this way.

   Because it is unable to contain cost growth, the 2010 Act, on top of our present system, creates the conditions for further government controls, especially price controls. How do we know? Look at the experience of single-payer countries. Leading observers of Canadian and European single-payer systems, sympathetic to the direction of the 2010 Act, criticize it precisely because it fails to "fully embrace the central lesson of international cost control experience. Effective cost control requires strong governmental leadership to set targets or caps for spending in the various sectors of medical care (hospitals, pharmaceutical, and physicians), either directly or through insurers."[66]

These observers deride as fantasy whatever cost control mechanisms exist in the 2010 Act and state unequivocally that, under that Act, "if medical costs are to be controlled, no substitute exists for constraining prices and capping expenditures." Their criticism of the 2010 Act is not that it provides for too much government control, but *not enough*. Their recommendation: nationalize the doctors and hospitals into great bargaining units under government budgetary control as the only way costs can be contained in a government-run health system. Anything else in a government-controlled health world, they point out, creates only "the illusion of painless cost control."

So no matter how it was packaged for political consumption, without changing direction completely, the 2010 Act leads inexorably to extensive further central government interference in the health market—prices, products, entry—precisely the features (as discussed later) long demonstrated to harm.

As with the formulation of the 2010 Act itself, this progression is concealed by most politicians, who can't

---

66 Marmor, Oberlander, and White, "The Obama Administration's Options for Health Care Cost Control: Hope versus Reality," *Annals of Internal Medicine*, 3/3/09.

admit to it. Indeed, the *New York Times* reported that Mr. Obama informed a group of "top business leaders" at the Business Roundtable that he is "an ardent believer in the free market" and his programs are not "big government socialism."[67] But words are one thing, deeds another; the truth may have been better put by one of *The New Yorker's* writers, who admitted to less beneficent aims, stating that "the purpose is to further redistribute income by putting health care further under government control, and in the process making the middle class more dependent on government. As the party of government, Democrats will benefit over the long run."[68]

Serious doubt exists whether, if the question were openly put, the American public or any substantial part of it would freely agree to place themselves under the extensive regime of government controls which the proponents of the 2010 Act created. Nonetheless, let us move now to an examination of the case for single-payer health care, and see if the claims made for it hold up to experience.

2. Analyzing the Case for Single-Payer Health Financing

A single-payer system is defined as "a universal coverage plan under which the government collects funds for health insurance and has a uniform plan for everyone in a given state or nation... The arrangements effectively eliminate private health insurance for basic coverage. Proponents believe it is the best way to reduce substantially

---

67 Peter Baker, "Obama Rejects Criticism of Agenda as Socialism," *N.Y. Times*, 2/24/2010. This was certainly untrue as to health care as pointed out above.
68 "Confessions of an ObamaCare Backer," 11/10/09, *WSJ*.

the rise in national health costs."[69] Canada is geographically the closest example, but Britain's NHS also fits the definition. Differences among these systems lie in the degree of control over pricing and service, with the NHS having almost complete control, and Canada's "Medicare" allowing the most choice. Under both, however, government sets budgets or prices for care at all levels and dictates what is covered and influences how it is delivered. It also provides all the funds, and patients none. Indeed, this is one of the system's goals and proudest points of advocacy.

The case for single-payer or government control rests on the belief that it is the only way to provide universal coverage and access—health care for all—while also containing costs to some level society deems acceptable. Proponents of single-payer systems rightfully extol the achievement of universality; everyone is covered and no one lacks at least the theoretical ability to call upon society to meet all ordinary and necessary health needs.

The problem comes in the fact that putting government in charge of pricing of course means political pressures dictate budgets, remuneration, what is covered and how it is treated, and investment into the factors of production—hospitals, clinics, physicians, etc. Individual choice over what to cover and how much to pay for it is lost or only allowed outside the system, if at all. This trade-off is justified as necessary to achieve universality. But as will be seen,

---

[69] Theodore R. Marmor, *Understanding Health Care Reform*, at 267 (Yale, 1994). Yale Professor Marmor has long been one of this country's leading proponents of a single-payer system like Canada's. He was the recipient of a five-year grant from the Canadian government for teaching and research on health care. His publications are relied upon here as representative of the arguments of single-payer advocates.

CHAPTER III: THE SINGLE-PAYER MIRAGE

this claim is false; alternative systems that preserve patient choice can also achieve universality.

Exhibit number one for proponents of single-payer systems is the large relative amount of gross domestic product (GDP) absorbed by health care expenditures in the US. Whereas single-payer systems from Japan to Britain to Western Europe spend on average about 9 percent of GDP on health care, the US spends 16 percent, and the rate of increase in the US far exceeds that in the other countries.[70] One proponent points out that "Canada's universal health insurance, a program administered by the ten provinces… manages to insure all Canadians for all 'ordinary and necessary' medical care, while spending about 30 percent less per capita than we do."[71]

The argument, therefore, is that we spend too much for what we get, and wastefully at that. It is certainly true that America's present quasi-socialized system forces evergreater increases in health care costs and that this is indefensible. But relative percentage of GDP spent on health care by various countries is at best an indirect and ambiguous measure of the virtues of relative systems of financing health care. It does not reckon any of the other costs and negative effects ushered in by the controls these other countries must insist upon.

As for waste, certainly that exists; this objection, however, is always made in competitive systems without recognition of the advantages duplication can bring. It is wasteful to have so much capacity to make cars. It is wasteful to have competing telecom providers building out wires and tow-

---

70 Bruce Bartlett, "Health Care: Costs and Reform—How we stack up against other OECD nations," (Forbes.com 07/03/09).
71 Theodore R. Marmor, *Understanding Health Care Reform*, at 2-3, 11.

ers throughout the countryside. But we are benefited by all that in better service and lower costs.

Also, as a generally wealthier society, Americans have a greater "taste" for health care, particularly high-cost, cutting edge technologies, and we are willing to spend more at the margin.[72] A richer society has more to spend, including on health care. America also probably outspends other countries on televisions, cars, and gourmet food, but no one would complain that this somehow justifies government dictating consumer tastes in those areas. Raw measures of consumption do not get at the drivers of unnecessary costs or reveal what underlying problems can best be corrected, or how.

Thus the issue is not simply costs as a percentage of GDP but whether the system for health care contains within it the ability to minimize costs while maintaining or enhancing service. As will be shown, single-payer systems do not.

Exhibit number two in the single-payer case is to contrast health outcomes in the US and elsewhere. The argument made is that you can get the same or better outcomes for less cost. Life expectancy and infant mortality are two areas where the US is seen as lagging many other countries; although the US has gained considerably since 1960, for example, other OECD (Organization for Economic Cooperation and Development) countries have exceeded our gains.[73]

Cross-national health outcome statistics have to be taken with a large grain of salt, however, both those favoring the US and those reflecting adversely. Especially notorious for creating misleading comparisons is the World Health

---

72 Goodman, Musgrave, and Herrick, *Lives at Risk*, at 6.
73 Bruce Bartlett, "Health Care: Costs and Reform," (Forbes.com 07/03/09)

CHAPTER III: THE SINGLE-PAYER MIRAGE

Organization, which "ranks" countries' health outcomes but includes political biases for socialized systems. Certain areas of health care may show well while related other areas don't; the example of Cuba discussed later—WHO ranks it number one in the world in doctor/patient ratio—is an egregious case in point. Despite the WHO plaudits, you don't see the world lining up for Cuban health care.

It is hard to capture the whole picture in selected tables and charts. For example, one of the reasons our infant mortality comparison lags is that fully one-third of ours comes in low birth-weight babies—the very existence of whom is due to superior technology and care. Both infant mortality and life expectancy track closer to genetic and cultural factors than to health care availability or quality.[74] Health care is only one factor amidst a welter of social, cultural, economic, and political tensions and differences.

One obvious contrast is the fact the US sports a hugely heterogeneous population with different attitudes and conditions while most OECD countries are relatively homogeneous. Many OECD countries spent a lot of resources and several world wars trying to eliminate their ethnic diversity. Our heritage as a nation of immigrants still casts a long shadow. The bottom line is that the case for single-payer systems based on health outcomes is caged with difficulties.

Another point of comparison with America that single-payer advocates use is the relative level of administrative costs. Pointing to Canada, for example, one such advocate notes, "There are no complex eligibility tests or complicated definitions of insured services. Administrative costs, as a consequence, are negligible by American standards."[75] First of all, as discussed later, such statements ignore

---

74   Goodman, Musgrave, and Herrick, *Lives at Risk*, at 49-58.
75   Theodore R. Marmor, *Understanding Health Care Reform*, at 186.

critical cost factors that are buried or lost in public reporting systems, and that if captured reveal public administrative costs to exceed those of private insurance companies. And while everyone agrees that a world without administrative costs would be delightful, administrative costs are not all negatives; sorting out false claims and ascertaining risks, for example, are mainstays of any insurance scheme that entails some costs. Eliminating fraud sifting shifts that function to public authorities or burdens other policyholders, and eliminating criteria for inclusion, while advancing equality at one level, destroys it on another; everyone is thrown into the same bucket insofar as risks are concerned. This means people are forced to pay for other people's risky lifestyle behavior, for example, which is a huge driver of increasing costs. Those who work hard to maintain weight or train themselves into good physical condition are forced to pay for the obese and unconditioned. Those who stay off narcotic drugs or high-inducing chemicals pay for those who don't, and so on.

Covering such lifestyle conditions harms both sides, reducing the incentive to alter harmful life choices, introducing moral hazard. The question with administrative costs is not just their level but also their function; are they appropriate to what they are supposed to be doing? In this regard, for-profit insurers have an advantage on not-for-profits, since the drive for profit focuses attention on reducing those costs that can be cut to achieve profit, and the fear of losing competitive advantage counsels against cutting costs just for the sake of it without regard to service.

Single-payer advocates urge other grounds to favor their system in addition to percentage of GDP, health outcomes, and administrative costs. These include: access to technology, cost containment, better overall quality, greater efficiency, better equity, better preventive care, curtailment of wasteful treatment, and expense. On close examination, none of these have been found to hold water.[76] In fact, the nature of single-payer systems requires unhappy trade-offs in quality to meet political restraints on costs.

Single-Payer Advocates Versus the American Individualist Tradition

Overall, it is hard to avoid the feeling that single-payer advocates tend to look at their favored system with rose-colored glasses, minimizing difficulties and negatives, while donning their horned skull caps for market-oriented approaches. Part of this is that they evince a more Euro-centric friendly attitude towards government bureaucracy and regulatory involvement in everyday life. Although ancient history to some, America was founded in revolt against government meddling in the pursuit by individuals of their economic life (remember the Stamp Act and Boston Tea Party), political life (faraway Parliament imposing laws), and religious life (prerevolutionary New England and Southern town governments were joined to the Congregational and Anglican Churches, respectively).

In all these areas, individual choice and freedom emerged as the primary virtue, superior to—indeed,

---

76 For a detailed examination of each of these grounds as well as the others, see John Goodman, Gerald Musgrave, and Devon Herrick, *Lives at Risk; Single-Payer National Health Insurance Around the World* (Rowman and Littlefield 2004), Sally C. Pipes, *The Top Ten Myths of American Health Care: A Citizen's Guide* (Pacific Research Institute 2008) and John C. Goodman and Devon M. Herrick, NCPA Report: "Twenty Myths about Single-Payer Health Insurance: International Evidence on the Effects of National Health Insurance in Countries Around the World," National Center for Policy Analysis (Dallas, Texas 2003).

compelling over—government control. The contrast with rigid European hierarchies restricting individual freedom and advancement was, and remains, pervasive.

This experience still shapes our negative attitude towards government control. And this attitude is not just some kind of xenophobia hiding flag-waving and foreigner-bashing. As pointed out first above, Europeans—largely lacking such experience and attitude—created welfare states that have led to severe relative decline in economic growth, and with it, reduced job creation and high long-term unemployment. The European sovereign debt crisis which began in 2010 involving successive bail-outs and debt restructurings of Greece, Portugal, Italy, and so on attests to the devastating negative long term effects of an excessive welfare state, a condition ushered in by generations of European promises, denial and delay. Thus attitudes born of different historical experiences have real-life connections and consequences.

With these considerations in mind, let us now turn to an examination of what a close look by economists at single-payer and other nationalized health care systems reveals.

3. An Overview of the International Experience: Characteristic Single-Payer Shortfalls

Prior to his election and early in his tenure, President Obama professed a lack of ideology and an interest in "what works," not just in health care but across the board. Everything was to be "reset" according to the best reason and evidence offer. As seen, however, the health care reform that issued in March 2010 took a distinctly

CHAPTER III: THE SINGLE-PAYER MIRAGE

anti-market, pro-government-control turn, seeking to emulate the British-European-Canadian model.⁷⁷ Yet it is clear from the evidence—highlighted by the revelations in the English white paper—that this is not a model that works in any sense most Americans can recognize and approve. Especially important is the trade-off of cost control versus diminishing quality of service, particularly through squeezing budgets and creating wait line rationing. Thus:

> [C]ountries with single-payer health insurance limit health care spending by limiting supply. They do so primarily by imposing global budgets on hospitals and area health authorities. Often there is a separate budget for high-tech equipment, to make doubly sure that high-cost procedures are curtailed. The consequence of making health care free, thus creating unconstrained demand, while limiting supply, is that demand exceeds supply for virtually every service. That, in turn, leads to rationing, usually by forcing patients to wait for treatment.⁷⁸

Governments are loath to publicize wait-list figures, so it is difficult to get exact numbers. But numerous sources give a good picture, and the result is uninviting:

> Everywhere it has been tried, the single-payer model has yielded inefficient service and lower-quality care. In Britain today, more than 700,000 patients are waiting for hospital treatment. In Canada, it takes, on average, seventeen weeks to see a specialist after a referral. In Germany and France, roughly half of the men diagnosed with prostate cancer will die from the disease, while in the United States

---
77 This is hardly surprising as Illinois state senator Obama was on record favoring a single-payer system.
78 Goodman, Musgrave, and Herrick, *Lives at Risk*, at 18.

only one in five will. According to one study, 40 percent of British cancer patients in the mid-1990s never got to see an oncologist at all. Such dire statistics have in fact caused many Western democracies with single-payer systems to turn toward market mechanisms for relief [Sweden, Australia, Canada].[79]

These numbers are getting worse over time, not better. By 2008, over one million Britons were waiting for hospital care. Another 200,000 were *waiting to get on a waiting list.* Canada, with only 33 million people, had 800,000 on wait lists. Fifteen years ago, in Canada the average wait between referral by primary care physician to specialist was nine weeks; by 2008, it was fifteen weeks. "Socialized systems ration services across the whole range of medical care. In Canada that means limited access to physicians, surgery, and other procedures needed by ordinary Canadians every day."[80]

Some of this decline in service can be directly attributed to government limiting what doctors and other providers get paid. "European governments also control costs by paying doctors far less than they would earn in a free market. On average, US physicians take home close to $300,000 per year. However, in Italy, the average doctor earns $81,414. In Germany, the average physician salary drops to just $56,455. And in France the salary is $55,000."[81] As noted before, it doesn't take a PhD to conclude that limiting incomes will limit the attraction and supply of suitably trained doctors—precisely the opposite result the system designers desired.

---

79 Cohen and Levin, "Health Care in Three Acts," *Commentary*, 2/2007 at 48.
80 Sally C. Pipes, *The Top Ten Myths of American Health Care*, at 125 (Pacific Research Institute, 2008).
81 Sally C. Pipes, *The Ten Top Myths*, at 131.

CHAPTER III: THE SINGLE-PAYER MIRAGE

The downward spiral of degeneration of service abetted by the upward spiral of costs is a perfect storm built into the single-payer world.

The world of national health care evidences considerable distance between myth and reality. To diminish rationing by waiting governments can only offset the necessity for increased investment in that area by declines in service elsewhere or rising costs. Systems of government control do not offer any escape from this conundrum. In their book, *Lives at Risk: Single-Payer National Health Insurance Around the World*, noted economists John C. Goodman, Gerald Musgrave, and Devon Herrick review in stark detail a number of such systems internationally, especially the English-language countries New Zealand, Australia, Britain, and Canada:

> The promise of national health insurance is that government will make health care available on the basis of need rather than ability to pay. That implies a government commitment to meet health care needs. It implies that rich and poor will have equal access to care. And it implies that more serious needs will be given priority over the less serious. Unfortunately, these promises have not been kept.
>
> - Wherever national health insurance has been tried, rationing by waiting is pervasive—with waits that force patients to endure pain and sometimes put their lives at risk.
> - Not only is health care not equal, if anything it tends to correlate with income—with the middle class getting more access than the poor, and the rich getting more access than the middle class, especially when income class is weighted by incidence of illness.

- Not only are health care resources not allocated on the basis of need, these systems tend to overspend on the relatively healthy while denying the truly sick access to specialist care and lifesaving medical technology.
- And far from establishing national priorities that get care first to those who need it most, these systems leave rationing choices up to local bureaucracies that, for example, fill hospital beds with chronic patients while acute patients wait for care.[82]

Where waiting lists are small, other aspects of health care suffer. The most common recipe is price control. Although variations among countries are pronounced, to contain costs all national health care systems from Japan to Taiwan to Germany to Britain to Switzerland to Canada share the need to suppress prices and fix charges, sometimes by bureaucrats but most often by regional bargaining between insurers, providers, and hospitals, under overall government budget control. Inevitably the most squeezed are the front line players—the doctors, hospitals, and other providers. In Japan, a huge book the size of a telephone book sets out the (low) price for every procedure. These efforts to contain costs, while making patients initially happy, reduce incentives to provide adequate trained personnel and services, and force pricing

---

82 Goodman, Musgrave, and Herrick, *Lives at Risk*, at 9. This work delves deeply into the underlying and often camouflaged statistics and facts of four English-speaking countries—Britain, Canada, Australia, and New Zealand—that are commonly used as points of comparison with our own. However, it also includes much about numerous other countries, particularly in Europe: Germany, Netherlands, Sweden, Norway. Thus it is an excellent, data-loaded resource for understanding the most relevant single-payer points of comparison.

CHAPTER III: THE SINGLE-PAYER MIRAGE

issues into the political arena, with politics playing the major role rather than individual needs. Inevitably, service suffers; there is no free lunch under nationalized systems as elsewhere.

Even Cuba's health care system—icon among some admirers of single-payer systems—displays a stark contrast between myth, official statistics, and bleak reality. The World Health Organization lauds its infant mortality rate (lower than that in the US on paper) while disregarding the large and growing maternal death rate; children live but mothers die in unsanitary "hospitals." Its vaunted doctor/patient ratio of one per 170 people, the best in the world, neglects the fact that over half of these doctors live abroad and seek to continue to do so (they earn twenty-five dollars per month at home and moonlight as taxi drivers or hotel workers). As for quality of training, very few can cut the mustard in the US; few who do make it to here can qualify as other than nurses. What about the highly touted equality? As in other single-payer systems, stark discrimination based on money and political power determines access. Those with influence go to the front of the line while the poor wait.[83]

As one reviewer of the Cuban scene concludes:

> The truth is that socialism and related forms of command-and-control technocracy work as well in the health care market as they do in every other. Which is to say, not at all. When better-heeled Americans start flying to offshore medical centers for their facelifts and bypasses (performed by expat American doctors) while poorer folk make do in ObamaCare's second tier, then perhaps the real lessons of the Cuban system will begin to sink in.[84]

---

83 Laurie Garrett, "Castrocare in Crisis," *Foreign Affairs* (July-August 2010).
84 Bret Stephens, Opinion, 7/12/2010, *WSJ.*

4. The English NHS—"Beacon of Progress"— Casts a Fading Light

The trouble with socialism is that eventually you run out of other people's money
MARGARET THATCHER

Along with Canada, the British National Health Service is the most often touted model for America. But as noted earlier, this is no longer tenable. The July 2010 white paper entitled "Equity and Excellence: Liberating the NHS" presented to Parliament by the government of England—the other parts of the Commonwealth are responsible for their own NHS legislation—admits that "the NHS simply cannot continue to afford to support the costs of the existing bureaucracy" because "the reality is that there is no more money." The white paper lists numerous areas where the NHS has fallen way behind other countries in health outcomes,[85] and admits that "the NHS has understood for some time the need to make extremely challenging improvements in productivity and efficiency." It admits that the costs of the NHS have been growing at 4 percent over inflation for six decades and have reached the point where they crowd out and diminish the other priorities of English life.[86]

---

[85] An August 2010 report on Britain's NHS found that malnourished patients who entered hospitals came out in greater numbers malnourished than entered. In other words, British hospitals' cutbacks on nursing and dietary services have stretched the ranks so thinly that basic nutrition is lacking. "Feeding the NHS, Starving Its Patients," Opinion Europe, September 1, 2010, *WSJ*.

[86] "Equity and Excellence: Liberating the NHS," submitted by the prime minister, deputy prime minister, and secretary of state for health, July 2010, to the Parliament of England, by "Command of Her Majesty" (available on the Internet).

CHAPTER III: THE SINGLE-PAYER MIRAGE

Margaret Thatcher's quip about running out of other people's money has come home with a vengeance.

The white paper's tenor and recommendations hardly set a tone favorable for single-payer advocates. It implicitly reflects a reality consisting of lack of patient control, bloated bureaucracies rationing care unequally, providers squeezed by ever-decreasing budgets, ever-lower quality, higher costs. To counter this, the document seeks a total revolution in all aspects of the NHS. Describing the neglect of patient wants, unfair discriminations, poor outcomes, and deteriorating service as well as ever-increasing costs, the white paper advocates a new system based on "patient power," where "money follows the patient" and where there is "no decision about me without me." Instead of "top-down control" by the NHS that created a "production-line approach to health care which measures volume but ignores the quality," the white paper recommends building from the "bottom up," starting with patients and their general practitioners. It frankly admits that the "top-down" socialism upon which the NHS was founded has led to bureaucratic bloat, neglect of patient needs, and decline of service quality.

Despite admitting that these conditions have been recognized for decades, the white paper reflects the first major redo of NHS since inception in 1948, itself a testament to the difficulty of altering systems of government control once established. Adopting the language of the patient-centered movement, the white paper sketches a series of radical restructurings, eliminating "top-down" controls in favor of creating "GP consortiums" at the local level that "in consultation with patients" will henceforth be responsible for allocating the taxpayer funding Parliament will still be providing.

105

Will it succeed? Since the government of England reflects the majority in Parliament, it is likely that the white paper's recommendations will be implemented in large part. But for reasons that will be described, these recommendations—falling far short of the "patient power" language of its conception—are a valiant effort to do the impossible. Prices are still controlled, regulations and mandates dominate, and the taxpayer is on the hook for everything. Reshuffling the bureaucracy into a "bottom-up" posture to save money asks GPs and their local authorities to become administrators, accountants, policymakers, politicians, and economists. It does nothing about the fundamental flaw; patients will still lack the individual power of the purse.

The British NHS is one of the most socialized health systems outside the communist world, the Grand Dame marking socialism's post-WWII zenith. Time has not been kind to the old lady. Admitting the desirability of promoting competition, increasing individual responsibility, enhancing patient power, and centering the system on actually helping the patient instead of administrative convenience surely moves the ball forward. But Britain's tragedy, reflected by the white paper's split personality, is that it is trapped in NHS's guiding principle—"free at the point of use and available to everyone based on need, not ability to pay"—which remains a compelling slogan but a formula for continuing fiscal crisis and decline of service.

Costs will continue their upward trajectory after an initial burst of savings from eliminating layers of bureaucracy and jobs throughout the system. The white paper is thus like Gorbachev's "glasnost and perestroika," a way station from the unsustainable to the unavoidable. Only freeing patients to build their own health care assets in health savings accounts or their equivalent truly "liberates the NHS" and the taxpayer and allows "the money to follow the patient" and "no decision about me without me" as the white paper seeks. Everything else affords the illusion of competition and cost reduction without the prospect of realistic attainment.

There is a way out. The Brits need not remain trapped in their ideology. The NHS is built on only one of several possible notions of equality. The first, to which the white paper nominally adheres, reflects the classic socialist creed that everyone be treated the same under all conditions. But as we have seen, eliminating private initiative and incentives in favor of total taxpayer funding and government control ushers in hidden discriminations, deteriorating quality, and increasing costs, which quickly undermine the goals set. Lacking any systemic means to lower prices and costs, no matter how bureaucracies are reshuffled, Britain will remain stuck in a cost/quality conundrum.

A different notion of equality—suggested by the white paper's emphasis on patient power and creating competition among providers—focuses on practical outcomes, not abstract ideology. Ensuring everyone has decent care that they can afford—such as through health savings accounts and vouchers, as sketched later—creates an equality based upon permanent values that, while not demanding unforgiving equal treatment, puts everyone on a higher plane without dragging down net social product. The British health system future need not remain bleak.

5. The Canadian Single-Payer System's Slow Morph Towards Free Markets

If the British model is no longer tenable, what about Canada? In Canada, the last sixty years have seen the nation-

THE BUMBLING COLOSSUS

alization of the health industry into sector bargaining units (hospitals, doctors, etc) that negotiate with the provinces under overall government budget control. This is government control "lite." Here are the mechanics:

> The federal government conditionally promises each province that it will prepay roughly 40 percent of the costs of all necessary medical care. The federal grant is available so long as the province's health insurance program is universal (covering all citizens), comprehensive (covering all conventional hospital and medical care), accessible (no limits on services and no extra charges to patients), portable (each province recognizes the others' coverage), and publicly administered (under control of public, nonprofit organization). All ten provinces maintain health insurance plans satisfying these criteria. The provincial ministry of health is the only payer in each province. There are no complex eligibility tests or complicated definitions of insured services... Annual negotiations between provincial governments and the providers of care determine the hospital budgets and the level of physicians' fees.[87]

This system achieves a high degree of satisfaction from the public, as registered by opinion polls (discussed later). But Canada is also starting to recognize the shortcomings of its own command-and-control dream. This came to a head in the courts. Privately set fees by doctors and private insurance were proscribed, to avoid a separate health system for the better-off, but by 2005 queues and poor service had gotten so bad someone sued to open up the market to private insurance, appealing to higher law, and the Supreme Court of Canada agreed. It held:

---

87 T. R. Marmor, *Understanding Health Care Reform*, at 186.

CHAPTER III: THE SINGLE-PAYER MIRAGE

The evidence in this case shows that delays in the public health care system are widespread, and that, in some serious cases, patients die as a result of waiting lists for public health care.[88]

When the courts start finding *constitutional violations of basic human rights* in the dire effects of systems of government control, even the most committed apologists of such things have to think twice.[89]

One sign of the malaise in the system is the exodus of Canadian doctors. Eighteen Canadian doctors leave for the US for every US doctor who leaves for Canada.[90] The squeeze on doctor pay required to keep budgets from exploding drains the system of its principal resource. The US provides a needed relief valve for Canadian doctors and patients and makes the adoption of a Canada-style system in America extremely problematic. Where do American doctors and patients dissatisfied with bureaucratic treatment and regimens go?

A historical parallel highlights the direction of change in Canada. In 1966, the premier of Quebec asked Claude Castonguay, "the father of Quebec Medicare," to head a commission to study the health system and make recommendations. The result? Quebec adopted publicly

---

88 *Chaoulli v. Quebec (Attorney General,)* 2005, 1 S.C.R. 791.
89 The Fraser Institute in Vancouver, a "free market"-oriented think tank, carefully tracks the doings and shortfalls of the Canadian single-payer system in numerous books, articles, and conferences. See www.fraserinstitute.org. Its output is a useful corrective to the encomiums of devoted single-payer advocates. See also Dr. David Gratzer, *Code Blue* (1999); David Gratzer, *The Cure: How Capitalism Can Save American Health Care* (2006, Encounter Books). For similar perspectives, see Regina Herzlinger, *Who Killed Health Care?: America's $2 Trillion Medical Problem —and the Consumer-Driven Cure* (2007, McGraw-Hill).
90 Sally C. Pipes, *Miracle Cure,* at 195.

financed health care, and by 1972, the rest of Canada had, too. In 2007, Quebec again asked Castonguay to head a commission and make recommendations. The result? Castonguay and the commission saw a deteriorating system in "crisis" and recommended moving to more private sector approaches.[91]

The Canadian experiment in trying to achieve low-cost, high-quality care for everyone falls short along predictable lines. Sally C. Pipes, a Canadian and longtime student of Canadian health care, summarizes the situation in her country as of 2004:

> Today, after thirty years of government intervention, the system suffers from:
> - long waiting times for critical procedures
> - lack of access to current technology
> - increasing costs to taxpayers and patients, and
> - a brain drain of doctors. [92]

These conclusions mirror those of other careful economists reviewing the international single-payer universe, including Goodman, Musgrave, and Herrick. They raise the question for single-payer advocates—do you really want us to proceed down the path to waiting lines, poorer service, diminished human and invested capital, fewer doctors, and ever-escalating costs? Have you really considered alternatives based on empowering patients like that offered here?[93]

---

91 Sally C. Pipes, *The Top Ten Myths of American Health Care, A Citizen's Guide*, at 138 (PRI 2008).
92 Sally C. Pipes, *Miracle Cure: How to Solve America's Health Care Crisis and Why Canada Isn't the Answer*, at 150 (Pacific Research Institute & Fraser Institute, 2004).
93 Some single-payer advocates seek to minimize the wait list problem, arguing that it is beneficial by weeding out the frivolous and un-

Progressive Idealism Cannot Repeal the Free Lunch Fallacy or the Regulatory Illusion

Earlier, it was possible for proponents of the Canadian system of nationalized health care to argue that "[m]ost of the negative effects predicted by economic theory and Canadian doctors—worrisome physician flight, rationing of lifesaving care, long queues, and technological obsolescence—have not emerged."[94] Clearly this early optimism needs to be modified on all counts. But the dream dies hard. Some Canadian single-payer proponents admit that rationing is a problem, but seek to minimize its significance: "Canada does ration medical care. So does the United States and every other country in the world. What counts is not the presence of rationing (or allocation) but the basis for and extent of restricted access to health care. The United States continues to ration by the ability to pay—a process largely determined by race, class, and employment circumstances."[95]

But this falsely equates the ills of government rationing, which harms everybody and destroys individual choice

---

necessary, or by otherwise helping sift through the casual for the needed. But it is doubtful such arguments diminish the anxiety and dread, not to mention loss of life, of those captured in these lines.

94 T. R. Marmor, *Understanding Health Care Reform*, at 186, 188. He does go on to say, however, that "At certain times and in some places, substantial waiting lists for selected surgical and diagnostic procedures occur...[and] there is no question that some expensive, high-technology items are not as available in Canada as they are in the United States."

95 T. R. Marmor, *Understanding Health Care Reform*, at 187. There is something disconcertingly retro in this depiction of America—like watching an old movie from the progressive era—after four decades of Medicaid, equal employment laws, affirmative action, and similar efforts to equalize and alleviate. Why not attack directly the more limited problems that remain instead of seeking to spread the injury to everyone that comes with government control?

and freedom across the board, with shortfalls for a relative few, which are amenable to a far less drastic solution than nationalization. Moreover, the relevant comparison is not with America's present inadequate and distorted system of quasi-government control and mandates; rather it is with a reimagined system based upon health savings accounts or their equivalent, supplemented by vouchers and the elimination of mandates and most controls on the substance of insurance coverage options. Under such a system, everyone—poor or not—has resources available for health care and insurance coverage for significant risks (which they are free to choose and exclude), and no reason is apparent why wait lists or rationing would need to be an issue.[96]

Canada achieved important goals in its effort to ensure everyone access to decent care. But the system it chose—government controls over most aspects of health care—leads inevitably to continuing tensions over high costs and

---

96 T. R. Marmor states: "Rationing can be a cruel and inefficient way of allocating scarce resources... But it is also, as any economist will note, one of only two ways of doing this. The other means of allocating goods and services is by price..." [mentioning the uninsured, the poor, and others unable to afford care under a pure price system—examples that are discussed above and that are corrected for in a HSA/voucher system]. He points out that even in a market-based system with financing for the poor, government will have to decide on what items of service are covered and what are not. "The point is that whatever our medical care system—whether it allocates medical services primarily by price or by nonprice means—tough decisions will have to be made as to who will have what and how much of it." T. R. Marmor, *Understanding Health Care Reform*, at 130. True, but it makes a big difference whether tough decisions are made by individuals for themselves and family or by bureaucrats for everyone across the board. The existence of tough decisions should not require eliminating the engine of economic progress that markets represent in favor of the bureaucratic state and politicized medicine.

lowering service. The Free Lunch Fallacy, which drew Canadians into the single-payer world to begin with, seduced the populace with the siren song of a presumed equality that unfortunately came a cropper when the nether side of the Regulatory Illusion began to reveal itself. Now the free lunch itself with its equality banner has become a national symbol for proud Canadians who wrongly fear that the only alternative to their declining dream is some cowboy version of free markets.

The title of this section, "the Canadian single-payer system's slow morph towards free markets," is provocative but intended to underline the evolution that all single-payer approaches necessarily take away from strict government control, of which the recent British experience with the NHS is representative. It is impossible to gauge the timing of such events. Who in 1950 could predict when and how the Soviet empire would collapse, or even if it would?[97]

More Administrative Cost Myths

A further word needs to be added on administrative costs. The Canadian, British, and European results raise doubts whether the claims of single-payer proponents that government-run health care is more efficient than private insurers can possible be true. This argument was often

---

97 At Harvard in the late 1950s and early 1960s, the specialists looked at the communist model—creators of Sputnik, atomic weaponry, and grand ten-year plans—as a possible economically efficient alternative to the West, ignorant of the real statistics (which were secret) and the tragedy of life behind the Iron Curtain, which was also largely concealed. The publication of Djilas' *The New Class* in 1957 began to open the eyes of many in academia to the depth and severity of the hidden realities of socialism and of course by the '70s and '80s the veil had largely lifted, the romance with socialism had paled, and the intellectual tables had turned.

made during the run-up to the 2010 Act. Certain sources put out statistics to the effect that Medicare and Medicaid only spend about two percent of their budgets on administration, so are significantly more efficient than private insurers, whose administration costs exceed that by a factor of seven or so.[98] Claims are made that administrative costs in nationalized systems are at similar levels to Medicare, and some countries permit only not-for-profit insurers as a result.

But the declining level of service and wait lists, or both, characteristic of nationalized systems are efficient only by harming patients; it is easy to eliminate administrative costs simply by putting everyone on a list to wait for service. Moreover, the statistics used to support government-run systems or not-for-profit insurers are misleading. Take Medicare, which sets lower prices for providers: by under-pricing for goods and service, huge off-budget costs are shifted to hospitals and doctors (and ultimately us), so that "it turns out that actually Medicare is not very efficient at all."[99] Studies that include all relevant administrative costs, not just those advocates choose to put forth, put Medicare at over 26 percent and private companies at 16 percent.[100]

So taking "profit" out of health care insurance—just as with drug manufacture or doctor's billings—turns out

---

[98] For example, the American Academy of Family Physicians puts Medicare's administrative costs at 4 to 6 percent compared to 15 to 20 percent in the private sector. Sally C. Pipes, *The Top Ten Myths of American Health Care: A Citizen's Guide*, at 102 (PRI 2008).

[99] John Goodman, "Five Myths of Socialized Medicine," *Cato's Letter*, vol. 3, number 1 (Winter, 2005).

[100] Council for Affordable Health Insurance Study (1994), cited in Sally Pipes, *The Top Ten Myths of American Health Care; A Citizen's Guide*, at 103 (PRI 2008).

not to be an advantage for anyone; it just reduces another incentive to lower costs while maintaining service.

6. The Masking of Single-Payer Deficiencies

It is a great historical irony, noted earlier, that just when Britain, Europe, Canada, and the rest of the developed world are starting to understand the mistake they made in substituting government for market approaches, the president and 2008-2010 Congress sought (successfully) to force us in the direction these other countries are moving away from. Thus in Britain, Australia, Canada, Germany, Netherlands, and Sweden, "…growing frustration with government health programs has led to a reexamination of the fundamental principles of health care delivery. Through bitter experience, many of the countries that once touted the benefits of government control have learned that the surest remedy for their countries' health care crises is not increasing government power, but increasing patient power instead."[101]

Why, then, do public opinion polls in socialized systems routinely show high approval levels? It is a paradox of the politics of medicine in socialized countries that people when polled are "happy" with their system and are slow to criticize even where objective evidence reveals that these systems are decaying and fall short.[102] These systems

---

[101] John Goodman, Musgrave, and Herrick, *Lives at Risk,* at 11. For the Netherlands, where at least one-third had private insurance, see Kieke Okma, "Health Care, Health Policies and Health Care Reform in the Netherlands," School of Public Policy Studies, Queen's University, Kingston, Ontario (March 2000).

[102] For example, polls routinely show Canadians favor their system to that of the US by 80 percent or more. But polls of Americans and Canadians about the quality of their own care show no differences. This suggests that, as elsewhere, much lies in the way the question is asked.

live a charmed life where failure is masked and criticism largely muted. Indeed, Goodman, Musgrave, and Herrick conclude that "[t]he failure of national health insurance is a secret of modern social science. Not only have scholars failed to understand the defects of national health insurance, too often advocates and ordinary citizens hold an idealized view of it."[103]

The most likely reason for this is that most people are simply ignorant of the truth; costs are hidden in the tax base and complex budgetary accounts. Then again, patients faced with lengthy waits and poor service are "conditioned for decades by a culture of rationing," so are docile and resigned to their fate.[104] The ideology of equality is promoted and widely admired despite obvious favoritisms. Poll results reflect national pride and belief in the ideology of equality more than some close judgment of costs and benefits. Canadians, for example, seem to equate their health system with their being "better than" America. These factors deflect popular attention from the deficiencies they experience and the way "the wealthy, powerful, and sophisticated—those most skilled at articulating their complaints—find ways to maneuver to the front of the rationing lines."[105]

This process is nothing more than the Regulatory Illusion at work. Having induced people into somnolence with

---

Questions eliciting 80 percent plus satisfaction rates likely reflect approval of the ideology of equality, not hardheaded analysis of how the system actually works. Nonetheless, one sees constant reference to questionably persuasive high satisfaction numbers.

103 Goodman, Musgrave, and Herrick, *Lives at Risk; Single-Payer National Health Insurance Around the World*, at 12.

104 This echoes the observation of F.A. Hayek quoted first above about dependency and government control.

105 Goodman, Musgrave, and Herrick, *Lives at Risk*, at 197-198.

the soothing promises of a free lunch, and having buried the truth under years of misdirection as to the true cause of the cost maelstrom, the regulatory apparatus continues with its self-justifications while its media and political friends continue to hold blinders over the facts. The truth is buried, costs are hidden, ideology of equality is promoted in the face of inequality, and opinion leaders make sure they benefit by getting prompt access (while others suffer the wait).

But the survival of such a system is fragile. Insisting on the pure equality upon which the system is rhetorically based would endanger the enterprise. Even before the white paper, some observers presciently observed about the NHS:

> If a member of the British Parliament, the CEO of a large British company, or the head of a major British trade union had no greater access to renal dialysis than any other British citizen, the British NHS would not last a week.[106]

Moving Beyond Single-Payer Mythology

Nationalized systems are like pushing on a balloon; no matter how hard costs in one part are depressed, the balloon pops out with costs or deteriorated service somewhere else. The law of supply and demand cannot be repealed by idealistic fiat. F.A. Hayek points out, "It may sound noble to say, 'Damn economics, let us build up a decent world'—but it is, in fact, merely irresponsible." [107]

---

106 Goodman, Musgrave, and Herrick, *Lives at Risk*, at 197; see also Sally C. Pipes, *The Top Ten Myths of American Health Care, A Citizen's Guide* (PRI 2008).
107 Friedrich A. Hayek, *The Road to Serfdom*, at 210.

Single-payer advocates complain that America's voluntary system "rations by price or income," where individual resources can make a difference in the care obtained. But they can only offer a system based ultimately upon coercion and limits where care is rationed by waiting lists or service is underfunded and suboptimal, and the rich and powerful get advantages anyway.

Having analyzed the roads to failure, now let's take a closer look at the basic principles a successful health care system should follow, and what a cost-effective, service-enhancing solution, which avoids "rationing by income" as well as "rationing by waitlist," looks like. The solution implied is not to radically rebuild health care along uncertain lines, but to look back at our historical strengths and build upon them.

CHAPTER IV:
Getting It Right: Principles to Follow in a Successful Health Care System

We now know what to avoid in reforming health care: single-payer and government control approaches, whether incrementally imposed by creeping legislation and regulation, as with the 2010 Act, or imposed wholesale, like the NHS. But what are the positive virtues or principles that we should follow to provide a stable, permanent foundation for good health care at reasonable cost?

First, *maximize individual incentives and responsibility, and market features.* Getting away from this leads to decline and failure. Costs matter, and only individuals provided with the tools to be "shoppers" for their own health care can drive lower costs, exploit competitive forces, and ensure high quality for themselves and their families.

Second, *make sure no one is left out.* Everyone should be able to take advantage of the benefits of modern health care regardless of income or health status. This sounds a lot like Britain's guiding principle for the NHS, but with a crucial difference, which is:

Third, *health care should not be free.* Putting it all on the taxpayer had good early returns in ravaged, post-war Europe and Britain, but the bloom is off the rose. The goal or promise of free health care is an especially pernicious illusion that ends up harming people far more than it helps.[108]

1. So What *Is* the Proper Role of Government in Health Care Finance?

How to reconcile these disparate, conflicting goals? We need to recognize that there is a critical role for individuals and business—largely free of regulation and government control—and a critical but limited role for government. It is a mistake to believe that government should have no role at all, for (as will be seen in Part B) government is critical to shaping the universe within

---

[108] These principles differ in some respects from those of leading American health policy experts who, dismissing individual- or patient-focused approaches such as here, advocate that the US adopt something akin to the Canadian model. For example, Theodore R. Marmor says: "Sensible reform should build on three fundamental principles. First, the three elements of the medical crisis—costs, access, and quality—are interconnected. We cannot solve one problem without attending to the other two. If we put all our emphasis on controlling health spending, quality and access may well suffer. If we focus solely on making sure that everybody has health insurance coverage, cost will rise and quality may erode. And if we do nothing but improve the (highly variable) quality of American medical care, fewer and fewer people will have access to more and more expensive services." The "we" is, of course, government, and the trade-off he describes is true of the single-payer, Medicare-Medicaid government-control world but not necessarily otherwise. He adds two beneficial principles for reform: 1) ability to have rapid implementation and 2) choosing a system that minimizes risk that the system will fail. T. R. Marmor, *Understanding Health Care Reform*, at 14-15 (Yale, 1994).

CHAPTER IV: GETTING IT RIGHT

which the participants in the health care market, as in other markets, can flourish.

One can give guidelines as to the major things with which government involvement should be concerned. It is important to avoid the Free Lunch Fallacy and the Regulatory Illusion, which have brought reforms centered on increasing government control over health care, such as single-payer systems and the 2010 Act. Government's role in health insurance should be limited to those things that 1) protect and reestablish a free and competitive insurance market, 2) fund the needy, 3) secure health care for those preexisting conditions that have become life certainties, 4) promote information, and 5) eliminate the distortions caused by earlier errors in tax favoring of employer-supplied coverage.

Harvard Business School professor Regina Herzlinger, a longtime analyst of health care systems, puts it this way:

> Government plays three crucial roles in any consumer-driven system; it oversees the solvency and integrity of participants, it provides transparency, and it subsidizes the purchase of important items for the needy.

When it comes to health care, the government should:

- Prosecute fraudulent providers, enrollees, and insurers and assure the financial solvency of insurers
- Use our tax money to subsidize those who cannot afford health insurance
- Require the dissemination of audited data about the performance of providers.[109]

---

109 Regina Herzlinger, *Who Killed Health Care*, at 214-215.

One essential element is missing from her list: eliminating mandates and controls on the content and coverage of policy choices. This is critical to achieving the goal of quality service for all. As economists Goodman, Musgrave, and Herrick point out, "Aside from an interest in encouraging catastrophic insurance, there is no social reason why government at any level should dictate the contents of health insurance plans." Through subsidy and tax policy, "the federal government's role should remain strictly financial." [110]

This approach sounds an old bell in a new tower. It reaffirms in the health care context what F.A. Hayek taught generally—that the "extended order of human cooperation" in commercial societies creates the conditions for government's limited role. Far from creating chaos or social Darwinism, commercial societies tend to order, minimizing of conflict, and peaceful relations, and provide the means to care for others. They extend as far as conflict-free turf permits and seek to extend ever further.[111] This insight is true across geography and culture and applies specifically to health care. All we need of government there—and it is a critical one—is to recognize its role in supporting competition, private incentives and choice, and directly funding those unable to pay.

So therefore, although much room for debate exists, we proceed here on the basis that the optimum health care system at this stage of history assumes the desirability of something approaching universal coverage (i.e., insurance) for all—the equality goal—ensuring there are minimal or no uninsured. The trick is to achieve this without falling into the trap exposed by the shortcomings of single-payer sys-

---

110 Goodman, Musgrave, and Herrick, *Lives at Risk*, at 231.
111 F. A. Hayek, *The Fatal Conceit*, at 11-16.

tems and other forms of government regulation and controls of markets. The payoff is large: solving the health care cost versus service dilemma not only ensures higher quality service for all but also frees the economy from wasteful expenditures, increasing productive investment and spurring job creation. Everyone benefits. How to do this?

Let a uniform minimum be secured to everybody by all means, but let us admit at the same time that with this assurance of a basic minimum all claims for a privileged security of particular classes must lapse, that all excuses disappear for allowing groups to exclude newcomers from sharing their relative prosperity in order to maintain a special standard of their own.

FRIEDRICH A. HAYEK[112]

---

[112] F. A. HAYEK, *The Road to Serfdom*, at 210

CHAPTER V:
The Solution—Free Up Insurance Markets, Provide Health Savings Accounts for All and Vouchers for the Needy

1. Health Savings Accounts (HSAs) Put Skin in the Game

By separating the patient/consumer from his or her health care wallet, the single-payer system removes the most powerful force for containing costs while maintaining high service levels—the incentive each of us has to tend our health *and* our resources. A better system places the money in the pocket of the individual, for it is the individual who has the greatest incentive to promote his or her own health and financial well-being. Government operates through rules, agents, and bureaucracies. No government bureaucrat or agent, no matter how suitably trained, educated, and taught, can possibly care as much or act according to our preferences as we do, since each of our situations is different.

Therefore, it is inherent in a government-run system that the incentive that only individuals possess to get the best service for the lowest cost gets lost. This shows up in the analysis we just saw of the unavoidable trade-off in single-payer systems between increasing costs on the one hand and declining service on the other. In order to reduce costs, single-payer systems must cut resources to providers. In order to ensure universal coverage, they have robbed themselves of the one thing that avoids this trade-off: the incentive the individual has to get the best for the least. What is needed is a system that preserves and enhances this incentive while also ensuring everyone is covered. To do this, we need to step away from the single-payer model and look at something quite different.

High-Deductible Coverage Puts the Incentives for Lower Cost and Better Service Back With the Patient

There is an approach that achieves this result and also reconciles and embodies all the principles of a successful health care system set out above while maximizing the proper roles of government and free markets. This approach is both bold and old: create a market for health services where patients are consumers who have the incentives to shop and save and be the targets for competition among providers of goods and services. To achieve this, consumers/patients need a measure of control over the resources they spend. We need to move the system from total so-called third-party payer (government- or employer-provided low- or no-deductible insurance) to one where people are in charge of their own health care expenditures.

The easiest way to do this is to make sure everyone has his or her own, tax-deductible health savings account (HSA), a legal structure that already exists and is in use, by which a bank account into which funds may be placed is tied by law to the owner of the account having a high-deductible so-called catastrophic health insurance policy connected with it. Funds put into the account receive a tax deduction and must be used only for health care, especially the costs of care below the deductible.[113]

Giving people control over their own health expenditures, including those below a certain moderately high deductible, provides the incentive needed for people to act as shoppers. Since contributions to HSAs are tax-deductible, and by law they must be linked to high-deductible coverage, they are the perfect vehicle to allow people to shop for services and products below the deductible as well as for insurance and are therefore essential to providing options and controlling costs. Of course, existing restrictions and limits on contributions would have to be lifted.

Federal Vouchers Provide Resources for the Needy

What about those unable to fund their own accounts? These folks should be made eligible for federally funded support with health care vouchers or their equivalent.[114]

---

113 Requirements and descriptions of HSAs are available on the Internet. Because of political pressures from those wishing us to go in the direction of government-controlled approaches, low limits on the amounts that may be put into these accounts have been enacted, and as a consequence, many banks have been discouraged from offering them. These restrictions, of course, need to be eliminated.

114 Voucher programs have been advocated before, most prominently in the debates surrounding Medicare reform in the late 1990s. Theodore Marmor, *The Politics of Medicare*, at 157-169 (2d Ed., Aldine De

These vouchers can be tailored to income levels so the cost of private insurance and the deductible is not a bar to anyone. They should be scaled to decline with income so as to thwart any disincentive to work. In one move, the system is changed to meet the goals set out above; people have incentive to control costs, and everyone is part of the system regardless of income.[115]

Shift Government Entitlements to the Same Structure

Medicare should also restructure to fund HSAs with tax-advantaged contributions for routine or predictable health needs. Medicaid and the Children's Health Insurance Program can follow, with special consideration to the low-income need for vouchers. All these should be phased in over time to allow adjustment to the new regime of responsibility.[116]

Gruyter 2000). But the system proposed here is more comprehensive: the whole universe of health care, public and private, is included in the HSA/voucher regime, and eliminating most mandates and controls on insurance is a key part of it.

115 For those whose health needs surpass the maximums in their "catastrophic" coverage, a community health fund could be created, funded by taxes or small charges on all insureds. This would prevent the threat of personal bankruptcy from unforeseen extraordinary health needs. To avoid creating an incentive for people to buy less than reasonably adequate coverage, however, such a benefit should not be available unless the patient has purchased maximum available coverage.

116 Leading economists agree with this approach. The reason is simple. "Having 'skin in the game,' unsurprisingly, leads to superior outcomes. As Milton Friedman famously observed: 'Nobody spends somebody else's money as wisely as they spend their own.' When legislators put other people's money at risk—as when Fannie Mae and Freddie Mac bought risky mortgages—crisis and economic hardship inevitably result. When minimal co-payments and low deductibles are mandated in the insurance market, wasteful health-care spending balloons." George

CHAPTER V: THE SOLUTION

Remove the Tax Distortions That Bind Us to Employment-Based Coverage

Critical as part of this shift is elimination of the tax bias favoring employer-provided (no- or low-deductible) coverage, moving it off center stage. Binding employees to their present employer because that is the source of health care coverage is a form of modern-day wage slavery. Instead, each person should control his or her own coverage regardless of by whom employed. If you get a better or different job elsewhere, there is no disincentive to change just to keep your health coverage intact. Because your coverage is your own, you decide what you want covered and how much to pay for it. Your choice of group or individual policies is not restricted by whatever your employer deems suitable.

Eliminating the huge and wasteful excess benefit costs on employers frees them up to invest capital productively, spurring job creation. Allowing employees and others power to act as shoppers for their own health care fosters individual responsibility and creates the needed drive for lowering costs across the system.

Breaking the Gordian knot of employer-based coverage is thus key to moving to a system based upon the educated patient/consumer. This can be done either by including employer payments for employee health care as income to the employee or by making all health care payments by individuals deductible to them, or both. As long as the playing field is leveled so no special benefit under the tax laws accrues by indirect payments for health care over persons paying for their own, people will be free to shift without loss of benefit to individualized HSAs.

P. Shultz, Michael J. Boskin, John F. Cogan, Allan Meltzer, John B. Taylor, "Principles for Economic Revival," 9/16/2010, *WSJ.*

Eliminate Most Government Mandates and Controls on Insurance Coverage

This switch to individually owned high-deductible coverage as a part of HSAs must be combined with an insurance market from which mandates and controls on the *content* of coverage have largely been eliminated. The huge accretion of these requirements at the state and federal level needs to be reversed. These mandates and controls drive up costs. They were put in to equalize, but vouchers do this far better. Companies will be free to offer, and people can choose, levels of deductibility and coverage with which they are comfortable. Solving the cost issue would be incomplete without also eliminating these myriad accumulated mandates, price and product controls, and cross-subsidies. These efforts to achieve fairness by imposing rules that skew risks and restrict freedom of market choice push costs ever higher in a crescendo of painful premium hikes. Begun as a political free lunch, the mandate policy turns into a disaster.[117]

Eliminate Barriers to Interstate Offering of Policies

Eliminated also should be barriers to interstate sales of health insurance, opening up a truly national market. No reason except parochialism exists for the continued fragmentation of insurance along state lines.

Mandates and controls on the provision of health insurance have traditionally been the province of state insurance

---

[117] Special attention needs to be made to the problem of non-renewal of a policy after claims. Policy length and non-cancellation rules can meet the objective here. Carriers take risks, as do insureds, and a rule balancing these interests serves all.

commissions, but with the federal revamping contemplated here, federal guidelines for state implementation are desirable for uniformity. The trick is to establish the minimum necessary for the HSA system to function effectively without opening the door to the kind of regulatory overkill we have now. The bottom line is that whatever rules are needed should aid individual freedom and choice, and should aid competition for the consumer's favor, not restrict these.

The high-deductible HSA approach provides the most desirable way forward out of our present dilemma. This has been tried elsewhere, albeit in small countries, with positive results. Singapore requires workers to put 6 percent of their salary into a personal medical savings account tied to a catastrophic coverage policy such as recommended here. South Africa, since 1993, has allowed a plethora of varying types of coverage, and health savings accounts have captured over 65 percent of the market.[118] Experience with both regimes has been very favorable.

Ironically and counterproductively, instead of promoting HSAs, the 2010 Act reduced their effectiveness by cutting by 50 percent the annual amount that may be contributed on a tax-deductible basis. The hostility to HSAs that this action evidences epitomizes the misconception of the enactment as a whole.

2. Vouchers Eliminate the Need for Mandates and Controls

With vouchers (or their equivalent), the prolix and confusing array of state mandates – numbering 1,961 as of 2008 – as well as those added by the 2010 Act, become as unnec-

---

118 Goodman, Musgrave, and Herrick, *Lives at Risk: Single-Payer National Health Insurance Around the World,* at 110, 243 (Rowman and Littlefield 2004).

essary as they are expensive. Eliminating them will allow the benefits of a free market—product innovation and premium/cost reduction—while providing health vouchers meets the desire for universal coverage and simultaneously eliminates the need for the prolix regulations. Health savings accounts allow the gradual tax-deductible and tax-free buildup of funds to pay the premiums for the high-deductible insurance that is tied to the HSA, as well as for the health costs below the deductible.

Eliminating mandates and controls that force unwanted cross-subsidies on unwilling premium payers allows natural risk pools to be created, which aligns risks with costs, incentivizes healthy behavior, and lowers cost for many. This freedom provides basic equity, for there is no fairness in requiring an older couple nearing retirement to pay for maternity coverage, or a teetotaler to pay for drug and alcohol abuse counseling, or people who go to great lengths to watch their weight to pay for the obese. The voucher program drains the force out of the argument that such cross-subsidies are fair to the poor so the burden on others is justified.

Getting rid of the mass of mandates and controls does not mean the elimination of all. The important ones to eliminate are those that interfere with the carriers' or consumer's judgments of risk and options to meet risk. Certain basic rules of the game, established in consultation with industry participants, may well be needed. For example, a reasonable requirement is that no company can cancel or fail to renew a policy if the risk for which it was purchased actualizes. This allows people to gain the advantage of the payments and risk coverage they choose. The market may well create such standards apart from law, as companies compete for the consumer dollar, in which case the redundancy is not harmful.

Another area for rules is the clarity of insurance coverage and conditions. No one should be misled into a false security. Actuarially sound minimum coverage guidelines as a part of the "catastrophic" coverage purchased as part of the health savings account can be developed and would be reasonable requirements. But all enforced cross-subsidies and dictates as to what should be included or not in coverage should go. Individuals, aided by private counselors of their choice, are the best judges of their own risk tolerance and needs.[119]

3. Information on Prices and Costs Must Be Available

Patients and other health purchasers cannot be effective buyers without adequate information on provider and manufacturer prices and costs. The question of how to best provide this has divided commentators. Regina Herzlinger suggests setting up a "Health Care SEC" to force hospitals, doctors, insurers, and other providers and payers to disclose relevant information on prices, costs, fees, and outcomes. "Nothing can work properly if those who create the goods and services are not measured on their performance."[120] Rep. Paul Ryan's "Roadmap for America's Future" (see *post*) advocates much the same thing. Better than a new

---

119 As with income taxes and financial investments, complexity can be overcome by private market advisors, the generation of which seems to be no hurdle wherever complex matters confront. And HSA-based high-deductible coverage is by definition simpler than today's prolix, mandate/control distorted coverage regimes.

120 Regina Herzlinger, *Who Killed Health Care?: America's $2 Trillion Medical Problem—and the Consumer-Driven Cure*, at 164, 234-239 (McGraw-Hill 2007).

agency, however, is requiring adequate disclosures and allowing private sources to compile, evaluate, and publish them. Failure to disclose could be tied to loss of benefits/payments or possible consumer fraud liability.[121]

Economist and *N.Y. Times* columnist Paul Krugman has raised the question whether people are competent to sort out varying insurance policy coverage terms and conditions. No doubt some complexity is involved. However, the world is full of insurance agents and brokers, and with some money included as a part of vouchers for paying for advice, there should be no dearth of people willing to provide these services as they already do in the private insurance market. Providing such advice is an example of the kind of information-based service that a voucher/support regime would readily encourage and help create.

4. The Special Case of Preexisting Conditions

Moving to HSAs for all reinstates health insurance to its historical and proper role as protection from the unexpected and unpredictable. But what about those whose health has already deteriorated into one of the many life-altering terminal or chronic conditions and for whom such health risks are not the unexpected and unpredictable but the expected and certain? There is a case here for government involvement because a social choice is being made to

---

[121] "Patient-centered" approaches follow the prescriptions set out above and are illuminating. Regina Herzlinger, *Who Killed Health Care?: America's $2 Trillion Medical Problem—and the Consumer-Driven Cure* (McGraw-Hill 2007); David Gratzer, *The Cure: How Capitalism Can Save American Health Care* (Encounter Books 2006); Goodman, Musgrave, and Herrick, *Lives at Risk: Single-Payer National Health Insurance Around the World* (Rowman and Littlefield 2004); Sally C. Pipes, *The Top Ten Myths of American Health Care*, (Pacific Research Institute 2008).

CHAPTER V: THE SOLUTION

ensure coverage, but the customary role of insurance is not present.

State insurance exchanges (stock exchange-like markets) for preexisting conditions make sense because actuarial techniques may still enable risk-sharing that private insurance companies may be willing to underwrite, albeit at an elevated price. Government will have to step up with vouchers to ensure the demand exists for the market to work and all persons are covered. The non-exchange private market should cover each person's health risks apart from the preexisting condition, i.e., everything except the certainty of cancer treatment, etc. There is no reason persons with preexisting conditions would not benefit as well as anyone else from the HSA-based approach; indeed, chronic health users should be sharper shoppers than more casual users, keeping the cost-effectiveness of the overall system at a maximum.

Many single-payer advocates look at the problem of preexisting conditions, as they do the problem of the 13 percent uninsured, and see failures requiring a total abandonment of the market-based approach and substitution of one of government control. This throws out the baby with the bathwater. There is no need to destroy the prospects for 87 percent to elevate those of 13 percent. Instead of our present process of gradual creeping mandates and controls (accelerated by the 2010 Act)—which strangles the baby slowly—we need to rid the system of the strangling vines and reintroduce the one thing proven throughout time and geography to work: competition in freed-up insurance markets. Part B describes the reasons and evidence for why this is so.

135

5. The Danger of Universal Coverage: Without Free Markets, It Becomes Another Huge Middle-Class Entitlement

There is another reason why mandates and controls should be eliminated in any voucher regime. To create universal coverage (by voucher or otherwise) as a part of existing arrangements—that is, without the elimination of mandates and controls that presently define and constrain the financing of health care—is really to create a new subsidy for the non-poor middle classes and would be highly counterproductive. The reason is that those who fall in the uninsured group are by and large not those who need the financial benefit of vouchers or tax credits to achieve coverage. Only a third of the uninsured are actually poor by any definition. The poor are already largely covered by Medicaid.

So who are the uninsured? According to Census Bureau figures, two-thirds of the uninsured in 2002 earned over $25,000 per year. Sixteen percent earned $50,000 to $75,000, and 16 percent earned $75,000 or more. Moreover, between 1993 and 1999, the number of uninsured in the below $25,000 group decreased 2 percent while that in the $50,000 group increased 57 percent, and in the over $75,000 group 114 percent.[122]

Thus clearly it is the relatively better off who are opting not to have insurance. The reason they are opting out is that the present system of mandates—especially guaranteed issue and community rating—"are a free rider's heaven," allowing the healthy to drop coverage until the crisis hits and then enroll.[123] The 2010 Act sought to address this

---

122 Goodman, Musgrave, and Herrick, *Lives at Risk*, at 218-219.
123 Goodman, Musgrave, and Herrick, *Lives at Risk*, at 220-222.

problem by requiring everyone to buy insurance or face a penalty. Even if this provision (and the Act itself) should survive constitutional challenge, adding enrollees in a world of soup-to-nuts coverage simply magnifies the cost problem at the heart of our current system.

We need to go in the other direction. Eliminating mandates and controls will eliminate these free riders and stop the growth of voluntary uninsured who rely on avoiding premiums until sickness calls. Freeing up insurance markets so competition thrives will drive down premiums for the vast majority (who are not chronically ill), thereby reducing the uninsured. Providing vouchers in amounts proportional to the average cost of treatment will ensure the chronically ill with preexisting conditions and the poor are covered as well. The key is high-deductible coverage in HSAs, free insurance markets without mandates and controls, and vouchers.

Since the uninsured problem is largely one for the non-poor middle classes, the cost control only free markets can ensure is critical to prevent reform being the greatest fraud in American history, where the middle classes are duped into supporting a new system where they are torn between the Scylla of the 2010 Act's nonexistent or illusory cost control and the Charybdis of single-payer global budgets or price controls set by government. The former leads to spiraling out-of-control premiums and taxation, and the latter leads to long queues and deteriorated service. Under either approach, everyone loses.

The conclusion seems unavoidable: only free insurance markets combined with HSAs and vouchers for the poor actually works—satisfying Galen's maxim ("first do no harm") by solving the health cost/service quality trade-off dilemma and meeting the needs of all.

6. The Three Cs and Q (Costs, Coverage, Controls, and Quality), and the Beauty of HSAs, Vouchers, and Free Insurance Markets

Why do HSAs, free insurance markets, and vouchers achieve the promised goal of universal coverage with lower costs and without degenerating quality, where our present system including the 2010 Act and single-payer approaches fail? I call it "the three Cs and Q." The three Cs are costs, coverage, and controls, and the Q is quality. The goal is to simultaneously lower costs, create universal coverage, and reduce or eliminate government controls (which, as seen, have adverse effects), while preserving or enhancing quality.

The beauty of HSAs is that by tying tax-favored accounts to high-deductible coverage, patients have skin in the game—they build up their own resources in these accounts to apply to health needs below the deductible, creating cost-consciousness, and the conditions are laid for them to become shoppers in a competitive environment. Insurance returns to its historic role—protect against the dire and unexpected. Eliminating mandates and controls on what health insurers can offer allows them to shape coverage according to real market demands and individual needs and desires, not some ivory tower or political conception of what is better for people in general. Eliminating state barriers to competition is a simple measure enhancing the competitive environment and consumer choice.

Together, HSAs and free insurance markets foster competition for the consumer dollar, driving down costs to everyone. Quality is enhanced because eliminating government controls on prices and products encourages providers to participate in the market (more doctors decide to stay or enter the profession, drug companies increase investment in research, carriers find ways to create new products).

7. An HSA-Based System with Vouchers is Best Suited for America

The program set out above represents a powerful advance for all Americans. It is *comprehensive*, including elimination of mandates and controls along with providing vouchers. It builds into the system a *permanent, systemic method* of cost control—realigning payment and decision-making in the proper hands, the patient's—through HSAs. It provides the basis for competitive forces to work in the quest by providers—hospitals, drug companies, doctors—energized by the profit-motive to serve instead of flounder and weaken. It puts incentives at the proper place at the core of the system—with the individual. It distances each of us from the reach of the bureaucrat and towards individual freedom of choice and action while undergirding the ability of all to participate. It is the proper system for America's traditions of individual liberty and solicitude for others.

And by separating employment and coverage, huge unnecessary costs are lifted from corporations and other job-creating entities, and economic growth is enhanced, a critical advantage in an era of possible jobless recoveries and slow job growth. Such a situation places pressures on politicians to expand credit and otherwise interfere in financial markets, to the detriment of sound banking and the economy. This is one way the right health care policy can help general economic conditions.[124]

---

124 See Raghuram G. Rajan, *Fault Lines: How Hidden Fractures Still Threaten the World Economy,* Ch 1 "Let Them Eat Credit" (Princeton University Press 2010). "Politicians have recognized the problem posed by rising inequality… Politicians have therefore looked for other ways to

The Opportunity to Change for Real Benefit

Although the 2010 Act moves us in the wrong direction, it also presents an opportunity. The cost explosion it builds in calls for—indeed requires—change, and under the federal constitution's supremacy and commerce clauses, all the above changes can be accomplished with the stroke of the federal pen, even as part of a single federal statute.[125] To do this is to modify the policy favoring state regulation of "the business of insurance" under the McCarran-Ferguson Act of 1945,[126] but only insofar as mandates and consumer restrictions are involved. The states still have an important role to play in supervising carrier investments and financial health and in implementing needed medical malpractice tort reforms.[127]

---

improve the lives of their voters. Since the early 1980s, the most seductive answer has been easier credit. In some ways, it is the path of least resistance... Politicians love to have banks expand housing credit, for credit achieves many goals at the same time. It pushes up house prices, making households feel wealthier, and allows them to finance more consumption. It creates more profits and jobs in the financial sector as well as in real estate brokerage and housing construction... Unfortunately, the private sector, aided and abetted by agency money, converted the good intentions behind the affordable-housing mandate and the push to an ownership society into a financial disaster."

125 *United States v. South-Eastern Underwriters Ass'n*, 322 US 533 (1944) (commerce clause allows federal regulation of insurance).

126 15 U.S.C. 1011-1015. The 2010 Act already demolishes this policy by extensive regulation of health insurers.

127 A note should be added on the role of tort reform. It is widely recognized that large malpractice awards drive up the cost of insurance for doctors and hospitals and add significantly to the rise in health care costs. Much writing exists on that subject. Various tort reforms have been attempted and others implemented in various states over the years without significant dent in the overall climate. What is most effective is a cap on pain and suffering damages, for this is the bulk of excess awards, although many other approaches are also feasible. Whatever

CHAPTER V: THE SOLUTION

Health policy experts point out that any change in our system must meet two additional basic requirements: ease of implementation and minimization of the risk of failure.[128] The system of health savings accounts and vouchers combined with freed-up insurance markets satisfies both criteria. In terms of implementation, there are these areas of primary concern: 1) timing and scheduling of HSA availability for Medicare and Medicaid, 2) how to calculate and fix the amount of subsidy in the voucher program, 3) what rules to implement for standard and minimum coverage to assure that all are protected, 4) how to structure the preexisting condition exchange market, and 5) how to publish and disseminate pertinent information on provider prices, costs, and quality.

With respect to the first, HSAs should be available immediately to most everyone. Anyone over some designated age, such as fifty-five, and under a certain income level should remain eligible for present Medicare based upon reliance, but the option of HSAs should be available. Regarding voucher amounts and scaling, much work has been done in this area over many years, starting with the "negative income tax" proposals of the late 1960s and recent work on patient-centered proposals.[129] As for rules of coverage, few are needed since reliance is upon the con-

---

health care system is in effect, tort reform is desirable and needed. The power of the plaintiff's personal injury bar to prevent political change has impeded needed reforms. Because tort reform is needed under any and all health care systems, it is not specially treated here, where the focus is on the larger questions of government versus individual control of resources and decision making, and how government can aid the individual. Whether to enmesh tort reform in the larger questions of HSAs and vouchers is a tactical choice others are better able to assess.
128 Theodore R. Marmor, *Understanding Health Care Reform*, at 136-145.
129 See e.g., Goodman, Musgrave, and Herrick, *Lives at Risk*, at 217-253.

sumer, but existing catastrophic coverage provisions can continue.

The second factor, the risk of failure of the new system, is minimized. This point is usually advanced as a reason to adopt a foreign single-payer system (in Canada, Britain, Europe, etc.), but this comparison is misplaced. For reasons set out above and again in Part B, the most relevant comparison is not foreign single-payer systems. Rather, we should look to our own history of freedom of individual choice before we began to distort health care with intrusive regulation. A shift to HSA-based individual responsibility — the contours of which are historically familiar — is not nearly as risky a change as that to a single-payer system, the deficiencies of which as seen above are substantial and predictable.

Follow the Least Invasive Procedure

A voucher/subsidy patient-centered financing approach such as here also meets the problem of the uninsured directly while single-payer schemes overshoot. Single-payer advocates find problems with the delivery of health care for some and use that to completely overturn the system that has worked for most, substituting something worse. This violates the cardinal rule of health itself: use the minimally invasive procedure that solves the problem. To overshoot – to throw out the baby with the bath water – is to harm the many in the name of helping a few. This violates what economists call "Pareto optimality" and common sense.

The principle – keep programs to the minimally invasive – applies across the board, not just in health care. If not enough African-Americans or students from relatively poor backgrounds are getting into college, the solution is not for the government to take over all of higher education. Rather, address the problem of minority admissions directly, in the most minimally invasive way. Perhaps specialized remedial efforts are warranted for those in need. Perhaps money to pay for the costs of college is required for those unable to pay. Education does not need to be free to everyone (which puts the entire burden on the taxpayer) just so a few get an opportunity they otherwise could not afford.

Single-payer advocates neglect such common-sense approaches—which they undoubtedly apply in every other area. Why do they fail to follow the minimally invasive procedure principle when it comes to health care? Why are they not just as shocked by the suggestion that government take over health care as by the suggestion government take over Yale and Harvard? [130]

---

130 A concise list of the proposals discussed in this section is in Appendix A.

B. The Regulatory Illusion: Why Government-Control and Single-Payer Failures are Predictable

CHAPTER VI:
First, Understanding the Benefits Markets Bring

We have seen how single-payer and other nationalized systems fail their patients and the taxpaying public and cannot live up to the ideals they profess. We have seen in Chapters IV and V the solution to the pitfalls of single-payer and other government-controlled approaches, a solution that opens up the health care door to all while providing a built-in means for cost containment and without a drag on job creation.

This part involves a broader excursion into relevant economics—theory and empirical findings—and brings it to the interested public, without technical detail or elaborate review of the studies themselves. It is designed to acquaint the reader with the foundations of sound economic thinking and then seeks to raise, and address, the most common and substantial objections and misperceptions people have to market approaches, at least as I understand them.

This chapter explains what a free market really implies, despite its sometimes bad press, and the benefits it can bring, and the following chapter on our experience with regulated industries and the findings of economic science in numerous studies of those industries makes plain why the shortfalls of single-payer and nationalized systems are easily predictable. Together they provide a deeper understanding of what is behind the everyday political rhetoric and a more complete explanation of why the solution sketched above that builds upon markets instead of seeking to replace them with government controls best satisfies the needs of the public. They lay the foundation for why it is imperative as part of any reform to rid the system of the accumulated morass of mandates and controls in the provision of health insurance and free up that sector so that everyone benefits.

1. People Talking Past One Another: Liberals Versus Conservatives

In thinking about these issues it is helpful to step back a bit and observe the public discussion. On health care as in other matters, liberals and conservatives, Democrats and Republicans, talk past one another. There is no real communication. This phenomenon is ubiquitous, so the battle is always engaged, never ameliorated. Liberals, those usually seeking greater role for government in the economy, and conservatives, those seeking a lesser governmental role, view the other as ill-informed or insensitive and somewhat villainous, wreaking obvious harm. Yet few stop to analyze this difference in attitude or get to the bottom. Partisan media feeds each side, digging the trenches deeper.

Perhaps the most astute analysis of this phenomenon is by George Stigler, the great Nobel Prize-winning economist. He writes:

> To the liberal the conservative's preoccupation with efficiency seems outrageous. The liberal sees a numerous fam-

CHAPTER VI: FIRST, UNDERSTANDING THE BENEFITS MARKETS BRING

ily supported by an ill-paid wage earner and asserts that an economy as rich as ours can afford to pay a meager $1.25 or $2.00 an hour [Stigler wrote in the 1960s] to this wage earner... A well bred liberal will not openly voice his doubts about the benevolence of a conservative, but it is difficult to believe that the liberal does not suspect that the conservative has greater love for profits than for people.

I venture to assert that the conservative is an earnest friend of man but that he looks at welfare in a less personal and restricted way than the liberal. When the price of wheat is raised by a crop restriction scheme, everyone can observe the benefit to the owner of the farm, and it is this benefit that catches the liberal eye. The conservative is troubled by two other effects of the crop restriction scheme: a tax has been levied on all consumers of bread; and the restriction scheme almost inevitably will lead to some waste of resources or, differently put, reduce the community's real income. These effects are obviously harmful to non-farmers.

...The conservative's preference for low prices, strong incentives to diligence and thrift and inventiveness, and similar attributes of efficiency and progress, has indeed a substantial advantage over the liberal's plan of assisting particular needy groups. There are many, many needy groups in a society, and some take a generation or two or even three before they catch the eye of the liberal, be he reformer or politician... The conservative's programs are designed to help everyone, even groups too poor to have a press agent.

These remarks are intended to illustrate a general proposition: the conservative opposition to intervention by either government or private monopoly is commonly stated in efficiency terms but could always be restated in terms of welfare, and especially the welfare of consumers. A conservative may be truly humane. It is fair to say that the conservative is compassionate for the great mass of the population which is moderately affected by each public policy, whereas the liberal is compassionate for the special, identifiable group which is most benefited or injured by the policy in question.[131]

Markets Achieve Efficiency, Which Delivers Maximal Benefits

As Stigler points out, morality and economics are a two-bladed sword: they cut in both directions and usually not in the direction moralists point to. A major question in economics is: what system or rules deliver the most benefits to the most people while minimizing harm to others and achieving basic equity? This centrally involves what economists call efficiency, which is a fancy word for the maximal use of resources without waste or decline in income, and the greatest possible job creation. In advanced societies, it is built on the division of labor, productivity increases, and competition. Together they maximize net social wealth. The division of labor allows each individual to do that which he or she does best and allows groups (companies) to produce what they can best. Productivity gains are the key to economic growth.[132]

---

131 George Stigler, "The Unjoined Debate," in *The Citizen and the State: Essays on Regulation,* at 6-7 (U. Chicago Press 1975).
132 Brian M. Riedl, "Why Government Spending Does Not Stimulate Economic Growth: Answering the Critics," 1/8/2010, *WSJ.*

CHAPTER VI: FIRST, UNDERSTANDING THE BENEFITS MARKETS BRING

Competition among people and enterprises reduces the cost of the good or service provided, ultimately to the level of the famous equation marginal revenue equals marginal cost. With characteristic wit, Stigler writes: "Competition may be the spice of life, but in economics it has been more nearly the main dish... In economic life competition is not a goal: it is a means of organizing economic activity to achieve a goal. The economic role of competition is to discipline the various participants in economic life to provide their goods and services skillfully and cheaply."[133]

Given time, "resources will tend to be put where they earn the most." This is important because only then will goods and services get into the hands that want them, in other words, achieve the greatest social good efficiently. The alternative is that some people with greater need or preferences lose out to those with less:

> The competitive structure of industry will lead to the establishment of competitive prices. Competitive prices are characterized by two main properties. The property of clearing markets is that of distributing existing supplies efficiently; the property of equalizing returns to resources is that of directing production efficiently...
>
> Since every buyer can purchase all he wishes of the good or service at the market price, there are no queues or unsatisfied demands (given the price). Since every seller can sell all he wishes at this market price, there are no undisposable stocks, other than inventories which are voluntarily held for future periods. The competitive price,

---

133 George J. Stigler, *The Organization of Industry*, at 5 (U. Chicago Press 1968).

then, clears the market—it equates the quantities offered by sellers and sought by buyers.

Whenever we find a persistent queue among buyers, we know that the price is being held below the level which clears the market, and which we naturally call an equilibrium price...

The importance of prices that clear markets is that this is the method by which goods and services are put in the hands of the people who most urgently wish them. If a price is held too low, some buyers who set a lower value on the commodity will get it while others in the queue who set a higher value get none. If the price is set too high, goods that buyers would be glad to purchase at a lower price go unsold even though (if a minimum price is set in a competitive industry) sellers would prefer to sell at this lower price.[134]

It is a distinctive property of markets and the price system, therefore, that they achieve the maximal distribution of resources—goods and services get into the hands of those who place the most value on them, by need or preference. Everyone has a different listing or schedule of needs and wants, and through price, markets get people what they want. People who complain that this leaves the distribution up to differences in income or wealth—at least at the upper and lower margins—have a point. But the critical question is, what system other than price and markets achieves the same maximal distribution? So far, the proponents of administrative or governmentally-controlled pricing (usually called

---

134 George J. Stigler, *The Organization of Industry,* at 9-10 (U. Chicago Press 1968).

CHAPTER VI: FIRST, UNDERSTANDING THE BENEFITS MARKETS BRING

"fair" pricing) have offered us only impoverished alternatives, which socialized countries and industries have amply demonstrated to impoverish their people and have taken generations to shake free of.

For most goods and services in life, therefore, competitive markets provide the optimal means. Where overriding concerns require government to assist the needy, the proper approach is not to throw out the market and substitute bureaucratic administering of prices, but to add to the market through careful provisioning of resources for the needy. This way, the advantages of markets are preserved and the benefits are enlarged. Health care is such an example.

The practical impact of moving away from markets and the price system, or interfering with them to "improve" them by regulation, is that there is a net cost to society, a loss of net social product, formally called a misallocation of resources. This has a very personal dimension; it ultimately leads to the very harms proponents of the regulatory regime seek to avoid: slower growth, fewer jobs, less people raised out of poverty—the effects of embracing a regime of relative impoverishment. Some wish this for political or ideological reasons or are propelled by a superficial morality or egalitarianism. But no amount of such moralizing can avoid the unmistakable truth that market efficiency creates relative betterment while regulatory regimes usher in relative decline and harms. The moral shoe is on the other foot, a fact that arrives often as quite a shock to the passionate deriders.

Extracting a General Approach to Policy

This suggests a general approach to public policy: that the interests of the whole of society, not just those of particular constituent parts, should be the guide, because that way favoritism among groups competing for political benefits—the power of special interests—is minimized, resources are allocated maximally, and the greatest good goes to the greatest number, usually including those least able to fend for themselves.

As Peter Boettke says, "Democratic government's natural proclivity is to concentrate benefits on the well-organized and well-informed interest groups in the short run and to disperse the costs across the ill-organized and ill-informed mass of voters and consumers in the long run."[135] This is a recipe for the domination of politics by special interests, since the incentive structure favors the few who care intensely over the many who care just a little.

To check this tendency, one can look in the initial instance at broad-based groups that bear most of the burdens of political interference as the best proxies for society as a whole. Taxpayers and consumers, one paying the costs of government and the other paying the costs of goods and services, stand out in this regard. The first, central question to ask, then, in assessing policy is, "How is the taxpayer or consumer affected?" Asking this question tends to cut against the tendency of government to favor particular interests or constituencies over others who may lack political "muscle." It raises the view to one approximating society as a whole. Claims from particular constituencies will still need to be addressed. But there is now a context for assessment of the claim.

For example, if the needs of the poor or other groups are compelling, government intervention should be done carefully and selectively, and then usually by direct subsidy, not forced cross-subsidies upon unwilling others, so

---

[135] Peter J. Boettke, "What Happened to 'Efficient Markets'?," *The Independent Review*, Vol 14, No 3, at 363 (Winter 2010).

the effort is transparent and cost/benefit can be reckoned. Looking at the broadest interest of society ensures that an eye is kept on government's core role—ensuring protection at home and abroad, supplying essential services, supporting competitive free markets, and, where all else fails, funding those in need without destroying incentives. I call this approach the "taxpayer-consumer perspective."

It involves recognition of two fundamental and well-recognized economic ideas. First, the economy is not a pie that, for example, can be just divided willy-nilly to take from the "rich" and give to the "poor"—at least without substantial harm to the whole—including the poor. Rather, it is a dynamic engine driven by individuals who are highly susceptible to disincentives and incentives.[136] Second, efforts by the well-meaning to improve by controlling business usually end up harming the very people supposed to be benefited. This is the "law of unintended consequences" in action.

Some Examples of How Neglect of the Taxpayer/Consumer Interest Brings Harms

Our health care and finance debacles exemplify neglect of the consumer-taxpayer perspective. In the finance crisis, it was precisely the government's well-intentioned effort to include in normal housing markets those who couldn't afford their own homes that brought the ship onto the rocks. HUD's affordable housing (AH) goals and scores that promoted the deterioration of traditional underwriting standards led to the proliferation of risky mortgages. In health care, it has been the WW II tax ruling exempting health care costs from employee income while allowing

---

136 "Principles for Economic Revival," George P. Shultz, Michael J. Boskin, John F. Cogan, Allan Meltzer, and John B. Taylor, 9/16/2010, *WSJ* (fact-based economics means attention to incentives and disincentives).

the company to deduct them, magnified by the more recent proliferation of state (and now federal) mandates and controls – limiting the risks that insurers could or could not include in their offerings to customers – that skewed incentives and has led to the escalating crisis of health care costs.

In both instances, policymakers were seduced by the Free Lunch Fallacy into adopting the Regulatory Illusion. They neglected the interests of the taxpayer and the consumer, who ended up picking up the tab for catastrophic costs. These politicians could have proceeded in a fashion that would not have brought about these harms. To provide affordable housing, the federal government could simply have built upon the existing structure of the FHA, whose primary mission is precisely that. Instead, politicians thought they saw a free lunch.

The route? Expanding credit through the private markets, by regulatory AH policies and requirements, both on GSAs and also on all major banks and mortgage originators and packagers through the Community Reinvestment Act and HUD Best Practices Initiative. This looked like a costless and easy way to quickly and vastly expand affordable housing *without putting any of it on the federal budget.* As President Clinton, who initiated the program, explained to the people, "This program will not cost the taxpayer one red cent." How foolish a prophecy that was became apparent in 2008 when the whole scheme unraveled and the financial crisis and deep recession ensued.

Avoiding the harms to all of us in exploding health care costs could have been effected similarly by adhering to the best interests of taxpayers and consumers. Step number one would have been to change the WW II tax rule so that the tax code no longer incentivized employees and unions to push employers to create no-deductible company-provided coverage. Doing this would have liberated the employee

CHAPTER VI: FIRST, UNDERSTANDING THE BENEFITS MARKETS BRING

from being tied to his present job for fear of losing coverage and would have allowed him or her to assess for self what coverage best suited needs and costs according to particular circumstances. A market for health coverage would have restarted.

Step number two would have been to stop the growth of mandates and controls on what must be included in everyone's coverage. This would have cut costs dramatically at one stroke as people could elect not to pay for the myriad lifestyle-induced conditions such as smoking, obesity, psychological counseling, drug and alcohol issues, and so on that today unnecessarily (by dictate of law) burden with increasing costs—indeed shock—individuals seeking coverage for self and family.

The material in this Part B on regulated industries reaffirms the failure of the regulatory approach as we have implemented it under the influence of old progressive thinking and posits as an operating rule of governance a strong presumption against regulation. But before getting to this material, let's clear out some of the underbrush that confuses many people about the presumed evils of markets, competition, and the drive for profit. These feelings underlie much of the hostility towards market-focused approaches to problems in society and are therefore important to address directly.

2. Greed is Not the Root of All Evil: It is Profit-Making Given a Bad Name

Early on, we should address the common complaint that greed (usually seen as fostered by capitalism and markets) is at the heart of economic problems and distress. But greed is a particular condemnation that short-circuits real analysis. Your greed is someone else's profit making. There is no principled way to define greed or legislate against it. Everyone in life seeks to make financial gain, to achieve security and a better life. If you cut legal or ethical corners––e.g., as a fiduciary who profits from a conflict of interest—you (hopefully) get nailed for that, both in the market and by legal and other authorities. Rules already exist against this behavior.

Short of crossing that line, everyone seeks more income if possible. To act otherwise is to harm your family, yourself, and the wider society that depends on gains in productivity and earnings. Adam Smith's famous "invisible hand" encapsulates this point -- the unintended consequence of the pursuit of one's self-interest leads to social gain.

Historian Edmund S. Morgan says it well:

> ….greed is simply one of the uglier names we give to the driving force of modern civilization. We usually prefer less pejorative names for it. Call it the profit motive, or free enterprise, or the work ethic, or the American way, or, as the Spanish did, civility…we have to ask whether we could really get along without greed and everything that goes along with it. Yes, a few of us, a few eccentrics, might manage to live for a time like the Arawaks.[137]

F.A. Hayek adds:

> It is hence hard to believe that anyone accurately informed about the market can honestly condemn the search for profit. The disdain for profit is due to ignorance, and to an attitude that we may if we wish admire in an aescetic who has chosen to be content with a small share of the

---

137 Edmund Morgan, *American Heroes* (Norton, 2009).

CHAPTER VI: FIRST, UNDERSTANDING THE BENEFITS MARKETS BRING

riches of this world, but which, when actualized in the form of restrictions on profits of others, is selfish to the extent that it imposes aesceticism, and indeed deprivations of all sorts, on others.[138]

Greed is an easy foil in which to dress envy and the self-interest of the denouncer. TV and the press need scandal the way poppy growers need addicts. Scandal and outrage sell. Undoubtedly there is much throughout the business world (as indeed the religious) that needs correction. But the fact of scandal is the exception that proves the rule. The business media features scandal the way the evening news highlights fires and murder. Neither proves, however, that free society should be overturned in favor of the bureaucratic state.

Indeed, the shoe is on the other foot. As George Gilder reminds us, greed is getting something for nothing—a condition not promoted by markets, in which participants are disciplined to try to serve the needs or wants of others, but by *government*, through which bureaucrats achieve power over others whether those others want it or not:

> Greedy and selfish people put comfort and security first. They turn to the state to give them the benefits that they lack the moral discipline to earn on their own by serving others. Greed, as I write in *Wealth and Poverty*, leads by an invisible hand to an ever-growing welfare state—not to wealth and capitalism, but to poverty and socialism.[139]

Returning to a freer market in health insurance will run into the popular view targeting insurance companies (along with their sister financial entities, banks) as the *bête noir*, the

---

138 Friedrich A. Hayek, *The Fatal Conceit: The Errors of Socialism*, at 105 (U. Chicago Press 1988).
139 George Gilder, *Wealth & Poverty*, at xxii (ICS Press 1993).

root of all evil. Especially during and after the financial crisis of 2008 and the run-up to the 2010 health care Act, the White House, Congress, and media vied among themselves to denounce the greed and heartless behavior of Wall Street and Big Insurance, the latter for the crime of seeking to raise prices, or charge higher rates to applicants based upon higher risk.

But those railing against market profit and greed have it backwards; instead, they should focus on the unhealthy conditions government extension into the economy promotes. In the health arena, insurance companies (as with other financial institutions) are no exception to the universality of benefit from profit seeking. They exist to make money. They do this on behalf of their shareholders (you and me). What insurance carriers offer is financial security (insurance) to their customers (you and me), in return for premiums. Governmental interference (usually well-meaning) in the form of mandates, cross-subsidies of one group by another, and restrictions on out-of-state sales, among others, drive up premiums. If premiums are too high, fewer of us can afford the security we want. More join the ranks of the uninsured or self-insured.

Government control of premiums, or the favoring of not-for-profit insurers (often part of foreign nationalized systems), just pushes the cost issues somewhere else in the system—deteriorated service, disincentivized providers, and the like. In the end, the patient and taxpayer suffer.

Frederich Hayek long ago pointed out the irony facing anti-market reformers: "We are ready to accept almost any explanation of the present crisis of our civilization except one: that the present state of the world may be the result of genuine error on our own part and that the pursuit of some of our most cherished ideals has apparently produced results utterly different from those which we expected."[140] The beginning of education, therefore, starts with ourselves—our ability to learn from the best evidence and alter our opinions accordingly, even our most highly cherished beliefs. With that thought, we now turn to a review of some basics in modern economics.

3. Adam Smith's Paradox and the Role of Competition

The way we protect ourselves against health risk is by choosing among competing carriers for the most advantageous pool of risks at the lowest cost to us, for our circumstances (which are infinitely variable). This requires 1) effective competition among carriers, wherever located, and 2) "economic freedom," the freedom of carriers to adjust pools and prices according to what maximizes their profit, which also simultaneously and necessarily maximizes the social good, i.e., the maximum numbers of people paying premiums according to their situation, in pools tailored to meet their needs. In other words, as long as there is competition, the insurance company's profits and the consumer's benefit go hand in hand.

Surprised by this assertion? You shouldn't be. It is Adam Smith's "invisible hand" at work. As he said of the tradesman and merchant:

---

[140] F.A. Hayek, *The Road to Serfdom*, at 10-11. Rep. Barney Frank, a Harvard graduate and leading Congressional proponent of forcing banks to lend to non-creditworthy borrowers—as such a key architect of the financial implosion of 2008—was candid enough to admit in his 2010 reelection campaign to "errors" wrought by good intentions to help increase homeownership for the poor, a view based on his own alleged deprived background. Whether or not genuine, the partial mea culpa was successful in deflecting voter anger at the enormous harms those "errors" created.

> ...by directing that industry in such a manner as its produce may be of the greatest value, he intends only his own gain, and he is in this, as in many other cases, led by an invisible hand to promote an end which was no part of his intention... By pursuing his own interest he frequently promotes that of the society more effectually than when he really intends to promote it.[141]

This is Smith's paradox—that the pursuit of self-interest leads to the social good. It is the central lesson of the free market, for only under conditions of freedom can people pursue their interests (and thus society's best enhancement) in the maximal way.

Samuel Gregg, director of research at the Acton Institute, elaborates:

> Adam Smith"s reference to the "invisible hand" perplexes some, but is simply a metaphor for the idea that through allowing people to pursue their self-interest, unintended but beneficial social consequences for others will follow. As individuals pursue profit, they unintentionally add to the sum total of the wealth in society, unintentionally allow people from different nations to come to know each other, unintentionally promote civility and peace, unintentionally allow others to benefit from more and better jobs, and unintentionally contribute to technological development. None of this means that commercial society does not afford opportunities for people to act altruistically. Rather, it is precisely because increasingly large numbers of people in a commercial society are able to accumulate sums of capital that exceed their immediate needs and acquired

---

[141] Adam Smith, *An Inquiry into the Nature and Causes of the Wealth of Nations*, Book IV, Ch 11, at p 477-78 (U. Chicago Press 1976).

responsibilities, they begin to develop opportunities to be generous to others.[142]

We (society at large) *want* insurance carriers (and banks, and oil companies) to make money, to profit. Otherwise they wouldn't exist and we wouldn't be offered the financial security, products, and services they provide.

4. Defining Terms: Free Markets Require Government Rules

There is a need to clarify terms to avoid confusion. People are often misled by the words "free markets," believing that the phrase implies anarchy without rules or restrictions of any kind. This is untrue. It also leads to the observation that "there is no such thing as a free market," and therefore that free market theory is absurd, since most markets have rules.

This apparent syllogism misses the point. As explained later, free markets are heavily dependent for their proper functioning upon rules, usually legislated but often imposed privately. It is not the existence of government rules themselves that marks the important difference between regimes of government control and so-called free markets; rather it is the nature and intent of the laws and regulations—whether their effect and design is to hinder and restrict competition and transactions or promote them. Thus markets are highly dependent for their efficient operation on often-complex sets of rules designed to foster transactions and facilitate free exchange.

Think of securities markets. Long before the SEC or any government agency thought up ways to follow legislative

---

142 Samuel Gregg, *The Commercial Society*, at 29-30 (Lexington Books 2007).

mandates, highly complex rules evolved among the participants governing the timing, manner, mode, and types of securities exchanged. These rules promote, not restrict, freedom of commerce.[143]

The important distinction between free markets on one hand and government-controlled markets on the other lies, then, in whether the rules imposed foster competition, transactions, and free exchange, or restrict them. In so-called regulated industries such as transportation before the Carter-era deregulation, the rules were restrictive of each of these. The ICC, CAB and other regulatory agencies imposed restrictions on what air, rail, barge, bus, and truck carriers could charge (pricing), where they could travel (entry), whether someone else could offer services in the market they served (competition), and what they could sell (product control). It is these types of rules that characterize what is referred to in the literature as regulated industries.

"Free" markets are free of such intrusive rules – and the concomitant agents of government armed with discretionary power to pick and choose among market participants and products and to skew optimal market outcomes, which accompany such rules. In "free" markets, the rules that exist are designed to foster, not restrict, transactions and to accept, not reject, open participation. In numerous industries in America – agriculture, banking and finance, communications (even after the ATT breakup), pharmaceuticals, and so on – numerous rules still restrict transactions, retard innovation, and restrict competition.

---

143 Ronald H. Coase, *The Firm, The Market and the Law*, at 9 (U Chicago Press 1990). It is a common mistake to point to the fact that all markets have regulations of some kind and conclude that therefore there is no such thing as a free market. The point is not the existence of rules, but their nature and tendency.

CHAPTER VI: FIRST, UNDERSTANDING THE BENEFITS MARKETS BRING

Health care used to be primarily a free market. Even before, but especially after, the 2010 changes, it has evolved into a highly regulated one, characterized by degrees of product control, price control, and restrictions on competition and entry. It is this evolution, and the harms it brings, that spurred this undertaking.

Transportation – and the railroad industry in particular – prior to President Carter's deregulations was a classic case of destructive economic regulation. Railroads could not give up unprofitable routes nor build prospective profitable routes without a certificate of convenience and necessity from the Interstate Commerce Commission. This allowed competitors to endlessly tie up such applications in expensive and drawn-out litigation. Rates could not be changed without similar approval, allowing rival shippers to seek competitive advantage by similarly gaming the system. Mergers between railroads were subject to exhausting and debilitating (often decade-long) hearings before the ICC.

The initial impulse for this regulation was popular distrust of "robber barons" and railroad stock manipulations in the late 1800s. But what happened over time was that the regulation choked off investment and lowered returns so that by the 1960s the railroads throughout America, with very few exceptions, were dying.

The Railway Labor Act put further nails in the railroad industry coffin. Enormous power accrued to the railroad unions, creating high and intractable labor costs. Although firemen were unnecessary once coal-fired boilers were replaced with diesel, and improvements allowed longer and longer daily runs, nonetheless railroads during the 1960s had to change crews every 120 miles, which a century before represented a full day's ride, just because the unions insisted on this sort of "featherbedding." Although no method of transportation is as efficient as steel wheels on track, the enormous benefits to society and the economy that the railroad presented were destroyed in a tangle of regulatory restrictions.[144]

President Carter ended all this by persuading Congress to deregulate the railroads. That the industry has come back from the edge of death is symbolized by the fact that in 2009 the Sage of Omaha, Warren Buffett, saw fit to cause Berkshire Hathaway to purchase Burlington Northern Santa Fe. This shows the industry has come quite a long way since, for example, the sale of the Chicago & Northwestern to its employees for a pittance ($50 million) forty years earlier.

5. It's Competition, Not Competitors, that Merits Our Protection

The essence of free markets can be stated in a phrase: it's not the individual firm or competitor that merits our social or economic interest or concern, it's *competition* itself—the freely evolving process that incentivizes innovation and change and revolutionizes markets and ways of life. People who think that the system exists to protect the likes of an AT&T, General Motors, or Citibank, or similar "rich fat cats," miss the point. We don't care as a society if, singularly, they succeed or fail; rather, it is the competitive arena that acts upon them that we do care about. In a free market, someone else, who better serves the needs or wants of consumers, will take their place or indeed is the occasion for their downfall. IBM failed to see the value in software and

---

144 The author had the opportunity to be a close observer of the railroad industry during the decades of the 1960s and 1970s.

CHAPTER VI: FIRST, UNDERSTANDING THE BENEFITS MARKETS BRING

handed its development and marketing over to Microsoft. IBM nearly failed selling computers and Microsoft became one of the world's most valuable companies.

In this, government has a critical role—in protecting free and competitive markets. It does this both by protecting against the creation of monopoly or combination (think Sherman Anti-Trust Act) and also, more significantly, in preventing the capture of *its own powers* by individual market participants or groups. For the real danger to the public comes less from private monopoly or combination, which history shows are unstable and temporary,[145] and more from the alliance of government, through agencies and bureaucracies that purport to serve the public interest, with particular market players, who thereby gain positions of privilege and protection that history shows tend to be stable and long lasting.

It is in the self-interest of an individual competitor to capture the levers of government for its own use—to exclude other competitors, allow fixed prices, secure privileges of one kind or another. This is what you see wholesale in certain Latin American countries, for example, and in Russia, where elite groups control both industry and government and ensure government continues their protected positions, protected against competition. These are stable and extremely hard to dislodge. This situation is the opposite of a free market. This is a market of limited entry and controlled pricing to the detriment of the consumer and

---

[145] The difficulty of policing combinations in the face of the lure each participant has to earn extra profits by cheating and selling outside the cartel arrangement has doomed the success of such efforts over time. George J. Stigler, "The Economic Effects of the Antitrust Laws," in *The Organization of Industry* (U. Chicago Press 1968).

producer and solely to the benefit of the privileged and their government patron.[146]

6. Are Free Markets Based on Selfishness at the Expense of Others?

Closely related to the mistake about greed is the mistake about self-interest. As Smith's paradox shows, morality and economics merge. If we benefit our fellows by pursuing our own interests, how much better that is than a program of forced charity or Sunday morning public spirit. Critics and those hostile to markets should recognize that morality is built into the so-called capitalist system—that although charity gets the press, the most effective way most people have of helping others is to do the best they can at the service or producing the product they do and that others desire and are willing to pay for.[147] This is called "working", and it is what all of us do most of our lives. It supports ourselves

---

[146] Some argue that in developing countries certain forms of "managed capitalism" are helpful in accelerating economic growth in the early stages of an export-driven economy. See Raghuram G. Rajan, *Fault Lines: How Hidden Fractures Still Threaten the World Economy,* Ch 2 "Exporting to Grow" (Princeton University Press 2010). But as Rajan notes, protection and subsidy are addictive, and the trick is how to turn off the faucet. The problem is that the protected and subsidized privileged few capture the political levers of power (or visa versa) to the detriment of the mass of the people. The experience of President Fujimori in Peru in the early 1990s and the contrast between Hong Kong and Singapore in the 1960-2000 era suggests that managed capitalism retards, not enhances, growth even in developing economies. Robert J. Barro, *Getting It Right: Markets and Choices in a Free Society,* at 21-43 (MIT 1996).

[147] Although few in commercial society can make charity their primary endeavor, nonetheless doing good for others and extending a hand where possible are all facilitated, not impeded, by commercial society.

CHAPTER VI: FIRST, UNDERSTANDING THE BENEFITS MARKETS BRING

and our families. We give our extra time, money, or both to others.

Although we get little moral credit for it, working carries an unrecognized, socially denigrated but extraordinarily high moral purpose. Morality—especially self-denial, discipline, honesty, civility, peace—is fostered by working. Working makes us part of the commercial interchange of the larger society. Missing this point, many people undermine the system in the name of improving it. As Yuval Levin points out:

> ...market players have a powerful incentive to consider what others will think of their actions, since they have to appeal to those others as customers. And the virtues most valued in sellers and buyers are precisely Smith's moderate virtues: prudence and thrift, honesty and reliability, civility and good order—in short, again: discipline. The market, as Smith saw it, is a powerful tool of discipline. It demands and rewards habits of peaceful order, and can spread these into the larger society.[148]

This idea, applied to collections of workers called companies, lifts the morality of the individual into the larger economic sphere. People get paid, and achieve success, because they supply others with some wanted service or product. In economic-talk, they are creating utility. Jamie Dimon, chairman and CEO of J.P. Morgan Chase, put it this way: "In a free market economy, companies grow over time because they are winning customers. These companies win customers and grow market share because they—relative to the competition—are doing a better and faster (and at

---

148 Yuval Levin, "Recovering the Case for Capitalism," 3 *National Affairs* at 127 (Spring 2010).

times less expensive) job of providing customers with what they want."[149]

It may come as a shock to those whose ingrained dispositions and ordinary reading material counsel them otherwise, but in this way the free market—popularly depicted as heartless—promotes virtues that, although certainly economic, are just as crucially matters of the spirit, values including lack of dependency, vigorous political expression, and élan. Self-interest – what we pursue by working, achieving success in our careers – is commonly confused with being selfish, but that is a fundamental misconception.

Self-Interest Includes Charity

Self-interest, as economists use it, the pursuit of gain and profit by work, is a broad concept paradoxically encompassing many virtues and objects not commonly conjured up by the term. Milton Friedman includes in self-interest "the whole range of values that men hold dear and for which they are willing to spend their fortunes and sacrifice their lives... It is the virtue of a free society that it nevertheless permits these [charitable, educational, and religious] interests free scope and does not subordinate them to the narrow materialistic interests that dominate the bulk of mankind. That is why capitalist societies are less materialistic than collectivist societies."[150]

Working, pursuing a career or profession or artistic interest, does not usually come to mind when thinking of self-interest in economics, but that is the core of what it is all about.

---

149 Jamie Dimon, chairman and CEO of JP Morgan Chase Bank, 4/4/2011, Letter to Shareholders, at 30, 2010, JPM Ann. Report.
150 Milton Friedman, *Capitalism and Freedom*, at 200-201. There is a close parallel between self-interest and "what one is interested in." Isn't someone interested in helping others through (say) his or her church pursuing his or her self-interest?

CHAPTER VI: FIRST, UNDERSTANDING THE BENEFITS MARKETS BRING

Much of the popular hostility towards free markets, capitalism, self-interest, and the like arises from confusion as to this simple everyday reality. To get along through life, each of us must earn enough to satisfy our needs – security, freedom, above all. We help ourselves by this effort and in the process help satisfy the wants of others – otherwise we would not last long in our job.

How much we take home, how much capital we accumulate, is a function of the degree we satisfy the desires and needs of others who are willing to pay us for what we are able to give or do through our work. Whether we become rich, poor, or land in some middle ground is of no moral consequence as long as we do our best in the effort to succeed. Someone who becomes rich is no less worthy nor more worthy than anyone else who performs a service or sells a good others desire.

Sinclair Lewis, Dickens, and other writers of the nineteenth and early twentieth centuries painted an indelible portrait of working and the commercial society as degrading to the individual and remorselessly squashing of personal initiative and opportunity. We all imbibed this in college, and many who take literature as their guide still argue this view. In fact, the exact opposite is true. It is not true of us as workers. Neither is it true of the entrepreneur, often considered to be the heart of the capitalist system. His or her risk-taking in the pursuit of the goal of providing a profitable service or product for others requires the essence of virtue—discipline, frugality, creativity, energy, self-denial. Why? An entrepreneur starts with an idea and through hard work, discipline, and an ear for what others want satisfies their needs. Or more likely fails.

The entrepreneur sacrifices or defers immediate gratification for longer-term goals. Greed is getting something for nothing, or taking advantage of others—the opposite of the behavior of the entrepreneur. Throughout the commercial world, where there is competition, greed is self-defeating. A greedy businessperson will cheat customers—until those customers take their business elsewhere. Ironically, the virtues at the heart of commercial life are the very virtues promoted from the pulpit and the hearth. As George Gilder puts it:

> Not from greed, avarice, or even self-love can one expect the rewards of commerce, but from a spirit closely akin to altruism, a regard for the needs of others, a benevolent, outgoing and courageous temper of mind... Not taking and consuming, but giving, risking, and creating are the characteristic roles of the capitalist, the key producer of the wealth of nations, from the least developed to the most advanced.[151]

The insights of Adam Smith and the best of economic science are hard for many to swallow. They are counterintuitive. We have a moralist perspective. We think, "People pursuing self-interest is bad; it is selfish. They should be made to do good."

But this lofty impulse leads to folly. Human nature seeks the betterment of self and family through profit seeking that, without intending to do so, aids others. This is a historical and universal truth. Max Weber, one of the founders of social science and the disciplines of sociology and political science, said: "The notion that our rationalistic and capitalistic age is characterized by a stronger economic interest than other periods is childish. The moving spirits of modern capitalism are not possessed of a stronger economic impulse than, for example, an Oriental trader."[152]

---

151 George Gilder, *Wealth & Poverty*, at 21 (ICS Press 1993).
152 Max Weber, *General Economic History*, at 355-6 (trans. by Frank H. Knight).

CHAPTER VI: FIRST, UNDERSTANDING THE BENEFITS MARKETS BRING

Western Liberation from Want was based on Freedom of Commerce

In fact, the so-called capitalist ethos evolved as an often-revolutionary way in contrast to the strict system of custom and status, bolstered by an established religion, which dominated social and economic life for a millennium after the fall of Rome. The new way was based upon an equality of opportunity rather than the equality of impoverishment and the status limitations of medieval times. R.H. Tawney describes this shift:

> The pioneers of the modern economic order were [Weber argued] *parvenus*, who elbowed their way to success in the teeth of the established aristocracy of land and commerce. The tonic that braced them for the conflict was a new conception of religion, which taught them to regard the pursuit of wealth as, not merely an advantage, but a duty... So far from poverty being meritorious, it is a duty to choose a more profitable occupation. So far from there being an inevitable conflict between money-making and piety, they are natural allies, for the virtues incumbent on the elect—diligence, thrift, sobriety, prudence—are the most reliable passport to commercial prosperity. Thus the pursuit of riches, which once had been feared as the enemy of religion, was now welcomed as its ally.[153]

Those who deplore what they see as rampant greed and self-interest throughout society or in some of its many niches and corners confront the danger that what they are implicitly urging is a return to the kind of static, rigid order from which mankind, at least in Western societies, achieved

---

153 R.H. Tawney, Forward to Max Weber, *The Protestant Ethic and the Spirit of Capitalism*, at 2-3 (Dover Publications 2003).

liberation. Those who urge enhancement of the regulatory and bureaucratic state must be cautioned lest they bring about the return of decline and the very equality of impoverishment and loss of the freedom that they now enjoy. Be careful what you wish for. Understand the benefits of the economic order we have before seeking to destroy or alter its essences.

There is a moral irony: societies built on "self-interested" commerce allow more to be done for others than societies built on traditional roles or ideal societies in which helping or eliminating the poor is their explicit goal. Efforts to legislate change in human nature, or morally improve it, as in the Soviet Union, Cambodia, North Korea, and Cuba, quite explicitly—but also in socialist and liberal societies that rely on government and laws to do the improving—are based on fundamental ignorance of Smith's paradox and the way modern commercial life fosters virtue and promotes security and peace.

Putting government bureaucrats in charge of economic life promotes greed—defined as getting something for nothing—by creating a privileged "new class" whose only claim to legitimacy is a talent for political advancement but who are rewarded with the material and other benefits of power over others. Such transformations have led to more spiritual and economic impoverishment and deaths in the twentieth century alone than all wars and disease.[154]

---

154 In this respect as in others, the advantage the rich or powerful take in a bureaucratized system mimics that long ago described in the '50s blockbuster, *The New Class* (Praeger 1957), by Milovan Djilas, denied his post as vice president of Yugoslavia and expelled from the Yugoslav Communist Party in 1954 for advocating "democratization." Djilas wrote this book while in Yugoslav prison for supporting the Hungarian uprising. The "new class" he described was the privileged bureaucrats

CHAPTER VI: FIRST, UNDERSTANDING THE BENEFITS MARKETS BRING

Personal Freedoms and Economic Freedoms are Indivisible

It is hard to reconcile free markets with dictatorship and other forms of governance denying individual political rights, although the Chinese and Vietnamese are certainly trying to give it a go. Over time, such monopolies are undermined by the rise of numerous private sources of power. One of the lessons of the Soviet-bloc experience is its vivid demonstration of the intimate—indeed intrinsic—connection between economic freedom on the one hand and political, intellectual, aesthetic, artistic, and religious freedoms on the other; repress economic freedom and all freedoms are at risk.[155]

As the quote from F.A. Hayek (at the beginning of Chapter I) reminds, the decay of the independent spirit fostered by communism occurs in democratic systems as well, wherever government control of an activity promotes attitudes of dependency. Studies reveal this exact phenomenon to occur under Britain's National Health Service, for example, showing how true this is even in a relative free society when people become subject to extensive government control.[156]

So those who define self-interest narrowly or conflate self-interest or profit seeking with selfishness and disregard for common humanity miss the point. In an extraordinary

and officials of the Tito socialist/communist regime, of which he had been a prominent member. His book was the first revelation by a prominent insider of the truth about the "classless society" on the other side of the Iron Curtain and was significant in opening the eyes of many on this side of the Iron Curtain who had come to believe in the myth.
155 Those needing reminders of this should watch the German movies *Das Leben der Anderen (*The Lives of Others) (2006) and *Der Tunnel* (2001).
156 John Goodman, Musgrave, and Herrick, *Lives at Risk*, at 197.

late work of great depth, Hayek described what he called the "extended order of human cooperation," revealing how profit seeking needs and breeds virtuous human interaction however simple or complex the society may be.[157] What Hayek describes is how freely interacting individuals in all societies, regardless of their stage of development, create beneficial links and connections based upon trade and commercial needs. Desert tent dwellers carry incense and myriad goods west to east and visa versa. Indian tribes in pre-Columbian America exchange cowrie shells and other prized goods and developed wampum as a monetary system to facilitate trade. The examples are endless.

The common requirements for such transactions were the ability to trust and safety. Thus virtues such as reliability, non-violence, and peaceful relations were important foundations for the society to flourish and progress. Wars, murder, and theft were common, but these worked counter to the basic needs of society, and one of the benefits of empire was its ability to combat predation and violations of person and property and bring about the conditions for facilitating trade.

Capitalism is not an "ism"

Although the change from religion- and aristocracy-dominated status societies is usually referred to as a change to capitalism, this word fails to capture the essence of the change. Yes, accumulations of capital were fostered and in turn allowed greater investment and greater job opportunities. But the creation of an "ism" to this process suggests something about it that was not true: that it was the conscious creation of a set of ideas, analogous to socialism. It is and was not at all like socialism. Socialism was the conscious

---

157 F.A. Hayek, *The Fatal Conceit*, at 11-28.

CHAPTER VI: FIRST, UNDERSTANDING THE BENEFITS MARKETS BRING

creation of a few people based on a clear set of ideas—government ownership of the means of production above all.

What is misleadingly referred to as capital"ism" evolved out of natural conditions of mankind, individuals trading and engaging in commerce for their mutual benefit across all nations and tribes and societies throughout time. It is the opposite of an ideology; it is a condition of the natural instincts of man.[158]

The importance of this observation is that those who seek to impose economic restraints and regulations on others in commercial life are fighting human nature, not working with it. Often without realizing it they are seeking to return us to a pre-1400s world of government-enforced stability and equality. They do this without recognizing that the trade-off was impoverishment and stagnation. Nevertheless, this impulse to create a riskless society by returning to pre-1400 type structures—governments that repress business freedom, individual enterprise, and initiative in economic life – in the name of some overriding ideology (equality, religion, etc) – is widespread and significant in everyday political life.

Often religions inadvertently foster this attitude by castigating greed and business profit. Radical Islam, as radical Christianity before it, explicitly seeks to return, by violence if necessary (as indeed it would have to be), to medieval conditions of security and government repression of individuality in spirit, ideas, and economic life. The cry against "profiteering capitalism" and "exploitative financiers" and

---

158 Successful societies work with, not fight or try to improve on, basic human instincts. "Exchange spurs growth because it is compatible with deep human intuitions." Jonathan B. Wight, "Public Policy, Human Instincts, and Economic Growth", *The Independent Review,* at 353 (Winter 2011); "Institutions that build on the basic instinct for self betterment (as in markets) have a much easier time in achieving success than institutions that oppose it (as in communism)."

the like is at root an expression of the desire for the security a static society brings, albeit without recognition of the downside cost in the decline of economic well-being, growth, progress, and freedom – things we take for granted but that implementation of policies designed to achieve equality and a riskless existence necessarily entails.

There is no getting around the unavoidable fact that commercial life entails commercial risk, and the kind of society required for commerce to flourish is one based on individual freedoms. Radical Islam perceives this fact and thus seeks to turn back the clock to medieval times. Those in our Western societies who seek similar goals, whether by increased regulation of business or socialism or anarchy, unconscious of the import of their demands and longings, are fellow travelers along the same road.

In politics and economics, this contest is most often centered on a debate about the role of self-interest. Much of the miasma can be cleared away by recognizing that the pursuit of self-interest is really just another way of saying that incentives matter; individuals seeking to advance their interests, broadly defined (and including charity and aid to others), are hindered or deflected by rules or conditions that create disincentives to their chosen course of action and are helped by rules or conditions that create incentives to that course. In this way, we are like an outboard motor, where the propeller is the urge of self-interest, and the rudder is the incentives that steer.

7. What is the Importance of Price in Free Markets?

Recognizing the central role of price in the economy and the correlative harm of interfering with free pricing is

CHAPTER VI: FIRST, UNDERSTANDING THE BENEFITS MARKETS BRING

central to understanding how free markets benefit society. The price of a good or service reflects in one simple bit of information the collective judgments of multitudes as to usefulness or utility. The price of corn, for example, dictates whether the consumer will choose it over something else at the market. Corn price is determined, at least in the initial instance, by supply and demand for livestock feed and human consumption. These in turn are affected by the price of fertilizer and farm equipment and labor. The price of fertilizer is affected by that for natural gas, the source for most ammonia, and mining for phosphorus, and so on.

Judgments by all users as to the relative utility of each of these and many other things is reflected in one simple bit of information: price. These judgments of utility are constantly shifting as technology, innovation, supply and demand factors in all relevant affected markets alter. No bureaucracy that displaces free pricing with "fair" or "just" pricing can read supply and demand and hence cannot create maximal social benefit. Any public agent attempting to act without freely negotiated price signals is creating wasted resources and lowering net social income. Gregg explains:

> An important component of competition's ability to send signals is the price mechanism—more specifically, prices that reflect the subjective valuation of different products by producers and consumers rather than prices fixed by legislative or judicial fiat. The advantage of free prices is that, as long as free competition exists, there is no room for arbitrary pricing. They will be a true measure of the scarcities in question.[159]

---

159 Samuel Gregg, *The Commercial Society*, at 67.

The fact is, it is not just hard, it is impossible for centralized government to determine prices properly so as to even approximate net social product: "When millions of people engage in economic exchanges, it is simply impossible for any one person to know everything about the particulars of these exchanges, including their own. Knowledge of such details is beyond the capacity of any one human mind."[160] This information-carrying function of price, reflecting the judgments of thousands or millions as to relative value, cannot be supplanted by any single bureaucrat or public servant, no matter how brilliant, well-meaning, and ably supported by legions of fact-gatherers. Resources are misapplied. Capital stock depreciates. Society's net wealth declines.

This was the principal reason why the Soviet experiment in displacing free prices failed so miserably, but the lesson applies just as strongly to the American or any other economy. Bureaucratic attempts to improve on the results of free markets inevitably fail, whether by benign European or American regulators or a Soviet commissar. Perhaps to only their own surprise, Soviet economic analysts discovered this the hard way:

> In their book, *The Turning Point*, Soviet economists Nikolai Smelev and Vladimir Popov focused on key factors which undermined the economy during the communist era. They concluded that Goskomsten, the agency responsible for setting prices, was simply incapable of setting and tracking prices on the myriad of goods and services under its purview.[161]

---

160 Samuel Gregg, *The Commercial Society*, at 66.
161 Robert Swerlick, "Our Soviet Health System," 6/5/2007, *WSJ*.

8. So Where Do We Start in Thinking About Health Care?

Understanding the essential working and virtues of markets and commerce lays the foundation for approaching the next subject, the effects of altering them by government action designed to interfere with market transactions. If you can't rely on castigating greed, and you can't try to change or reform human nature, and regulating prices is harmful and counterproductive, how *do* you start to think about issues like health care? Where *should* we look for underlying causes of ballooning costs, decreasing service availability, deteriorating quality, and the like? What is the best way to do something about them?

It turns out that careful examination into this subject shifts focus to ourselves and our political operatives in government; to the *well-intentioned but often counterproductive net of laws, agencies, and regulations* our politicians passed perhaps long ago and continue to pass—perhaps with the best of intentions—that confine and regulate our business and economic activity and that misalign incentives, in the misguided effort not to facilitate transactions but to improve on outcomes that competition and markets otherwise provide. As we shall see, careful empirical work confirms theory: markets, while not perfect, work far better than usually assumed. Market failure theories, upon which most regulatory regimes on industry are premised, have proven dry and unfruitful.[162]

Instead of seeking more layers of regulation and bureaus, commissions and agencies, careful attention to

---

162 *Market Failure or Success; The New Debate*, edited by Tyler Cowen and Eric Crampton (Independent Institute 2002), discussed later in Part C, thoroughly sets out various market failure theories and their empirical refutations.

the removal of existing, largely counterproductive laws and regulations throughout all layers of government—both in health care financing and in other areas—realigns incentives and offers the best hope of liberating the economic engine of America and each of us as well, and fixes along these lines is where the real net gain for society begins.[163]

The High Cost of Regulation: A Hidden Tax

The power of the Free Lunch Fallacy is that it makes us forget the invisible harms that regulation ushers in. It is therefore important at the outset to recognize that regulation, even putting to one side its effect on the economy, is not cost free. It is often referred to as a hidden tax. Compliance, enforcement, monitoring, and other

---

163 For a time during the 2008-2010 financial crisis, deregulation was the whipping boy of those seeking to alter America down a more Eurocentric path. These voices were aided by misdiagnosis of the ills confronting America. Whatever the temporary political advantage such voices gained, the overwhelming weight of evidence continues to demonstrate not the failure of deregulation but the continuing failure of the regulatory state. This is not to say that deregulation has always had an easy or successful path. Most industries deregulated in this country (e.g., trucking, railroads, airlines, oil and gas) have been unalloyed successes, as have those in Britain. Experience with deregulation of the savings and loan industry in the 1980s showed that it is much harder to deregulate successfully in the financial area, especially if only part of the business is deregulated and part remains under controls, and much better to avoid intrusive regulation in the initial instance. As in all cases, attention must be paid to incentives and disincentives, and especially to the role government regulations play in distorting or undermining these. In the savings and loan area in the 1980s, relaxing the types of investments allowable while maintaining government guarantees on deposits let inadequately trained personnel chase pie-in-the-sky construction projects with other people's money. The lesson is not to reregulate or stop reforming controls but to pay attention to how the package of new rules incentivizes ordinary market behavior.

CHAPTER VI: FIRST, UNDERSTANDING THE BENEFITS MARKETS BRING

inherent aspects of regulation are expensive. Often they create barriers to entry sufficient to keep new entrepreneurs from competing. So those whose reflex reaction to a problem in the economy is to say, "Well, just regulate it," are assuming something that is factually untrue—that the cost of a regulatory scheme is not a significant burden to the public.

Cumulatively, these burdens are enormous, creating a drag on employment, jobs, income, and growth. "Although the total does not appear anywhere in the federal budget, the multitude of rules, restrictions, and mandates imposes a heavy burden on Americans and the US economy. According to a report recently released by the Small Business Administration, total regulatory costs amount to about $1.75 trillion annually, nearly twice as much as all individual income taxes collected last year."[164] Just this fact alone should give rise to a presumption against regulation. As we shall see, this presumption is confirmed by economic analysis of the effects of regulation on industries apart from just compliance costs.

Of course, certain kinds of regulation are helpful in structuring economic activity. How to tell what regulation is beneficial and what is not is the subject of a following chapter. But it is critical (and bears repeating) to appreciate the deadweight burden and drag on the economy—especially on small business, the most powerful source of job creation—simply from the cumulative effect of excessive regulation. One of the most comprehensive and thorough recent analyses of the costs of regulation on our economic life, noted above, fleshes out the raw numbers:

---

164 James Gattuso, Diane Katz, and Stephen Keen, *Report,* Heritage Foundation (2010), noted in 10/29/2010, *WSJ,* "Federation Feature."

The findings in this report indicate that in 2008, US federal government regulations cost an estimated $1.75 trillion, an amount equal to 14 percent of US national income. This obviously represents a substantial burden on US citizens and businesses... Had every US household paid an equal share of the federal regulatory burden, each would have owed $15,586 in 2008. By comparison, the federal regulatory burden exceeds by 50 percent private spending on health care, which equaled $10,500 per household in 2008. While all citizens and businesses pay some portion of these costs, the distribution of the burden of regulations is quite uneven. The portion of regulatory costs that falls initially on businesses was $8,086 per employee in 2008. Small businesses, defined as firms employing fewer than twenty employees, bear the largest burden of federal regulations. As of 2008, small businesses face an annual regulatory cost of $10,585 per employee, which is 36 percent higher than the regulatory cost facing large firms (defined as firms with five hundred or more employees).[165]

---

[165] Report funded by the federal government's Small Business Administration, "The Impact of Regulatory Costs on Small Firms," by Nicole V. and W. Mark Crain, at pp. iv, 6 (September 2010, Lafayette College): "Unlike most fiscal actions taken by government, the costs of regulatory actions are relatively hidden. For example, consider the activities, products, and services consumed by a typical household on a typical day. The costs of government regulations get stirred into the indistinct mixture of countless economic forces that determine prices, costs, designs, locations, profits, losses, wages, dividends, and so forth. Isolating the contribution of regulations to one's daily routine requires more than simply looking at the sales receipts, for example, as in the case of government sales taxes. A comprehensive list of regulatory influences that affect one's daily existence is indeed extensive and overwhelming to track or sum up. Yet, knowledge of the cumulative consequences of regulatory actions, and how these are changing, provides important information to assess and evaluate the performance of a political-economic social system." *Id.*, at 1.

CHAPTER VI: FIRST, UNDERSTANDING THE BENEFITS MARKETS BRING

Not only is this hidden cost or tax enormous, but it is also growing faster than inflation. "The combined federal burden—federal receipts plus regulatory costs—reached $37,962 per household in 2008, an increase since 2004 of nearly $6,900 per household. The combined federal burden is growing at a real annual rate of 5.5 percent." And the impact falls disproportionately upon small firms—the very engine of job creation we should aim to insulate from such burdens.[166] And of course, ultimately the cost falls on us.

This analysis reveals that much of the political impulse to increase regulation starts on a false premise of cost-free change; each incremental step is enacted without appreciation of the overall impact on the taxpayer/consumer. The harm to the economy from economic regulation of a single industry can often be seen quite clearly—railroads before President Carter's deregulation in 1980 is a sharp example, characterized by declining investment, aging rolling stock and track, paltry stock values – the result of regulatory constraints found in the ICC and the Railway Labor Act. When the totality of economic regulation throughout the economy is considered, the effect is like piling loads of lead on a mule. The animal may not break until the last load is lifted on, but the pace will slow and the ultimate failure becomes inevitable.

Because no one is looking at the totality, when the breakdown comes, there is general surprise, false culprits are furiously hunted down, and, usually, more regulations are piled on top of the existing burden in the wholly fal-

---

166 Crain and Crain, "The Impact of Regulatory Costs on Small Firms," Id., at 46, 57. "Overall and on almost every regulatory frontier, compliance costs place small businesses at a competitive disadvantage. The cost disadvantage confronting small business is driven by environmental regulations, tax compliance, and occupational safety and health and homeland security regulations."

lacious belief that somehow this way the burden and fear will be alleviated. Instead, a greater disaster is built in for the future.

It's not just Costs, it's Dependency

It is easy in thinking about the dollar costs of regulation to forget the most important cost, which has been briefly noted before – the dependency which the people fall into of reliance on government and its regulators instead of their own independent thinking and spirit. How easy it is to just say, "Well. the government says it's OK" instead of doing the obviously safer or better thing right at hand. This point is so ubiquitous and everyday we often miss it. As noted previously, even the designers and engineers for the Titanic, knowing better, chose to rely on existing regulations, resulting in far too few life rafts for safety in the event of catastrophe.

That's why we began this exercise with the quote from F.A. Hayek, who nearly alone and early keenly appreciated the interior personal decay which the administrative state fosters in its subjects. Germany has also dramatically experienced this phenomenon when, after the Wall fell, millions of citizens of the former East German paradise found themselves without the tools to readily reintegrate into commercial society.

Crises Promote Bad Policies

Times of economic crisis compound the problem of excess and misguided regulation. Crises spawn cries for immediate action by government and provide the opening for marginal or otherwise-sidelined voices to dominate dis-

CHAPTER VI: FIRST, UNDERSTANDING THE BENEFITS MARKETS BRING

course and political action. Rarely are the products of such times productive or healthy for the economy.

The 2008-2010 economic recession and financial crisis is a case in point.[167] Misconceiving the causes of the freeze-up in lending and unwilling to face the consequences that recognizing the truth would mean for their careers, politicians crafted legislative "solutions" that, far from helping the economy, only created burdens it may take decades to overcome. The 2008 "stimulus" of $787 billion or more gave tax rebates that people used to pay down debt instead of spending and fed dollars to already over-padded public employment, thus simultaneously taking money out of the productive private sector, creating a huge debt overhang that taxpayers know will be theirs to reckon with, and making harder the readjustment of public payrolls to reality.[168] The Dodd-Frank

---

[167] For a detailed exposition of government's role in creating the 2008-2010 economic crisis, see the analysis of how government intrusion to push homeownership distorted and ultimately crippled our financial system, Raghuram G. Rajan, *Fault Lines: How Hidden Fractures Still Threaten the World Economy*, Ch 1 "Let them Eat Credit" (Princeton University Press 2010). For targeted examples of harmful political intrusion, see, e.g., Jeff Jacoby, "Frank's Fingerprints are all over the financial fiasco," 9/28/08, *The Boston Globe*; Peter Walliston, "Barney Frank, Predatory Lender," 2009, *WSJ*.

[168] As pointed out before, substitution effects neutralized any net spending by individuals or government; individuals paid down debt, and state and local governments substituted federal grants for ongoing debt issuance. "The bottom line is the federal government borrowed funds from the public, transferred these funds to state and local governments, who then used the funds mainly to reduce borrowing from the public. The net impact on aggregate economic activity is zero, regardless of the magnitude of the government purchases multiplier. This behavior is a replay of the failed stimulus attempts of the 1970s." John F. Cogan and John B. Taylor, "The Obama Stimulus Impact? Zero," 12/9/2010, *WSJ*. See also Gary Becker and Kevin Murphy, "There's No Stimulus Free Lunch," 2/10/09, *WSJ*.

"Wall Street Reform and Consumer Protection Act" of 2010 did nothing about the real causes of the financial crisis—the government-spurred push on banks and GSEs (Fannie, Freddie, Ginnie, FHA, VA, etc.) to make mortgages to non-creditworthy homebuyers through "affordable housing mandates"—and instead counterproductively heaped additional unnecessary regulatory burdens on banks and deprived them of needed sources of revenue.[169]

The 2010 Act on health care followed this same pattern, misdiagnosing the ills and legislating in the wrong direction. It made worse the growth of generations of well-intentioned but harmful mandates, cross-subsidies, and controls, which leaves us, as Sally C. Pipes puts it,

> Mired in a quasi-socialist medical system that distorts incentives to provide good health care, while degrading the doctor-patient relationship.[170]

Not only was the folly of these measures observable in hindsight, but they were also eminently foreseeable. Our country has rich experience with the failures of exactly the

---

[169] "What made the recent financial crisis distinctive was that because of affordable-housing requirements and other policies, half of all mortgages in 2008 were subprime or otherwise risky loans. When the bubble deflated, they began to default in unprecedented numbers. If government policy had not encouraged the origination of these mortgages, we would not have had a financial crisis." Peter J. Wallison, "A Way Forward for the Mortgage Market," 2/15/2011, *WSJ*. For detailed analysis see the *Report of the Financial Crisis Inquiry Commission*, but especially the powerful dissent and critique of the majority by Peter J. Wallison, at www.fcic.gov/report (January 2011). See also Peter Wallison, "The Dodd-Frank Act: Creative Destruction, Destroyed," 8/31/10, *WSJ*.

[170] Sally C. Pipes, *Miracle Cure: How to Solve America's Health Care Crisis and Why Canada Isn't the Answer*, at 107 (Pacific Research Institute 2004).

CHAPTER VI: FIRST, UNDERSTANDING THE BENEFITS MARKETS BRING

type of legislation that the 2008-2010 period called forth, and amply persuasive evidence exists of the failure of the approaches taken to achieve their objectives. Having seen in Chapter III how single-payer systems create common failures to meet the needs of patients and taxpayers, let's now see how the regulation approach has fared in the many other industries and markets in which it has been imposed—and how predictable the failures of single-payer and government-controlled systems are.

The progressive view of government is, if it moves, tax it; if it keeps moving, regulate it; if it stops moving, subsidize it.

RONALD REAGAN

CHAPTER VII:
Experiences with Regulation: How it Ends Up Protecting Select Private Interests at the Expense of the Public

1. **The Long, Unhappy History of Populist Regulation of Industries**

Health care is a group of industries and markets, so it is very relevant to see how efforts to regulate other markets and industries both in America and elsewhere have fared. If government control has proved ineffective or counterproductive in other industries, this is a powerful cautionary tale for those seeking further government regulation of health care. Although some wish to rely on impoverished market-failure theories, discussed later, to justify treating health care differently, the fact is there is nothing unique about health care markets (except perhaps for the extent of interference already); general findings and principles of economic behavior apply specifically to health care, and such is the experience around the world.[171] Incentives matter in health care as elsewhere. The costs of regulation burden as elsewhere. Therefore, no discussion of health care systems is really complete without examining the experience with regulated industries across the board.

We have already pointed out the relevance of the financial crisis and the Dodd-Frank Act to the health care question and seen how the same mistake was made there and in the 2010 Act. This section starts with some history of the regulatory approach and its legacies—an examination of the most active regulatory period, the New Deal, where most of our current agencies of government and schemes of economic regulation began.

2. The New Deal as a Model

Most advocates of today's regulation of the health care economy look to the New Deal's government interferences in the economy as inspiration. But despite its usually favorable press in the colleges and among academic historians (e.g., Arthur Schlesinger, Jr.: *Age of Roosevelt*, 1957; Professor David M. Kennedy: *Freedom From Fear*, 1999), numerous careful studies have now exposed the New Deal legislation as an economic failure unnecessarily prolonging high unemployment and retarding growth.

---

171 This discussion of regulation puts to one side the special problem of public utilities, where entry is restricted by law and prices controlled in the name of alleged economies of scale, disruption, and other factors, e.g., protecting against endless digging up of streets to lay gas pipes or filling the skies with electric wires on poles. But even here, studies of electric and other utilities cast doubts on the benefits of regulation in this area. George Stigler, "What Can Regulators Regulate? The Case of Electricity" *The Citizen and the State*, at 61; Harold Demsetz, "Why Regulate Utilities?" *Journal of Law & Economics* (April 1968).

CHAPTER VII: EXPERIENCES WITH REGULATION

The market crash was in 1929, but five years later, after numerous efforts to improve by government intervention into the economy, unemployment remained high. "From 1934 to 1940, the median annual unemployment rate was 17.2 percent. At no point during the 1930s did unemployment go below 14 percent."[172] The argument some make—that perhaps the New Deal kept America from the even more devastating effects of outright socialism—is faint praise, especially for the millions of unemployed who had to suffer through an unnecessary decade of well-meaning, contradictory experiments by political actors and their cohorts, most brilliant and from the finest schools, who were nonetheless ignorant of economics and blind to the harm they wreaked.

Nor did huge widespread government spending increases help. "As a cure for the Great Depression, government spending didn't work. In 1933, federal government outlays were $4.5 billion; by 1940 they were $9.4 billion, FDR more than doubled federal spending, and still unemployment remained stubbornly high."[173] Big spending programs designed without concern for their long-term productivity, promoted by Lord Keynes, proved to be a false path that did not raise America out of its downturn.[174]

---

172 Jim Powell, *FDR's Folly: How Roosevelt and His New Deal Prolonged the Great Depression*, at vii (Crown Forum 2003).

173 Jim Powell, *FDR's Folly*, at xiii. Roosevelt's own Treasury secretary, Henry Morganthau, admitted the administration's failure to the House Ways and Means Committee in April 1939: "Now, gentleman, we have tried spending money. We are spending more than we have ever spent before and it does not work... I say after eight years of this administration we have just as much unemployment as when we started...and an enormous debt, to boot." Phil Gramm, "Echoes of the Great Depression," 10/1/2010, *WSJ*.

174 In a twist of historic irony, the Obama administration allowed this same mistake to be made in promoting the so-called stimulus pack-

Careful later analysis revealed the real culprits prolonging high unemployment were increased taxes, tariffs, and the tight money policies of the Federal Reserve, assisted by the climate of uncertainty promoted by Roosevelt's constant political business-bashing. Business is reluctant to invest not knowing what to expect from changing government regulations or new laws, especially those aimed at reducing their profits.[175]

---

age of some $800 billion plus in 2009-2010, which mainly fed political constituencies and gave ineffectual tax rebates without concern for long-term productivity gains. The result has been to create a huge debt overhang (threatening future tax increases), failure to increase jobs where needed in the private sector, and increase the growth of government at the expense of the economy. Contrary to administration claims of large benefits to the economy by flawed multiplier analyses based upon outmoded, oversimplified Keynesian models, no such multiplier developed. As Noble Laureate Gary Becker and Kevin Murphy concluded, "We believe a multiplier well below one" is likely. Becker and Murphy, "There's No Stimulus Free Lunch," 2/10/09, *WSJ*. Others believe the multiplier to be zero or below. Harvard Professor Robert J. Barro, "Magic Multipliers," 2 *Hoover Digest*, at 37 (Spring 2009). As comparisons with Euro-zone countries that did not adopt such large stimulus spending both during the New Deal period and during the 2008-2010 period shows, both Roosevelt and Obama significantly harmed working Americans by targeting the wrong ills and enacting the wrong spend and tax solutions. Phil Gramm, "Echoes of the Great Depression," 10/1/2010, *WSJ*.
175 Milton Friedman and Anna Schwartz, *A Monetary History of the United States, 1867-1960*, at 11, 688-700 (Princeton Univ. Press 1971 ed.); Burton Folsom, Jr., *New Deal or Raw Deal: How FDR's Economic Legacy Has Damaged America* (Simon & Schuster 2008); Gene Smiley, *Rethinking the Great Depression* (Ivan R Dee 2002); Robert Higgs, "Regime Uncertainty: Why the Great Depression Lasted So Long And Why Prosperity Resumed After the War," *The Independent Review* 1, no. 4, at 561-90 (Spring 1997); Robert Higgs, "Recession & Recovery: Six Fundamental Errors of the Current Orthodoxy," *The Independent Review* 14, no. 3, at 465-72 (Winter 2010).

CHAPTER VII: EXPERIENCES WITH REGULATION

The depression of the 1930s became "The Great Depression" because it was so prolonged. Economists Harold Cole and Lee Ohanian squarely blame the New Deal:

> Why wasn't the Depression followed by a vigorous recovery, like every other cycle? It should have been. The economic fundamentals that drive all expansions were very favorable during the New Deal. Productivity grew very rapidly after 1933, the price level was stable, real interest rates were low, and liquidity was plentiful. We have calculated on the basis of just productivity growth that employment and investment should have been back to normal levels by 1936. Similarly, Nobel Laureate Robert Lucas and Leonard Rapping calculated on the basis of just expansionary Federal Reserve policy that the economy should have been back to normal by 1935.
>
> So what stopped a blockbuster recovery from ever starting? The New Deal. Some New Deal policies certainly benefited the economy by establishing a basic social safety net through Social Security and unemployment benefits, and by stabilizing the financial system through deposit insurance and the Securities Exchange Commission. But others violated the most basic economic principles by suppressing competition, and setting prices and wages in many sectors well above their normal levels. All told, these anti-market policies choked off powerful recovery forces that would have plausibly returned the economy back to trend by the mid-1930s... Our research indicates that New Deal labor and industrial policies prolonged the Depression by seven years.[176]

---

176 Harold Cole and Lee Ohanian, "How Government Prolonged the Depression," 2/2/2009, *WSJ*.

Jim Powell nicely summarizes the New Deal programs, their objectives, and economists' evaluations of their actual effects. Just with reference to agricultural programs, for example, he points out how conflicting policies undermined any hoped-for gains:

> The Agricultural Adjustment Act forced food prices above market levels, in an effort to help farmers, but higher food prices hurt everybody who wasn't a farmer. The National Recovery Administration forced up prices of manufactured goods, hurting farmers who had to buy farm tools and equipment. Agricultural allotment policies cut cultivated acreage, while the Bureau of Reclamation increased cultivated acreage. Relief spending helped the unemployed, while corporate income taxes, undistributed profits taxes, Social Security taxes, minimum wage laws, and compulsory unionism led to higher unemployment rates. New Deal spending was supposed to stimulate the economy, but New Deal taxing depressed the economy.[177]

Public perception and reality are far apart when it comes to the New Deal. Professors Burton and Anita Folsom, students of economic history, point out the anomaly:

> 'He got us out of the Great Depression.' That's probably the most frequent comment made about President Franklin Roosevelt, who died sixty-five years ago today. Every Democratic president from Truman to Obama has believed it, and each has used FDR's New Deal as a model for expanding the government.

---

177 Jim Powell, *FDR's Folly*, at 5, 263-274.

CHAPTER VII: EXPERIENCES WITH REGULATION

It's a myth. FDR did not get us out of the Great Depression—not during the 1930s, and only in a limited sense during World War II.

Let's start with the New Deal. Its various alphabet-soup agencies—the WPA, AAA, NRA, and even the TVA (Tennessee Valley Authority)—failed to create sustainable jobs. In May 1939, US unemployment still exceeded 20 percent. European countries, according to a League of Nations survey, averaged only about 12 percent in 1938. The New Deal, by forcing taxes up and discouraging entrepreneurs from investing, probably did more harm than good.[178]

After the War, President Truman tried to get Congress to enact Roosevelt's ideas for a "New-New Deal" set of federal programs, fearing as Roosevelt did a return of New Deal-era stagnation and high unemployment. Instead, (a predominantly Democrat) Congress, weary of failed efforts

---

[178] Burton Folsom, Jr., and Anita Folsom, "Did FDR End the Depression? The Economy Took Off After the Post-War Congress Cut Taxes," 4/12/2010, *WSJ*; based on Burton Folsom, Jr., *New Deal or Raw Deal: How FDR's Economic Legacy Has Damaged America* (Simon & Schuster 2008). As economist Paul Godek points out: "One message we're hearing often from Washington is that recent increases in government spending have averted another Great Depression. That's nonsense. If such policies had any coherence there would have been no Great Depression (when government spending grew); the US economy would have collapsed following World War II (when government spending plummeted); and the US, not to mention Greece, would now be experiencing a boom like no other. As many observers of the economic scene have noted, private investment and hiring are suppressed by economic and political uncertainty. Such uncertainty is generated by unprecedented government intervention, massive increases in government spending, and anticipated tax increases. This is what the policies undertaken during the 1930s, those that sustained the Great Depression, should have taught us." *Opinion*, 7/23/2010, *WSJ*.

to lower unemployment by spending, rejected these overtures. It cut taxes instead and spurred a prolonged period of sustained economic growth.

Most New Deal Economic Regulation Was a Bad Deal for Taxpayers and Consumers

Despite the evidence, the New Deal's market/industrial regulatory schemes have been sold to Americans as a great success story, and many of these programs—having created built-in constituencies—persist to this day. But the failures of these as aids to the general welfare are not new information.

Even the most highly regarded government agencies have been exposed as of dubious value. Take the regulation of new investment securities by the SEC. The SEC mainly enforces information-disclosure laws on corporations, a seemingly unquestionable good. But ordinary people untrained in accounting and finance find 10-Ks, 8-Qs, and the like essentially unreadable, although their purpose is to "protect the investor." These required statements appear to lack real benefit and involve much unnecessary cost.

In a path-breaking study, George Stigler tested whether they really did act to protect the investor. He measured the value of new issues of shares in industrial companies before and after the legislation relative to the overall market. The conclusion? "These studies suggest that the SEC registration requirements had no important effect on the quality of new securities sold to the public."[179] In other words, "the SEC did not appreciably improve the experience of investors in the new securities market by its expen-

---

[179] George Stigler, "Public Regulation of the Securities Market," in Stigler, *The Citizen and the State*, at 87 (U. Chicago Press 1975).

CHAPTER VII: EXPERIENCES WITH REGULATION

sive review of prospectuses."[180] But despite solid evidence of ineffectiveness and cost, the laws go on without change: the politicians are quieted, lawyers and accountants are happy, and the public proceeds in ignorance of the true state of affairs—at a considerable drain to the taxpayer and investor who must support with taxes and fees the ever-growing legion of highly paid bureaucratic enforcers.

That's not all. Close study reveals that a hidden effect of the securities legislation was to protect certain powerful investment banking incumbents: "The Securities Act pursued socially useful goals. In particular, its disclosure requirements..." [Other provisions] "benefited investment banks, particularly high-prestige investment banks, and likely raised costs to issuers and investors... A closer look, in light of the competitive conditions in the underwriting market in the 1920s, shows that even the Securities Act was a likely source of rents for the firms it subjected to regulation."[181]

A series of events—prime among them the Madoff and Stanford Ponzi schemes that percolated for decades under the nose of SEC personnel—have brought into the public eye the questionable ability of the SEC to perform its supposed principal function: protect the investor. But the politicians' response is not to question the structure of government intervention but rather to hire up accountants and lawyers and pile on ever more costly controls and requirements in addition to those of negligible help that are already on the books.

---

180 George Stigler, "Can Regulatory Agencies Protect the Consumer?" in *The Citizen and the State*, at 185.
181 Paul Mahoney, "The Political Economy of the Securities Act of 1933," in *The Journal of Legal Studies*, at 30-31 (January 2001) ("the net effect was to reduce competition among investment banks.").

The Food and Drug Administration (FDA) is another agency with high popular regard but questionable net social utility.[182] At an average drug development cost of $500M to 2B only a few giant firms can compete, as many drugs fail the three-phase gauntlet intended to ensure safety and efficacy. Regulations creating such huge barriers to entry call for clear evidence showing net social benefit, but instead, the evidence points in the other direction.[183]

If the evidence of careful studies shows that serious question exists whether such generally applauded agencies as the SEC and FDA add net benefit, you can easily see how it is that so many government economic regulatory agencies fail the same test. Ronald H. Coase, Nobel Laureate, reviewing a number of the detailed studies in the economic literature as long ago as 1974, concluded:

> I have referred to studies of the regulation of natural gas and drugs. But there have also been studies of the regulation of many diverse activities such as agriculture, aviation, banking, broadcasting, electricity supply, milk distribution, railroads and trucking, taxicabs, whiskey labeling, and zon-

---

[182] Sam Pelzman's careful studies of its lack of effectiveness—principally by increasing development costs and delaying helpful drugs—have suggested the public would fare better if it disappeared. The cost to dying and needy patients in delayed treatments may far outweigh the occasional benefit in ferreting out harmful ones. Sam Peltzman, "An Evaluation of Consumer Protection Legislation: The 1962 Drug Amendments," *The Journal of Political Economy*, 1973, 81(5), pp. 1049-91; Daniel Klein, "Policy Medicine versus Policy Quackery: Economists against the FDA," *Knowledge, Technology and Policy*, vol. 13 (2000). Other examples abound in the economic literature.

[183] J.A. DiMasi, R.W. Hansen, and H.G. Grabowski, "The Price of Innovation: New Estimates of Drug Development Costs," *Journal of Health Economics* 22, no. 2 (2003) at 151-185 (estimates average capitalized drug development cost through approval to be $802M).

ing. I mention only studies with which I am familiar; there are doubtless many others. The main lesson to be drawn from these studies is clear: They all tend to suggest that the regulation is either ineffective or that, when it has a noticeable impact, on balance the effect is bad, so that consumers obtain a worse product or a higher-priced product or both as a result of the regulation. Indeed, this result is found so uniformly as to create a puzzle: One would expect to find, in all these studies, at least some government programs that do more good than harm.[184]

Studies like these reveal that the principal effect of populist regulation of markets is not to benefit the public but to harm it, to bring on a host of negatives—increase costs of doing business, slow income and economic growth, retard the best use of capital and labor, misdirect the young into less-productive professions and occupations, promote attitudes of dependency, and cater to the dominance of society by powerful labor unions and state-protected and subsidized business.[185]

3. Recent Adventures with the Regulatory Illusion: The Financial Crisis

As Professor Raghuram Rajan (former chief economist for International Monetary Fund) nicely shows in his *Fault Lines*, contrary to popular tarring of the banks, it is clear that the risky subprime and Alt-A market which underlay

---

184 Ronald H. Coase, "Economists and Public Policy," in *Essays on Economics and Economists*, at 61 (U. Chicago Press 1994).
185 "The difference between the actual operation of the market and its ideal operation—great though it undoubtedly is—is as nothing compared to the difference between the actual effects of government intervention and their intended effects." Milton Friedman, *Capitalism and Freedom*, at 197.

the financial crisis "was driven largely by the government or government-influenced money." Government incentives and pressure on banks to make risky loans to the poor operated on the unwise theory that a relatively small proportion of poor risks intermixed in the vast array of collateralized debt obligations would be a free lunch—no one would notice the pollution. They didn't, until suddenly they did. The 2008 seize-up proved this approach to be extremely shortsighted.[186]

In fact, the financial crisis of 2008 and ensuing deep recession are classic examples of how apparently well-motivated people can cause immense harm to the entire populace by the rush to regulation. The Report of the Financial Crisis Inquiry Commission, set up by President Obama to form the basis for understanding the crisis as well as any possible legislation, was issued in January 2011. But the legisla-

---

[186] Raghuram G. Rajan, *Fault Lines: How Hidden Fractures Still Threaten the World Economy,* Ch 1, "Let Them Eat Credit" (Princeton University Press 2010). "As more money from the government-sponsored agencies [Fannie Mae, Freddie Mac, FHA] flooded into financing or supporting low-income housing, the private sector joined the party... [Edward Pinto, former chief credit officer of Fannie Mae] estimates that in June 2008, the mortgage giants, the FHA, and various other government programs were exposed to about $2.7 trillion in subprime and Alt-A loans, approximately 59 percent of total loans to these categories. It is very difficult to reach any other conclusion than that this was a market driven largely by the government, or government-influenced money... Some progressive economists dispute whether the recent crisis was at all related to government intervention in low-income housing credit. This certainly was not the only factor at play, and to argue that it was is misleading. But it is equally misleading to say it played no part. The private financial sector did not suddenly take up low-income housing loans in the early 2000s out of the goodness of its heart, or because financial innovation permitted it to do so—after all, securitization has been around for a long time. To ignore the role played by politicians, the government, and the quasi-government agencies is to ignore the elephant in the room."

CHAPTER VII: EXPERIENCES WITH REGULATION

tion (the so-called Wall Street Reform and Consumer Protection Act, popularly referred to as Dodd-Frank in honor of its principal sponsors) was rushed through and enacted in the summer of 2010, months before the Commission had even held hearings, much less issued a report.[187]

When finally issued, the majority apparently saw it as their purpose to justify post facto the Dodd-Frank Act already enacted, and they issued a majority report with analysis blaming the usual culprits—mortgage underwriters, banks, CDOs, MBSs, homeowners, lax regulators, unregulated actors, greed—virtually everyone involved in creating, acquiring, disseminating, and buying mortgages. But a net cast so wide lacks credibility in an analysis of the cause of the crisis. These factors had been involved for a long time, in some cases decades, so why did they all come a cropper at a specific date, September 2008? The eight commissioners who relied upon such a laundry list really just identified the participants, not the cause.

The dissent by Peter J. Wallison analyzes all this and sets forth a lucid, wholly credible scenario consistent with Professor Rajan's analysis.[188] Beginning in 1992 at the outset of the Clinton administration and continuing on into the Bush years, legislation directed HUD to establish affordable housing goals for the government-sponsored enterprises (GSEs), Fannie, Freddie, Ginnie, as well as

---

187 The Wall Street Reform and Consumer Protection Act ("Dodd-Frank") neither helpfully reforms nor protects the consumer. In its extraordinary prolixity (848 pages of impenetrable delegation of responsibility to bureaucrats) it asks so-called experts in agencies to create at least 243 rulemakings and 67 studies to suggest further rulemakings. These are the same experts who guided and fostered the financial crisis to begin with.
188 *Financial Crisis Inquiry Commission, Dissenting Statement of Peter J. Wallison* (January 2011), available at www.fcic.gov/report.

the FHA and, ultimately, through the Community Reinvestment Act (CRA) and HUD "Best Practices Initiative," for the entire mortgage industry. These goals, scores, and other forms of federal pressure forced a degeneration in underwriting standards and drove the creation of the huge supply of nontraditional mortgages (subprime, Alt-A, "liar loans"), which ultimately broke the back of our financial world when the housing boom peaked in 2007-2008. Wallison concludes:

> This analysis lays the principal cause of the financial crisis squarely at the feet of the unprecedented number of NTMs [nontraditional mortgages] that were brought into the US financial markets by government housing policy. These weak and high-risk loans helped to build the bubble, and when the bubble deflated they defaulted in unprecedented numbers. This threatened losses in the PMBS [private mortgage-backed securities] that were held by financial institutions in the US and around the world, impairing both their liquidity and their apparent stability.
>
> The accumulation of 27 million subprime and Alt-A mortgages was not a random event, or even the result of major forces such as global financial imbalances or excessively low interest rates. Instead, these loans and the bubble to which they contributed were the direct consequence of something far more mundane: US government housing policy, which—led by HUD over two administrations—deliberately reduced mortgage underwriting standards so that more people could buy homes. While this process was going on, everyone was pleased. Homeownership in the US actually grew to the highest level ever recorded. But

the result was a financial catastrophe from which the US has still not recovered.[189]

The motivation for these affordable housing (AH) goals was pure: to increase the number of people who owned their own homes, seen as promoting virtue and progress. Indeed, the percentage of Americans who owned their own homes increased from 64 percent to 69 percent as a result of these government policies. By 2005, HUD and other federal housing leaders crowed that the purposes of the effort had been achieved and the programs were an outstanding success.

The joy was short-lived, and the result was tragic. By 2010, most of the people who bought homes under the lowered underwriting standards that the law and HUD promoted had been foreclosed upon or otherwise defaulted. By 2010, the national percentage of homeownership was back to 64 percent. The harm to the banking industry and untold millions of homeowners and investors who lost their jobs, homes, wherewithal, and sacred honor is incalculable and is enduring.

The Government's Own Analysis Confirms This View

In a securities fraud complaint filed December 16, 2011, against former top officers of Fannie Mae and Freddie Mac, the SEC revealed that its investigation affirmed Mr. Wallison's analysis. Moreover, Fannie Mae and Freddie Mac admitted to the facts and admitted responsibility. The complaint details the growing size of these agencies' portfolios of subprime, Alt-A, no-documentation, and similar low-quality mortgages, starting in the mid-1990s, to satisfy government AH policies,

---

189 *Financial Crisis Inquiry Commission, Dissenting Statement of Peter J. Wallison*, at 483.

which they bought, packaged, and sold out into the market, giving assurances they were a small portion. In fact, these low-quality loans were magnitudes greater than stated, often by factors of ten or more. This deception misled the banks, the market, investors, and regulators, compounding the ultimate harms since no one realized the danger—particularly to the banks—until it was too late.[190]

Thus the financial crisis exemplifies several features that are major themes here. First, it was intrusive government regulation in the initial instance, pursued for apparently well-motivated reasons, that principally caused the crisis and the enormous harms by undermining traditional underwriting standards so that persons to whom the market would not otherwise have lent money could live in houses they owned. The benefits were short-lived and the damage incalculable. The politicians and administrators who promulgated the AH policies were seduced by the promise of a political and economic free lunch—that by regulating private banks and GSEs to force them to give mortgage loans ever farther down the risk spectrum, great public benefits could be achieved and the costs would be hidden among

---

190 Fannie and Freddie led private lenders into the subprime market. In July 1999, for example, Fannie and Countrywide Home Loans signed an "affiliation agreement" whereby Countrywide procured low-documentation loans for Fannie to fund and package. See SEC news release and accompanying complaint, dated and filed 12/16/2011, at http://www.sec.gov/news/press/2011/2011-267.htm. Then they lied about it. "Fannie Mae and Freddie Mac executives told the world that their subprime exposure was substantially smaller than it really was," said Robert Khuzami, director of the SEC's Enforcement Division. "These material misstatements occurred during a time of acute investor interest in financial institutions' exposure to subprime loans and misled the market about the amount of risk on the company's books."

CHAPTER VII: EXPERIENCES WITH REGULATION

private players and be invisible. They were blinded by and in turn fed a classic Regulatory Illusion.[191]

Second, when the time came to examine the cause and understand what happened, the forces that propelled the crisis in the first place ensured that the cover story exonerated them and maintained their political fortunes. History was rewritten to favor the politicians and their administrators who, luckily for them, gained power in the 2008 elections.

In retrospect, aware of the Free Lunch Fallacy and Regulatory Illusion, it is relatively easy to design a program that satisfies the goals sought by regulation while avoiding its harms. If non-creditworthy borrowers are to be the subject of government policy to be enabled to buy their own homes, any such policy should not be undertaken by regulation of banks with the intent to achieve a free lunch by lowering traditional underwriting standards across the board but should be directly made by the FHA or other such government agency in a totally transparent fashion.

---

191 "The decision by Fannie and Freddie to embrace no-doc lending in 2004 opened the floodgates of bad credit. In 2003, for example, total subprime and Alt-A mortgage originations were $395 billion. In 2004, they rose to $715 billion. By 2006, they were more than $1 trillion. In a painstaking forensic analysis of the sources of increased mortgage risk during the 2000s, "The Failure of Models that Predict Failure," Uday Rajan of the University of Michigan, Amit Seru of the University of Chicago, and Vikrant Vig of London Business School show that more than half of the mortgage losses that occurred in excess of the rosy forecasts of expected loss at the time of mortgage origination reflected the predictable consequences of low-doc and no-doc lending. In other words, if the mortgage-underwriting standards at Fannie and Freddie circa 2003 had remained in place, nothing like the magnitude of the subprime crisis would have occurred." Charles W. Calomiris, professor of finance, Columbia Business School, "The Mortgage Crisis: Some Inside Views," 10/27/2011, *WSJ* (analyzing emails among Freddie Mac risk officers).

This lesson is directly applicable to the subject at hand here, health care systems. The parallel is that efforts to change market outcomes for health care, if desired, should be done by supporting directly those unable to afford such care, not by taking over the whole system, as with single-payers, or regulating providers to force them to bend to government mandates and skew market outcomes.

The Cumulative Effect of Bad Laws

Regulating one industry badly creates many harms but it is the cumulative effect of multiple regulation and destruction of markets that brings an economy to its knees. Andreas Bergh and Magnus Henrekson of the Research Institute of Industrial Economics in Sweden point out the case of Sweden—once the poster child for the welfare state—which increased its size of government welfare benefits, of which health care is a large part, and went backwards fast, from fourth in the world in per capita GDP to seventeenth in twenty-three years. They raise a caution for Americans who look favorably on the expansion of such government-run programs:

> Americans eat out more and hire people to clean their homes, take care of their children, or mow their lawns. Swedes, who have less money to spend after taxes, will do such work themselves. Raising government spending and taxes would cause Americans to behave more like Swedes, hurting the entire US service sector and throwing many—mainly working class Americans—out of a job... Many Americans argue that the US could safely increase its spending share from roughly 32 percent of GDP to 37 percent to 38 percent of GDP. The evidence suggests otherwise. The US needs to acknowledge the trade-off between government size and economic growth. A larger government sector may

CHAPTER VII: EXPERIENCES WITH REGULATION

decrease some economic inequality, but will ultimately leave Americans sharing smaller pieces of a smaller pie.[192]

Recognizing the intimate tie between an overly regulated health care system and slower economic growth, always important, is especially important in hard times with high unemployment, particularly persistent long-term rates[193] that have proven impervious to huge government efforts to stimulate.[194]

The election of President Obama saw a remarkable revival of the New Deal as model, in apparent disregard

---

192 Andreas Bergh and Magnus Henrekson, "Lessons From the Swedish Welfare State—New Research Shows Bigger Government Means Slower Growth. Our Country is a Prime Example," 7/10/2010, *WSJ*.

193 See Raghuram G. Rajan, *Fault Lines: How Hidden Fractures Still Threaten the World Economy*, Ch 4, "A Weak Safety Net," (Princeton University Press 2010), which describes the lengthened time before job loss recovery starting in the 1990-1991 recession (twenty-three months) and showing up in the 2001-2002 (thirty-eight months to restoration of job losses) and the 2008-2009 recessions (still struggling to recover as of 2010).

194 Brian M. Riedl, "Why Government Spending Does Not Stimulate Economic Growth: Answering the Critics," 1/8/2010, *WSJ*: "Government's effect on economic growth is determined by its effect on productivity and labor supply... Only in the rare instances where the private sector fails to provide those inputs in adequate amounts is government spending necessary. Government spending on education, physical infrastructure, and research and development, for instance, could increase long-term productivity rates—but only if government invests more competently than businesses, nonprofit organizations, and private citizens would have if those investment dollars had stayed in the private sector. Historically, governments have rarely outperformed the private sector in generating productivity growth. Thus, mountains of academic studies show that government spending typically reduces long-term economic growth." See also Gary S. Becker, George P. Shultz, and John B. Taylor, "Time for a Budget Game-Changer," 4/4/2011, WSJ ("extensive governmental efforts to stimulate the economy and reduce joblessness by spending more have failed to reduce joblessness.")

or ignorance of the overwhelming economic evidence showing its harmful effects and flawed promises. The 2010 Act, single-payer systems, and the like follow this well-worn path of failure in pursuit of the Free Lunch Fallacy and the Regulatory Illusion, yet the White House and Congress proceeded as if this knowledge does not exist. Instead, they relied on old progressive panaceas and limited or obsolete paradigms or ideas.[195]

It has been observed that President Roosevelt and his Brain Trust were "utterly ignorant of economics...apparently unaware that such policies had been tried before in many other countries—and failed."[196] Whatever role economic advisors played, one is led to conclude that despite his public speeches lauding free markets, President Obama, trained as a lawyer and community organizer, together with the leaders of the 2008-2010 Congress, shared the same infirmity.

---

195 One such outmoded idea is the Keynesian notion that increasing aggregate demand by any form of government spending (Keynes' famous example of paying people to dig ditches and others to fill them up again) will have a multiplier effect of about 1.5 as the Obama administration projected—that is, it will increase economic output by half again the amount spent. To the contrary, Professor Robert J. Barro of Harvard has calculated based upon the best evidence—large changes in spending driven by shifts in war and peace—that the actual multiplier is closer to zero, and no more than 0.8. The Keynesian model proposed in *The General Theory* has been shown inadequate, yet top government officials still employ it. As Barro says, "The financial crisis and possible depression [of 2008-2010] do not invalidate everything we have learned about macroeconomics since 1936." Robert J. Barro, "Magic Multipliers", 2, *Hoover Digest* at 37 (Spring 2009). Because government spending has negative effects on private investment and spending, a dollar government spends is less than a dollar added to GDP and probably has a negative effect.

196 Jim Powell, *FDR's Folly*, at 5.

The IQ Fallacy, Intellectual Arrogance, and the Law Review Perspective

The educated electorate is often drawn to high intelligence as the supreme quality for top political office. But without the right kind of experience and education, the brightest bulb in the room will lead into the closet. It is a particular trap to believe that brilliant academic resumes correlate with wisdom in real life policy formation.

The assumption is that sheer brilliance is all that is needed to craft good policy, and remove from business experience gives objectivity. I call this the "Law Review Perspective," the belief that bright people with high IQs lacking any particular knowledge or life experience in a field (thus "uninfected" by crass commercial interest) can nonetheless sort out and solve problems in the best fashion. President Obama, whose signal experience was as president of the Harvard Law Review, exemplifies this attitude, having often spoken of his belief that he and a few chosen top aides can craft the best policies and his pride at being "the smartest person in the room."

This attitude is a setup for disaster. It is true that law review editors—high in IQ and with two years of law training under their belts—are trained to break down problems and reassemble them and to spot issues, and this allows them to participate in the highest level of legal analysis, able to help inform judges and perhaps a few others. But wisdom in the broader world is not generated in law review offices, nor does the specialized intelligence useful in writing blue books translate to substantive social policy.[197]

---

[197] This is not to disparage the two wonderful years the author spent on the University of Chicago Law Review.

Self-regard based on IQ without grounding in the business or economic world is particularly dangerous to popular welfare when combined with belief in the purity of one's own good intentions and the impurity of those who disagree. When the Law Review Perspective is combined with what Thomas Sowell calls "the vision of the anointed" (see Chapter VIII, *post*), a high danger to sound public policy exists.

4. Regulatory Capture and the Continuance of Failed Programs

Serious errors of policy are not redeemed by good intentions. The consequences of reenacting failed policies are too harmful—and permanent. This is especially true with government programs. Milton Friedman points out how bad programs generate a life of their own:

> In our own country, one social welfare program after another has turned out to have effects opposite to those that were intended by the well-meaning people who supported them. Good intentions alone are not enough. Government employees, no less than employees of private business, will put their own interests above the interests of others. Calling them public servants does not alter that fact… Government spending thus acquires a momentum of its own from two sources: the tolerance of the public as it seeks to achieve its objectives by spending more money and the expansion of programs that start small.[198]

It is an unfortunate fact that government employees lack the incentives that private employees have to cut costs.

---

[198] Milton and Rose Friedman, *Tyranny of the Status Quo*, at 38-39 (1984).

CHAPTER VII: EXPERIENCES WITH REGULATION

A private employee is promoted, paid, and given bonuses on the basis, in part, of contributions to the profitability of the enterprise. But:

> Bureaucrats, alas, are not. In fact, they are highly disincentivized to increase efficiency and to innovate. In business a penny saved is a penny earned, the savings flowing directly to the all-important bottom line. But in a bureaucracy, a penny saved is a penny likely to be cut from next year's budget. And prestige in a bureaucracy comes not from profit but from the size of one's budget. So even accidental savings are likely to be suppressed with make-work.[199]

Bemused by the promise of a political and economic free lunch, the Regulatory Illusion propagates itself as government agencies grow ever larger regardless of social benefit. The vast literature since the 1950s on the theory of public choice—which applies economic principles of self-interest to politicians and bureaucrats—confirms this phenomenon; so-called public servants seek to expand their benefits and their realm through expanded government, regardless of harm to the public that may result.[200]

---

199 John Steele Gordon, "Incentives vs. Government Waste," 5/14/2010, *WSJ*.
200 Goodman, Musgrave, and Herrick, *Lives at Risk*, at 187-200. An early father of public choice theory was Anthony Downs, whose *An Economic Theory of Democracy* (Harper Row 1957) elaborated on the application of economic principles to political choices. This analysis also tells us why well-intentioned calls for increased pay for already well-paid government employees to improve the performance of government are bound to fail. It is not in the nature of government agencies to self-immolate. The problem is not a lack of "the best and the brightest"—indeed, glittering resumes are what many agencies already sport. Efforts to change incentives to encourage diminishing agency size and scope are no more likely to succeed than efforts by idealists to change human nature. The tyranny of the status quo is not so easily overcome.

Other analyses highlight other facets of this phenomenon. Milton Friedman suggests that the middle classes, with the lion's share of the votes, ensure public programs are to their benefit: "The elementary fact is that almost all government programs are either a complete waste and help nobody, or they benefit the middle and upper-middle classes at the expense of both the very poor and the very rich."[201] Economists call this Director's Law of Public Income Redistribution after Aaron Director of the University of Chicago Law School, the father of law and economics.[202]

Someone benefits from regulation, just not those intended by people of good will who promote the legislation. As Stigler and others have shown, the Securities Acts and their recent add-ons lend little or no benefit to investors, but are a rich source for fees to lawyers and accountants from all those trapped in the net of SEC jurisdiction. Indeed, lawyers themselves often refer to these as the "Full Employment for Attorneys and Accountants Acts." More generally, economists and political scientists have come to recognize how the regulation of markets tends to end up being captured by incumbent interests—management, labor, and related professionals —and the resulting governmental regulators co-opted by them.

After studying electrical utilities, stocks, and other examples of market regulation, Stigler concludes that, rather than being in the public interest, "as a rule, regulation is acquired by the industry and is designed and operated for

---

201 Milton Friedman, *Bright Promises, Dismal Performance*, at 73 (Harcourt Brace 1983).
202 George Stigler, "Director's Law of Public Income Redistribution," *Chicago Studies in Political Economy*, at 106 (U. Chicago Press 1988).

CHAPTER VII: EXPERIENCES WITH REGULATION

its benefit."[203] From involvement in drafting the legislation to selection of administrators to on-going communications regarding rules and interpretations, existing market players shape the contours to their benefit and in the process make harder efforts by newcomers to compete. This is why private markets are preferred to public regulation:

> The superiority of the traditional defenses of the individual—reliance upon his own efforts and the power of competition—lie precisely in the characteristics which distinguish them from public regulation. Each of the traditional defenses is available and working at all times—self-interest and competition are never passing fads. Each of the traditional defenses is available to individuals and small groups—changes in policy and adaptation to new circumstances do not require changes in the ponderous, expensive, insensitive machinery of a giant state. It is of regulation that the consumer must beware.[204]

Other groups that benefit from regulation are the political and bureaucratic classes, who expand their areas of influence and patronage. The bottom line: both in theory and in evidence, the path of government regulation is most often the road to public harm, not public salvation.[205]

---

203 George Stigler, "The Theory of Economic Regulation," in *The Citizen and the State: Essays on Regulation,* at 114 (U. Chicago Press 1975)
204 George Stigler, "Can Regulatory Agencies Protect the Consumer?" in *The Citizen and the State: Essays on Regulation* at 188.
205 The history of fraternal/friendly societies in England, the U.S., and Europe further demonstrates how concentrated pressure groups can use political power to create intrusive economic regulation benefiting them, but harming patients and consumers in the process. These societies were organized on self-help principles along local or trade lines, and achieved a high point in the nineteenth and early twentieth centuries. These met the need for health and other kinds of insurance for their members, including for poorer laboring people, and their

None of this would have been news to Adam Smith. He was cynical when dealing with the idea that politicians and bureaucrats are holy men invested with pure public spirit: "It is the highest impertinence and presumption…in kings and ministers, to pretend to watch over the economy of private people, and to restrain their expense…they are themselves, and without any exception, the greatest spendthrifts in the society."

And of those who argued that business should serve public interests, he noted: "I have never known much good done by those who affected to trade for the public good. It is an affectation, indeed, not very common among merchants, and very few words need be employed in dissuading them from it."[206]

5. The Illusion of Benefit from Failed Programs

There are, of course, certain cases where government involvement does a good job in promoting social progress: national defense, expressways, dams, satellites, land-grant

---

rise and decline echoes themes sounded here. They solved the usual problems of excess claims, moral hazard (taking on more risk because insured), and adverse selection (higher risks tend to seek insurance) by charging different premiums for risk and by social pressures such as neighbors in "visiting committees." These societies sought to provide good medical care at low cost, which drove down medical prices. In England, the doctors organized and in 1911 backed compulsory health insurance legislation, which promoted commercial insurance companies over the societies. Doctor incomes doubled. This legislation spelled the demise of the societies, which remained popular but blew away with the winds of socialism and the 1948 creation of national health insurance. Pavel Chalupnicek and Lukas Dvorak, "Health Insurance before the Welfare State; The Destruction of Self-Help by State Intervention," 13, *The Independent Review*, at 367 (Winter 2009).
206 Adam Smith, *Wealth of Nations*, at 478.

colleges, public health research, Sherman anti-trust laws, certain information-forcing laws—but these *do not involve control by government agents of industry prices, products, or entry*. These areas of relative success and the natural vitality of our economy tend to obscure from the public mind the fact that it is the market, not government regulation, that drives progress, and this confusion leads to the false conclusion that it is the regulation that benefits and that all is well in the regulatory state. Milton Friedman concludes:

> The greater part of the new ventures undertaken by government in the past few decades have failed to achieve their objectives. The United States has continued to progress; its citizens have become better fed, better clothed, better housed, better transported; class and social distinctions have narrowed; minority groups have become less disadvantaged; popular culture has advanced by leaps and bounds. All of this has been the product of the initiative and drive of individuals co-operating through the free market. Government measures have hampered not helped this development. We have been able to afford and surmount these measures only because of the extraordinary fecundity of the market. The invisible hand has been more potent for progress than the visible hand for retrogression.[207]

Thus the delicious irony: people see progress and mistakenly ascribe it to the very government measures that have served to retard it over what would be without those measures. Philosophers have a name for this common logical fallacy: *post hoc ergo propter hoc* – after the thing therefore because of the thing.

---
207 Milton Friedman, *Capitalism and Freedom,* at 199-200.

6. How Do You Tell What Regulation to Avoid and What to Keep?

Certain types of laws and government regulations are helpful for the proper functioning of markets. All markets—not just exchanges—operate better if supported by basic rules of the game that protect physical security, property rights, individual incentives for advancement, and the ability to contract freely. This is not to deny that commerce can flourish under anarchic or stateless conditions as long as the return to productive activity is sufficient.[208] But there is no doubt that regulations or customs that encourage participation in commercial life and go beyond the informal means anarchy allows do further support its flourishing. It is helpful to know that the party with whom one is dealing is subject to legal constraints encouraging performance of your contract. It is helpful to be protected from theft, fraud, and other depredations on the fruits or subjects of your efforts or commerce. It is helpful if private property is protected. It is helpful if disputes can be settled short of resort to arms.

These items form the basic rule of law, and without them, commercial life would suffer and be limited in scope. Courts or customary arbiters or both fill a necessary role. Lawyers and courts are sometimes less important than informal commercial means. In Boston, for example, during the heyday of the wool and cotton trade in the late nineteenth century, one individual, a Norwegian immi-

---

208 David Skarbek, "Self-Governance in San Pedro Prison," *The Independent Review*, Vol. 14, No. 4, Spring 2010, at 569. Skarbek notes, "Somalia's relative economic performance has improved during its period of statelessness," and his study of economic life in a largely self-governing Bolivian prison demonstrates how people lacking government can nonetheless prosper.

grant named Peder Olsen, my great-grandfather, rose to become the highly regarded settler of disputes as to quality and price whom other merchants of cotton, wool, and other fibers would turn to. Most disputes never reached the courts.

Market-Promoting Rules

Markets need rules of the game, but of a special sort, especially given the ongoing costs of compliance with regulation. As the example of stock or commodity exchanges shows, commerce and exchange are promoted by rules that encourage and foster transactions and preserve incentives for individual advancement. Such exchanges have numerous rules (usually self-adopted) regulating the activities of the traders: times of day, terms of settlement, what can be traded, and the like. Ronald Coase notes, "It suggests, I think correctly, that for anything approaching perfect competition to exist, an intricate system of rules and regulations would normally be needed... The explanation for these regulations: that they exist in order to reduce transaction costs and therefore to increase the volume of trade."[209]

The best regulation, of course, is industry self-regulation, as with exchanges; government need not be involved. Standardized weights and measures are another example of mostly beneficial rules. But the important thing about these rules, whether privately or publicly created, is that they arise out of the needs and interests of the business and its consumers, and promote commerce and competition, not restrict them.

---

209 Ronald H. Coase, *The Firm, The Market, and the Law,* at 9.

These items do not create the Regulatory Illusion, nor promise a free economic or political lunch. They assist commerce and help effectuate transactions by lowering their costs. Consumers and taxpayers benefit, as do all those whose welfare is advanced by economic growth, including the jobless, who now have greater job opportunities.

7. Restraints on Competition and Prices are Not Beneficial

So if we know what sorts of laws or regulation are helpful, then what types of laws or regulation are harmful? Certainly we know the answer in part: particularly harmful are those industry-specific laws that hamper or prohibit competition and entry into the market (think the alphabet agencies, like the now-eviscerated CAB and ICC), constrain new entrants and old (FCC), eliminate or reduce consumer choice of product or service (FDA), set prices (Department of Agriculture), effect wasteful subsidies (farm supports), add deadweight costs without compensating benefit (SEC), or otherwise seek to interfere with the functioning of market prices and competition. Each of these measures reduces individual incentives for advancement.

The harms of such interferences are well understood and accepted. Stigler notes, "For long periods the tradition of economic theory has been opposed to protectionism, minimum wage legislation, price and production controls and 'just' (non-rational) prices... The general theory still says that these policies are inefficient and hence undesirable."[210] It is this form of legal imposition by government that is referred to here and elsewhere as undue

---

210 George Stigler, "Economic Theory and Economic Policy," in *Essays in the History of Economics*, at 27 (U. Chicago Press 1965).

regulation. Much of the New Deal was of this sort, and we are still living with it.

Why there Is a *Strong Presumption Against* Regulation

If in case after case empirical evidence shows efforts to improve the workings of the economy by government economic regulation of prices, products, and entry fail to achieve their stated goals and create more harm than good, then the case for intrusive regulation of *any* industry is a hard one to make. (See Appendix B for a discussion of whether banking and the environment are exceptions). As discussed, regulation is not free: even disclosure requirements, for example, drive up costs and make life harder for new entrants and consumers and must be carefully designed not to interfere but to assist markets.

Fundamentally, the reason why intrusive market regulation—the core of the Regulatory Illusion—harms society is that it reduces the area for individual effort and initiative by imposing hurdles to innovation and entry that impede the creative flow of energy and imagination freedom of commerce fosters. This freedom of "personal economic enterprise" has been sometimes described as so fundamental, even without regard to U. S. constitutional doctrine, that all societies should recognize it as a universal right:

> Experience shows us that the denial of this right, or its limitation in the name of an alleged "equality" of everyone in society, diminishes, or in practice absolutely destroys the spirit of initiative, that is to say the creative subjectivity of the citizen. As a consequence, there arises, not so much a true equality as a "leveling down." In the place of creative initiative there appears passivity, dependence, and submis-

sion to the bureaucratic apparatus which...puts everyone in a position of almost absolute dependence.

This point echoes that by Friedrich Hayek quoted at the beginning of Chapter I, but the source is not a Chicago or Austrian economist. It is, perhaps unsurprisingly, no less a moral authority than Pope John Paul II.[211] The deeper lesson is that the regulatory state, shorn of its various politically promoted pretenses to moral superiority (to promote equality, reduce unfairness, temper rapacious greed, help the poor or impotent, etc), is exposed to a rather simple criticism—its profound and harmful effect on basic human nature and needs, by creating dependency and undermining personal economic enterprise, which is a key driver of social progress and moral good.[212]

Innovation creates new industries and jobs, and regulation stifles innovation. As Eric Schmidt, the CEO of Google, put it after experiences tussling with Congress and

---

211 Papal encyclical *Solicitudo Rei Socialis*, by Pope John II. I am indebted to Peter Wehner of the Ethics and Public Policy Center for this reference.

212 Economist Hernando de Soto recounts an experiment in setting up a business in Peru before the Fujimori reforms of 1992. It took nearly a year of filling out forms and seeking licenses, and ten bribes (out of many more requested), to open a small business in Lima. This is described in Robert J. Barro, *Getting it Right: Markets and Choices in a Free Society*, at 38 (MIT 1996). In Egypt, de Soto found in a 1997 study published in 2004 that "To open a small bakery, our investigators found, would take more than five hundred days. To get legal title to a vacant piece of land would take more than ten years of dealing with red tape. To do business in Egypt, an aspiring poor entrepreneur would have to deal with fifty-six government agencies and repetitive government inspections." Hernando de Soto, "Egypt's Economic Apartheid," 2/3/2011, *WSJ*. Then people wonder why progress is nonexistent and unrest always just under the surface. This unrest broke out across the Arab world in January-February 2011. It remains to be seen whether the new governments will deal with the regulatory morass at the root of their economic stagnation.

the administration's efforts to regulate Google and the Internet:

> Regulation prohibits real innovation, because the regulation essentially defines a path to follow. This by definition has a bias to the current outcome, because it's a path for the current outcome.[213]

Because—even apart from compliance costs—extensive government regulation so rarely if ever helps and has so many observed harms, wisdom counsels that it be enacted only in extreme circumstances where the case is unambiguous and promising alternatives are exhausted. Otherwise, it is wise to operate with a *strong presumption against* government regulation, based on a healthy skepticism that its promises will be achieved, and the insight from history that beneficial outcomes are rare. This is a disposition, or attitude, not a rigid ideology or belief, and is founded on both understanding of the benefits of markets and the overwhelming detailed studies demonstrating the harms and costs of numerous regimes of intrusive economic regulation and control.

The question is, then, does the 2010 Act satisfy the presumption against government regulation? Have the high burden of necessity and the exhaustion of promising alternatives been met? After examining the single-payer universe, the experience with regulated industries, and the HSA-based voucher alternative described, the answer is clearly no.

---

213 "Google Speaks Truth to Power," L. Gordon Crowitz, 10/24/11, *WSJ*.

C. Meeting Complaints, Criticisms, and Other Objections

We have now seen how our health care system puts us on a treadmill of rising costs and decreasing quality (in Chapters I and II), what the international experience in health care – especially Britain, Canada and Europe – reveals once the myths are stripped away (Chapter III), what the proper principles guiding a redone health system are (Chapter IV), what a program designed to bring true "patient power" and the forces of competition and individual responsibility looks like (Chapter V), what the power of free markets delivers (Chapter VI), and how the regulatory state promises much and delivers little, making single-payer and government-control approaches predictable failures (Chapter VII).

The result is not happy for the proponents of government-controlled health care, and clearly shows that the patient power advocates – recently supported by the English Government's official White Paper admission of failure of the NHS – advance the only real path to a better future.

This could end the story. But there are still voices of doubt favoring government-control which advance ideas and views based on various notions of the perceived failures of free or open markets. Any effort at a complete treatment of the subject at hand requires some discussion of at least the most prominent of these views. To that end, this Chapter addresses these points and additional objections not treated earlier to the program advanced here and elsewhere of HSAs, vouchers and freed-up insurance markets.

CHAPTER VIII:
Critics of Free Markets Rely on Failed or Unsupported Theories

Don't let the rain come down / My roof's got a hole in it and I might drown.

1960's FOLK TUNE

1. Health Care is Not a Market Failure

Some have asserted that our health care system is an example of hypothesized market failure, requiring government regulation to correct inherent shortfalls between private enterprise and the optimal social product.[214] This idea is not new, and indeed "[t]he economic justification of government intervention usually rests on a claim of market failure."[215] The importance of this concept is that it forms

---

214 See e.g., Theodore Marmor, "Market Failure," *The Washington Monthly*, April 2000 (critical review of Richard Epstein's *Mortal Peril: Our Inalienable Right to Health Care?*). This is also often uncritically asserted in the editorial pages of the NY Times.

215 *Market Failure or Success: The New Debate*, ed. by Tyler Cowen and Eric Crampton, at 3 (Independent Institute, Edward Elgar 2002).

the basis for justifications of government control; if there is no market failure, health policy experts must deal with the principles and findings of economics described here. If there is market failure, they feel free to disregard or diminish them.

Historically, market failure theories rested on assumptions about public goods and externalities, which created free riders. A public good is indivisible, such that its benefits cannot be limited to persons who pay for it. A classic example is national defense; your neighbor is protected even if he does not value the good enough to voluntarily pay for it. If only those willing to pay do so, everyone else is a free rider external to the transactions of suppliers and payers, yet benefiting without contributing to the expense. This is a sound justification for possible government involvement, for only by taxing everyone for defense can free riders be eliminated and those who benefit carry the cost. The modern development of this theory came from Paul Samuelson and Kenneth Arrow, both of whom received Nobel Prizes in economics.

Both Samuelson and Arrow, however, sought to extend the theory of public goods (based upon the externality that strangers to the transaction can free ride) beyond narrow confines until they virtually eclipsed all of markets everywhere. This created the basis for loose arguments promoting government intervention willy-nilly. Finally this approach came a cropper. As a plain example of a public good, Samuelson had pointed to lighthouses, for which there was no perceived way to limit the use to those who paid a fee, thus promoting free ridership by others.

But Ronald Coase, in a famous article, demonstrated that just such a private fee system in fact operated successfully, and more efficiently than a public operation because of the institutions that developed whereby merchants and other interested parties were able to effect policies. This empirical work undercut the rationale and generality of the public goods theory, which has since retreated to its proper limits, such as for national defense, which is truly indivisible.[216] Coase also exposed the unfruitfulness of the emphasis on externalities proposed by Paul Samuelson, upon which much of the theoretical justification for government regulation in various areas has rested.

The original market failure ideas did not appear to extend to health care, which is a consumer-based market evidencing supply-and-demand factors, the absence of "natural monopoly," and not characterized by public goods or burdensome externalities. Free riders are not a problem inherent in health care, based as it is in individual doctor-patient relationships. Nor is there any inherent reason the American consumer/patient is incompetent to make decisions, guided by relevant medical advice, in his or her own self-interest. Information, now largely suppressed and unavailable, can be made open and available. So the traditional case for market failure based on public goods and free riders seems generally inapplicable to health care.

Since the original theory of market failure was sketched in the 1950s and 1960s, additional bases for market failure have been suggested, usually premised on an assumption of imperfect information by consumers or "information asymmetry." It is to these new or additional theories that

---

216 Ronald H. Coase, "The Lighthouse in Economics," 17 *The Journal of Law and Economics,* at 357-376 (October 1974). Previously, Paul Samuelson had written in his popular textbook, *Economics; An Introductory Analysis,* that lighthouses are an example of an indispensible function of government, like national defense and police, because of the external effect that some ships can take advantage of their provision without paying. Coase proved this assertion to be wrong.

one must look when seeking a basis for the market failure hypothesis that single-payer advocates assume when making their arguments.

The intellectual case for health care as a market failure requiring governmental intervention rests largely on an article published in 1963 by Ken Arrow, building on earlier work by A.C. Pigou.[217] Arrow differentiates health care from other markets on the basis of five features: unpredictable needs and demands, licenses to practice creating barriers to entry, trust relationship between doctor and patient, asymmetrical information (doctor knows more than patient), and lack of cost transparency (insurers pay after service, patient lacks knowledge of costs). He draws the conclusion that since these five factors differ from or are not part of the ideal of perfect competition in markets, a case exists for government to intervene to regulate relations. Arrow's analysis is still relied upon as justification for government control in health care and is relied upon further by those who seek to impose price and budget controls, such as in single-payer systems. In its heyday in the 1960s and 1970s, even many solid economists accepted the analysis as appropriate and persuasive.

The Nirvana Approach and Free Lunch Fallacies

This is no longer the case. Arrow's assumptions and analysis have been examined critically and found wanting, and they are no longer seen as providing a basis for the government interventions that he advocated and others imposed in the earlier era. In the first place, the five fac-

---

217 Kenneth Arrow, "Uncertainty and the Welfare Economics of Medical Care," *American Economic Review* (December 1963).

CHAPTER VIII: CRITICS OF FREE MARKETS

tors he identified are in no way unique to health care. Most markets in fact operate with much of these limitations, yet competition allows prices to decline and services and products to improve as providers compete to fill the consumer's wants. Information on medical care and providers has proliferated with the Internet, and more can readily be done; patient ignorance is not a necessary part of the health care scene. Trust is a factor in most markets, yet competition flourishes without regulation. Insurance carriers have not left large areas without; products have multiplied to cover myriad uncertainties not thought of in 1963, and carriers seek out new uncertainties to price risk wherever a profit seems possible. So, on the face of things, Arrow's suggestions appear to have been refuted by experience.[218]

In addition, Arrow's approach rests upon a fundamental flaw. He contrasts existing health market conditions with Pareto optimal ideals (leading him to find inefficiencies justifying government intervention). This is an example of what noted economist Harold Demsetz calls "the nirvana approach," where failure is always found by contrasting some existing market with some ideal state. Demsetz criticized Arrow's method of analysis directly in his classic 1969 article, "Information and Efficiency: Another Viewpoint:"

> The view that now pervades much public policy economics implicitly presents the relevant choice as between an ideal norm and an existing "imperfect" institutional arrangement. This *nirvana* approach differs considerably from the *comparative institutional* approach in which the relevant choice is between alternative real institutional arrangements. In practice, those who adopt the nirvana viewpoint

---

[218] Avik Roy, "Health Care and the Profit Motive," 3 *National Affairs*, at 40-45 (Spring 2010).

seek to discover discrepancies between the ideal and the real and if discrepancies are found, they deduce that the real is inefficient. Users of the comparative institutional approach attempt to assess which alternative real institutional arrangement seems best able to cope with the economic problem; practitioners of this approach may use an ideal norm to provide standards from which divergences are assessed for all practical alternatives of interest and select as efficient that alternative which seems most likely to minimize the divergence... The nirvana approach is much more susceptible than is the comparative institutional approach to committing three logical fallacies—*the grass is always greener fallacy, the fallacy of the free lunch*, and *the people could be different fallacy*.[219]

Demsetz examines Arrow's method of analysis closely (in the related field of new knowledge generation) and finds it perfectly exemplifies all three of the logical fallacies associated with the nirvana approach. For each of Arrow's factors, Demsetz shows how nothing in Arrow's logic suggests the advantage of government over market solutions:

Given the nirvana view of the problem, a deduced discrepancy between the ideal and the real is sufficient to call forth perfection by incantation, that is, by committing the grass is always greener fallacy. This is usually accomplished by invoking an unexamined alternative. Closely associated in practice with this fallacy is the fallacy of the free lunch. An example of the latter is given in Arrow's discussion of

---

219 Harold Demsetz, "Information and Efficiency: Another Viewpoint," set out in *Market Failure or Success: The New Debate*, edited by Tyler Cowen and Eric Crampton, at 107 (The Independent Institute, Edward Elgar 2002), originally published in *The Journal of Law & Economics* 12:1 (1969).

the difficulties posed for the competitive system by uncertainty [quoting at length from Arrow].

Although Arrow locates some interesting facets of real world market functioning, his utter failure to contrast these with any alternative institutional arrangement vitiates his suggestion of improvement by government intervention. Imperfections are never reckoned, and the grass is always greener in Arrow's contrasted perfect world of government control. This world also presents a free lunch, since the asserted imperfections in the market economy magically disappear in his hypothesized nirvana. Such a conclusion is, of course, unreal. This approach also leads to "the people could be different" fallacy, since if only people acted differently, there would be no need to try to improve them or avoid moral hazards. But human nature is not so readily changed.

Although Demsetz's critique was aimed at Arrow's analysis of how markets invest in information generation and dissemination, it applies directly to Arrow's analysis of health care, in which he proffered and relied upon the same nirvana approach. Lacking a real-world alternative against which to contrast, Arrow was moved to advocate government control-type solutions based on unfounded assumptions:

> If he were to compare a real socialist system with a real capitalistic system, the advantages and disadvantages of each would stand out, and it would be possible to make some overall judgment as to which of the two is better. But Arrow compares the workings of a capitalistic system with a Pareto norm that lends itself to static analysis of allocation but, nonetheless, is poorly designed for analyzing dynamic problems of production. He finds the

capitalistic system defective. The socialist ideal, however, resolves static allocation problems rather neatly. But this is only because all the dynamic problems of production are ignored. The comparison of a real capitalistic system with an ideal socialist system that ignores important problems is not a promising way to shed light on how to design institutional arrangements for the production and distribution of knowledge.[220]

Whether the subject of analysis is information generation or health care, the comparison of an existing system with an ideal is not a promising basis for grounding a critique of markets or launching into a program of single-payer or other form of government control. Arrow, and generations of health policy experts following his lead, leapt from weak or insufficient theories of market failure to proposing programs of government control without recognition of the infirmities in the approach and the fact that they have moved far out beyond the area of sound analysis.

By contrasting the ideal with the real instead of two real alternatives, Arrow not only committed an egregious logical error, he also performed a disservice, the implications of which—given the use made of his papers to implement policy—are profound.

Even apart from its nirvana infirmities, market failure fails both as economic theory and in the light of empirical analysis. Years ago George Stigler commented, "In truth I consider both the complex theory of welfare economics—for that is what we call the economic analysis of market failures—and that blend of hope and cynicism which passes for

---

[220] Harold Demsetz, "Information and Efficiency: Another Viewpoint," in *Market Failure or Success: The New Debate*, at 116.

CHAPTER VIII: CRITICS OF FREE MARKETS

political wisdom to have been infertile and obfuscatory."[221] This judgment has only been reaffirmed and strengthened in the years since.

Economists delight in striking out on new ground, and market-failure theorists are no exception. But so far, no one has successfully raised a market failure theory that sustains rigorous empirical analysis. In their volume, *Market Failure or Success: The New Debate*, economists Tyler Cowen and Eric Crampton set out in full the major works proposing new or additional areas of market failure and proposed theories explaining them, including works by George Akerhof and Paul David, as well as by Nobel Laureate Joseph E. Stiglitz. They also include the works by others refuting the empirical basis for these theories.[222]

To the original areas of hypothesized market failure have been added in recent years approaches based on asymmetrical information (one party knows more than the other), which was one of the bases for Kenneth Arrow's article arguing that health care is a possible area of market failure. A classic example given by the new failure theorists of asymmetry in information is the applicant for life insurance, who knows far better than the company what risks to predict. According to the theory, carriers, aware of this asymmetry, should charge a premium over market-clearing levels, creating inefficiency justifying government intervention. But empirical analysis reveals this assumption to be false.

Another basis suggested for possible market failure is where "network effects" occur, for example where an initial entrant

---

221 George Stigler, "The Economists' Traditional Theory of the Economic Functions of the State," in *The Citizen and The State*, at 103.

222 *Market Failure or Success: The New Debate*, edited by Tyler Cowen and Eric Crampton (Independent Institute, Edward Elgar 2002), economists at George Mason University.

garnering a large market share may be able to set standards for the industry and perpetuate its position although better alternatives exist. This inefficiency is also urged as a ground for government intervention. But again, empirical analysis reveals no such inefficiency to exist. Neither of these new theories (nor any other market failure theory yet proposed) is much of a basis for building a case for market failure.[223]

The Failure of Market Failure

The essays on market failure theories in *Market Failure or Success* leave the reader with an unequivocal conclusion: whether the area of inquiry is "lemons"—poor used cars—life insurance, credit markets, wages and cyclical unemployment, the defeat of Beta by VHS, consumer protection laws, health care, or other areas in which market failure theorists have proposed their conditions to exist, careful attention to real-world conditions refutes these claims time and time again.[224]

---

223 Tomohide Yasuta, "Food Safety Regulation in the United States: An Empirical and Theoretical Examination," 15, *The Independent Review*, at 209-11 (Fall 2010), confirms this analysis as applied to food safety (the FDA and other departments). Like Demsetz, he finds that the claims of market failure and imperfect information rest on false comparisons of existing conditions with an idealized state of perfect information, which does not exist whether regulation is or is not in place. As he shows, "the imperfect information theorists assume as a matter of fact the existence of market failure. However, careful reasoning and real-world observation reveal that this assumption is false," and that the studies justifying regulation on these bases are systematically flawed. This is because "[e]conomic efficiency, projected by cost-benefit analysis, cannot be achieved because of regulators' inherent inability to distribute benefits among consumers according to each consumer's demand. Government intervention, claimed to correct market inefficiency, creates a new situation of inefficiency." Yasuta, *id.*, at 221.

224 For an analysis of earlier theories, see *The Theory of Market Failure: A Critical Examination*, ed. by Tyler Cowen (George Mason U. Press 1988).

This is not to say that this conflict is over; as long as open questions remain, someone will attempt to fill the gap. Like Cassandra, market failure theory predicts and finds market failures everywhere. There is, in this view, hardly a nook or cranny of life where the beneficial influence of an omniscient state would not improve upon the state of affairs created by markets. But while markets are not perfect and there is always room for improvement in almost all areas of economic life, the call of market failure advocates leads most often not to small-scale alterations in the conditions or laws governing relations but to government and bureaucratic interposition into the heart of the matter.

Although Arrow's analysis of health care has been thoroughly discredited, it is still a star in the firmament of the doggedly overcommitted old progressive. Paul Krugman, for example, who writes for the *N.Y. Times* and recently also received a Nobel Prize for other work, cites Arrow's analysis and relies upon it for his numerous prescriptions advocating government spending and intervention. Promoting this view may satisfy some of the paper's readers, but it does them a disservice.

Misconceiving Economic Ideas and Theory for Social Goals

If, on the other hand, by market failure health policy experts are not referring to the economic concept discussed above but simply mean that everyone is not able to participate in the health care market to the extent desired, and these advocates are not attempting to follow Arrow's analysis to justify something grander, then the matter sits differently. They are making a social choice that some people should be enabled to participate who might not otherwise do so.

Indeed, this is the premise of the health care proposal advanced here—that in today's world, society should aim for universal coverage. This goal implies a limited role for the federal government in financing health care availability for those otherwise unable to do so, which is why we have included a voucher regime. But to say that the benefits of the market in health care should be extended to those not covered is very different from saying the health care market should be dismantled or eliminated or so curtailed by government control as to be unrecognizable. To go from seeking to extend the benefits of the market to all to advocating a single-payer or other system of government control that destroys the market is to make an illogical leap, unjustified by the social goal of universality.

If you make a social choice that everyone should have refrigerators, you provide funding for those without; you don't seek to have the government make and distribute refrigerators or otherwise control the market for them. If you want to give the poor access to higher education they otherwise can't afford, you provide them funds; you don't nationalize the universities.

Universality implies government financing of those unable to participate—extending and building on the market—not the wholesale abandonment of the system that, for all its flaws, has brought the highest level of benefit to the most people not only in America, but also around the world.

The Interrelationship of Vouchers, HSAs, and the Elimination of Mandates and Controls

But a caveat here is necessary. A voucher regime instituted without also ensuring countervailing market forces would feed the demand side and just further raise costs. So that is why the existing health insurance mandate/control labyrinth must simultaneously fall, and information proliferate, so competition can serve to drive down prices towards marginal cost. The market for health care that this country formerly had can be reestablished, but these three interrelated steps must occur: health savings accounts, vouchers, and a free market in insurance.

To see market failure in today's system of poor patient information, omniscient doctors, and spiraling costs—largely a product of mandates, controls, and low- or no-deductible company policies and Medicare—is to confuse the cause and the effect. The reason American health care does not function well as a market is not hard to find: the system has grown so dependent on tax breaks for employer-sponsored coverage and interlaced with government interference—which distorts incentives, drives up costs, and buries information about choices—it is remarkable any individual choice continues to exist. It is, as many have noted, government failure, not market failure.

So the merits of the single-payer case and that for government control of health care, shorn of loose rhetoric about market failure, reduce down to the claim that such systems will deliver similar or better care at less cost. As we have seen above, they do the opposite, delivering poorer service levels, intolerable or growing costs, or both.

2. Does the Existence of Externalities Justify Government Intervention?

Although not appearing to apply to health care, one principal justification for government intervention relied upon by welfare economists is the concept of externalities briefly discussed above and worth further attention. The term was coined by Paul Samuelson to describe the effects on those not party to a transaction. A farmer raises hogs on land he buys for that purpose and sells them to bacon lovers. But the noise and smell of hogs annoy his neighbor, who is not a party to the sale. The prominent welfare economist A.C. Pigou explained his cure for this problem of externalities:

> It is plain that divergences between private and social net product...cannot, like divergences due to tenancy laws, be mitigated by a modification of the contractual relation between any two contracting parties, because the divergence arises out of a service or disservice rendered to persons other than the contracting parties. It is, however, possible for the State, if it so chooses, to remove the divergence in any field by "extraordinary encouragements" or "extraordinary restraints" upon investments in that field.[225]

Stigler mocked this approach with the comment: "Again, there would be no loss in content, and perhaps some gain in form, if the last sentence were rewritten: 'It is, however, ridiculously simple for his Serene Omnipotence, if it pleases him, to remove the divergence in any field by 'extraordinary encouragements' or 'extraordinary restraints' upon investments in that field.'"[226]

Contrary to Pigou and his modern compatriots enamored with the theory of externalities as a reason for government intervention, Coase points out:

> It is easy to show that the mere existence of "externalities" does not, of itself, provide any reason for govern-

---

[225] A.C. Pigou, *The Economics of Welfare*, 4th ed., p.192.
[226] George Stigler, "The Economists' Traditional Theory of the Economic Functions of the State," in *The Citizen and the State*, at 113.

ment intervention. Indeed, the fact that there are transaction costs and that they are large implies that many effects of people's actions will not be covered by market transactions. Consequently, "externalities" will be ubiquitous. The fact that government intervention also has its costs makes it very likely that most "externalities" should be allowed to continue if the value of production is to be maximized... The ubiquitous nature of "externalities" suggests to me that there is a *prima facie* case against intervention, and the studies on the effects of regulation which have been made in recent years in the United States, ranging from agriculture to zoning, which indicate that regulation has commonly made matters worse, lend support to this view.[227]

As Coase explains, effect on others is just another factor of production, and the concept of externalities is completely unnecessary; the problem can be addressed by conventional market methods and common law. Thus in addition to the fact it does not apply to health care by its own terms, the theory of externalities as a basis for government intervention sweeps too broadly to be a useful idea in practice.

3. Is the Free Market Model Based on Unrealistic Claims about Human Nature?

Modern economics is heavily invested with the idea of rational behavior. Many people naturally recoil at this assumption of rationality in the pursuit of self-interests characteristic of economic theory—the insistence that aggregate market behavior acts "as if" the participants are rational and have rational expectations, even though individual households or people may and do often act irration-

---

[227] Ronald Coase, *The Firm, the Market, and the Law,* at 26-28.

ally. Many question whether a discipline can truly inform that is built on rationality when we all know how irrational each of us can be. Nobel Laureate Gary Becker puts it this way:

> To many the word [rational] suggested an outdated psychology, lightning-fast calculation, hedonistic motivation, and other presumably unrealistic behavior. As economic theory became more clearly and precisely formulated, controversy over the meaning of the assumptions diminished greatly, and now everyone more or less agrees that rational behavior simply implies consistent maximization of a well-ordered function, such as a utility or profit function.[228]

Nevertheless, irrationality persists in decision making, and it was one of Becker's contributions to point out that both rational and irrational decision making are limited by "opportunity sets"—the amount of goods or services available at a price—so that "irrational units would often be 'forced' by a change in opportunities to respond rationally."

> Even irrational decision units must accept reality and could not, for example, maintain a choice that was no longer within their opportunity set. And these sets are not fixed or dominated by erratic variations, but are systematically changed by different economic variables: a compensated increase in the price of some commodities would shift consumption opportunities towards others; a compensated increase in the price of some inputs would shift production opportunities towards others; or a compen-

---

[228] Gary Becker, "Irrational Behavior and Economic Theory," *The Economic Approach to Human Behavior*, at 153 (U Chicago Press 1976).

sated decrease in the attractiveness of some occupations would shift employment opportunities towards others. Systematic responses might be expected, therefore, with a wide variety of decision rules, including much irrational behavior.[229]

So it appears that even irrational behavior or motives may often need to conform to overall dictates of rational market behavior and the discipline that markets impose. Nevertheless, it remains true that deep insights into individual human behavior in making choices are elusive and unsettled; psychology and economics remain tablemates, not bedfellows. But this does not put the knife into economic theory, for the discipline does not need to await the next Sigmund Freud to gather its insights. While each of us may remain a bundle of unfathomable contradictions, certain common behaviors prove compelling. Ronald Coase points out that shortfalls in understanding individual motivations can await resolution:

> In the meantime, however, whatever makes men choose as they do, we must be content with the knowledge that for *groups* of human beings, in almost all circumstances, a higher (relative) price for anything will lead to a reduction in the amount demanded. This does not only refer to a money price, but to price in its widest sense. Whether men are rational or not in deciding to walk across a dangerous thoroughfare to reach a certain restaurant, we can be sure that fewer will do so the more dangerous it becomes.[230]

---

229 Gary Becker, "Irrational Behavior and Economic Theory," at 167.
230 Ronald H. Coase, *The Firm, the Market, and the Law,* at 4 (italics added).

The study of economics goes on and bears fruit because behaviors follow patterns that are predictably rational in that underlying sense.

4. Does Behavioral Economics Invalidate Free Market Economics?

The most recent challenge to the primacy of standard "rational man" economics comes from proponents of the newly hatched discipline of behavioral economics, given visibility when President Obama announced his belief in it and appointed one of the leaders in the field, Cass Sunstein, a former colleague at the University of Chicago Law School, to be his "regulatory czar" at OMB in the White House, overseeing all new regulatory initiatives.

This theory, elaborated by Richard Thaler of the University of Chicago Business School, focuses on the irrationality of much decision making—or what Herbert Simon referred to as bounded rationality—and seeks to identify those irrationalities or imperfections in choice that are predictable so as to mold regulatory responses to "nudge" behavior in directions deemed more desirable by those with presumed superior knowledge and with access to the reins of power.

At its base is the old belief that markets are arenas for some to prey on others. As Thaler says, "There is no reason to think that markets drive people to do what's good for them. Markets also drive people to do what's good for the people selling."[231] He has coined the phrase "libertarian paternalism" to try to capture their focus on enhancing freedom while shaping regulation to improve outcomes, as

---

[231] "Can Behavioral Economics Save Us from Ourselves?" *University of Chicago Magazine*, 2/05/2010.

Thaler puts it, "to create forgiving environments" for people to make better decisions.

Sunstein and Thaler, recognizing the ill effects of regulation described in Chapter VII, advocate turning away from mandates and controls. They argue that instead "better governance requires less in the way of government coercion and constraint, and more in the way of freedom to choose. If incentives and nudges replace requirements and bans, government will be both smaller and more modest. So, to be clear: *we are not for bigger government, just for better governance.*"[232] An example: research reveals that people are irrationally reluctant to save for their retirement by putting away regular monthly deposits into their 401(k)s. The behavioralist's answer? Enact a rule making monthly deposits the default option so employees have to actively opt out. Most will not, so the goal of retirement savings is met even though they might otherwise prefer to spend the money.[233]

Better Regulations or Less Regulation

Time will tell if the behaviorists have something to add beyond simply tinkering at the edges of economic theory and multiplying the stacks of regulations and the opportunities for bureaucratic aggrandizement. There is little doubt that its supporters also support the foundational work described in Chapter VII showing the adverse nature of the regulatory approach wherever tried. The behaviorist approach, however, appears to brighten the eyes of the regulatory crowd. It is easy for "nudge" to morph into "shove."

---

232 Thaler and Sunstein, *Nudge,* at 14 (Penguin 2009) (italics in original).
233 *Nudge,* at 111.

The danger is that, regardless of benign intent, it offers the prospect of an almost endless panoply of opportunities for government intrusion into people's lives under the humble but misleading notion that by eschewing mandates and direct controls in favor of default rule changes, subtle incentives and disincentives, people can be manipulated into doing what government wants (live "better") without compulsion. Regulation that should be eliminated may be maintained in new dress.

By 2012, the Obama administration's "Regulatory Czar", Cass Sunstein, had left the White House to return to academic climes without leaving any noticeable impact on the size of the ever-burgeoning Federal Register (the home for federal regulations).

The swollen elephant may have been simply too big a mouthful. It is yet to be proven that behaviorists' emphasis on individual decision making improves upon traditional economists' focus on aggregate or group behavior, where for example information asymmetries can cancel out and persons with special skills or lacking them nonetheless find useful roles through market sifting. Economists George Loewenstein and Peter Ubel point out that "behavioral economics has spawned a number of creative interventions… [but] is being asked to solve problems it wasn't meant to address." Its suggestions should "complement, not substitute for, more substantive economic interventions. If traditional economics suggests that we should have a larger price difference between sugar-free and sugared drinks, behavioral economics could suggest whether consumers would respond better to a subsidy on unsweetened drinks or a tax on sugary drinks. But that's the most that it can do."[234]

---

234 George Loewenstein and Peter Ubel, "Economics Behaving Bad-

CHAPTER VIII: CRITICS OF FREE MARKETS

And while traditional economics has produced reams of solid empirical evidence and can point to multiple cases of success, there is doubt if many of the findings of behaviorists are real; as Gary Becker says, "There is a heck of a difference between demonstrating something in a laboratory, in experiments, even highly sophisticated experiments, and showing that they are important in the marketplace. Economic theory is not about how people act in experiments, but how they act in markets."[235]

Markets discipline people in a way that transcends individual irrationalities. No business will last long buying at a dollar and selling at seventy-five cents, regardless of individual peculiarities.

The "rational man" theorem is therefore not understood as a statement of the individual in his ordinary life (although Gary Becker's work has vastly extended the range of the analysis of advantages and disadvantages) but in the group world of the economic marketplace. One does not last long selling at a loss. And further, as Ronald Coase points out, whether it is rational or not for a single person to cross a dangerous thoroughfare for a chicken sandwich, we can be certain fewer will do so the more dangerous it becomes.[236]

---

ly," 7/14/2010, *N.Y. Times*.
235 Quoted by Andrew Ferguson in "Nudge, Nudge, Wink, Wink: Behavioral Economics—The Governing Theory of Obama's Nanny State," 4/19/2010, *The Weekly Standard*, at 23.
236 Ronald H. Coase writes: "I have often wondered why economists, with these absurdities all around them, so easily adopt the view that men act rationally. This may be because they study an economic system in which the discipline of the market ensures that, in a business setting, decisions are more or less rational. The employee of a corporation who buys something for $10 and sells it for $8 is not likely to do so for long. Someone who, in a family setting, does much the same thing may make his wife and children miserable throughout his life. A politician who

5. What Accounts for the Persistence of Anti-Market Belief?

It ain't what you don't know that gets you into trouble. It's what you know for sure that just ain't so.

MARK TWAIN

Market failure, behavioral economics, welfare economics, moralists, and their like prove to be weak reeds for supporting government intervention. What is astounding is that such critics of sound economics and advocates of the moral approach to health care persist in the face of empirical contradiction and the absence of sound theoretical foundation. Examples of continuing folly abound. Two leading academics who support government-controlled health care opined during the run-up to enactment of the 2010 Act that:

> There is no stronger indictment of American private insurers or better example of *the profit motive's corrosive influence on medicine* than rescission [when carriers rescind a policy based on misrepresentation or non-disclosure of major health issues]... It also illustrates how difficult a task it will be to transform the business practices of *an industry that profits from discriminating against sick people.*[237]

This view, of course, confuses the role of insurance with guaranteed coverage. Insurance companies profit by satisfying the wants and needs of their customers, who in turn

---

wastes his country's resources on a grand scale may have a successful career." R.H. Coase, "Comment on Thomas W. Hazlett, Assigning Property Rights to Radio Spectrum Users: Why Did FCC License Auctions Take 67 Years?" 41, *Journal of Law and Economics*, 577-580 (1998).

237 Theodore Marmor and Jonathan Oberlander, "Health Reform: The Fateful Moment," *N.Y. Review of Books*, 8/13/09 (emphasis added).

CHAPTER VIII: CRITICS OF FREE MARKETS

want to be able to choose coverage pools according to individual perceptions of risk and need. Forcing into your pool bad risks or persons who insist on poor lifestyle choices is the opposite of satisfying customer wants, yet that is precisely the outcome that government mandates and controls require. Self-styled old progressives of the sort represented really advocate the abolition of true insurance in favor of government financing for all, a result seen earlier to bring about far worse effects than the problem of inadequate coverage itself that these advocates seek to remedy. The cure they propose is overkill—far worse than the disease.

The attitude expressed in the quote above and the government-control policies advanced by these authors echo early New Deal optimism about the ability of "the best and the brightest" to redeem the rest of mankind by enlightened (and greatly expanded) government agencies improving by intervention imagined rude market behavior and callousness. This view—denigrating free markets and elevating government control—appears to be uninfected by the reams of empirical findings modern economics has developed showing the failure of that particular dream. Their sense of being on the high moral ground gives popularity and longevity to what would otherwise be a failed point of view.

The World According to Keynes

Why is this view so widespread, especially among the educated elite of university teachers, the student population, service professionals, the art world, media ownership, and reporters? Supported by Smith's paradox in the world around them, they proceed to disregard it along with the mountain of evidence of ineffective and costly regulatory schemes. No doubt much of the reason for this lies in widespread acceptance of popularized Keynesianism, derived from the writings and articles of the later John Maynard Keynes that, especially in *The General Theory of Employment, Interest and Money* (1936), promoted government control over business and caused him to be seen as the intellectual godfather of the New Deal. Prior to the thirties, Keynes spoke for a conventional classical economics. The thirties brought him more in line with Marx in his disdain for and blindness to the critical and positive role profit, price, and interest rates play in signaling and directing economic activity in the marketplace.[238]

Generally credited with inventing or at least elaborating the macroeconomic concepts of aggregate demand, aggregate supply, marginal propensity to consume, multiplier effects, etc, in common use today, Keynes nonetheless was guilty of gross errors in his specific recommendations for regulating business (to eliminate profit), driving interest rates to zero (a prescription for combating deflation, which instead spurs inflation), government control of the alloca-

---

[238] Keynes' legacy has been far less destructive than Marx's and unlike Marx, Keynes' contribution to modern economics is profound. Perhaps the most thorough analysis of Marx's thought and contributions is economist Thomas Sowell, *Marxism: Philosophy and Economics* (William Morrow & Co, New York 1985). Sowell concludes: "Despite the massive intellectual feat that Marx's *Capital* represents, the Marxian contribution to economics can be readily summarized as virtually zero. Professional economics as it exists today reflects no indication that Karl Marx ever existed... In professional economics, *Capital* was a detour into a blind alley, however historic it may be as the centerpiece of a worldwide political movement... The supreme irony of Marxism was that a fundamentally humane and egalitarian creed was so dominated by a bookish perspective that it became blind to facts and deaf to humanity and freedom... People who could never be corrupted by money or power may nevertheless be blinded by a vision." *Marxism*, at 220-1.

CHAPTER VIII: CRITICS OF FREE MARKETS

tion of capital instead of banks and companies (socialized banking everywhere shown to lead to demise), and numerous others.[239]

Most people educated through college imbibe the whiskey of government control from later-day Keynes without realizing the drunken stupor into which following this path has been amply shown since 1936 to lead those governments that adopt his theories. Keynes died in 1946, and, as Warburg Professor of Economics at Harvard Robert J. Barro points out, and as shown above, much has been learned since then that invalidates much of what Keynes was seeking to promote. While Keynes' macroeconomic concepts are useful and ubiquitous, many of Keynes' ideas and specific recommendations, and especially his views on government control of business and capital allocation, have long been shown to be hugely counterproductive.[240]

---

239 For an excellent dissection and analysis of Keynes' errors, distortions, evasions, mistakes, and sheer paradoxes, see Hunter Lewis, *Where Keynes Went Wrong: And Why World Governments Keep Creating Inflation, Bubbles and Busts* (Axios Press 2009), and Allan H. Meltzer, professor of public policy, Tepper School at Carnegie Mellon University, "Four Reasons Keynesians Keep Getting It Wrong," Opinion, 10/28 /2011, *WSJ* ("Most now recognize that more than a trillion dollars of spending by the Bush and Obama administrations has left the economy in a slump and unemployment hovering above 9 percent.").

240 Add to those his views on unalloyed government spending, which we now know subtracts from private spending and investment, i.e., a multiplier below one, probably below zero. Counterexamples to the Keynesian free spending hypothesis abound. "After a significant economic contraction in 2001, Turkey embarked on a new path of rapid fiscal consolidation. By the end of 2002, growth was 6 percent and by 2004, 9 percent. Rather than slowing the economy further, government tightening was associated with strong and almost immediate growth. More recently, Estonia, which experienced almost a 20 percent contraction by the end of 2009, instituted fiscal reforms. Among them was a 10 percent reduction in government operating expenses and a flattening of the pension growth trajectory. In 2010, the year following the

Once again, the 2008 financial crash and resulting economic recession provides a ready example. The root cause of these, as shown before, was precisely the kind of government interference with the allocation of capital advocated by Keynes (incentivizing and penalizing banks to make mortgage money available to non-creditworthy borrowers, pumped up by low interest rates from the Federal Reserve)—a kind of long-term legacy from 1936 that destroyed the legatee in 2008.

For all Keynes' admitted brilliance and ironic depredations on private risk-taking, profit-making, and pricing, his solutions have proven to bring unemployment, inflation, sovereign debt crises, stagflation, prolonged recession, and more. The misallocations of capital that result from his policies usher in harm not only for this generation, but for the next and next, not only in this country, but across the globe.[241]

The Liberal Professoriat Impedes Its Own Goals

The widespread predominance among especially the liberal arts and social science professoriat of hostility to free

---

reforms, growth had already turned positive, to around 3 percent, and it is forecast to be above 6 percent for 2011." Edward P. Lazear, professor of economics, Stanford University, "The Euro Crisis: Doubting the Domino Effect," 10/31/2011, *WSJ.* These examples reaffirm that "The financial crisis and possible depression [of 2008-10] do not invalidate everything we have learned about macroeconomics since 1936. [Rather than spending,] more focus should be on incentives for people and businesses to invest, produce, and work." Robert J. Barro, "Magic Multipliers," 2 *Hoover Digest* at 41 (Spring 2009).

241 There is an interesting historical parallel between Keynes' shift to government-control ideas and the rise of Mussolini's somewhat similar approach. Both opposed capitalism and socialism. Both developed in the late 1920s-early 1930s, when fascism was admired widely by many in the intelligentsia. See Joshua Muravchik, *Heaven on Earth: The Rise and Fall of Socialism,* at 144-171 (Encounter 2002).

markets and belief in outmoded and weak government-control views (what economist and author Thomas Sowell calls "the vision of the anointed") has received much recent documentation and comment.[242] This bias compounds itself by repetition and is reinforced by media pandering to customer prejudices.[243]

Professor Jonathan Haidt, a social psychologist at the University of Virginia, read a paper to the Social Psychology national convention in 2011 in which he described this phenomenon as follows: "The fight for civil rights and against racism became the sacred cause unifying the left throughout American society, and within the academy." This shared morality both "binds and blinds... If a group circles around sacred values, they will evolve into a tribal-moral community. They'll embrace science whenever it supports their sacred values, but they'll ditch it or distort it

---

[242] See, e.g., Neil Gross and Solon Simmons, "The Social and Political Views of American Professors," September 24, 2007 (working paper at http://www.wjh.harvard.edu/~ngross/lounsbery_9-25.pdf); Daniel B. Klein, Carlotta Stern, Andrew Western, "Documenting the One-Party Campus," *Academic Questions*, Vol. 18, No. 1 (2004) (study of six fields in the humanities and two universities in California show overwhelming registration in the Democratic party, "negligible" in Republican or independents); John F. Zipp and Rudy Fenwick, "Is the Academy a Liberal Hegemony: The Political Orientations and Educational Values of Professors," *Public Opinion Quarterly*, Vol. 70, Issue 3 (2006).

[243] Thomas S. Kuhn, in his *The Structure of Scientific Revolutions* (Univ. of Chicago Press 1962), describes how professors and others who have spent lifetimes or significant commitments pursuing particular aspects of an existing "paradigm" resist against all odds the coming of a new and different way of thinking that throws the importance and relevance of their life's work into question. Such, for example, was the reaction of the tenured and ensconced professoriat to the innovations of Darwin, Einstein, Freud, and others throughout the history of science. The same resistance to unwanted or threatening ideas exists throughout the social sciences and literary establishments.

as soon as it threatens a sacred value."[244] Ditching science, especially economic science, because it threatens a sacred value or favored political party or view, does seem to characterize the attitudes displayed by many among this otherwise highly intelligent and select group.

No doubt insulation from normal market forces accounts partly for the overwhelming dominance of government-control thinking in the universities. Such insulation is akin to European aristocratic privilege, a protected group or class largely freed of economic necessity and able to look down on trade as avaricious. (Substitute for landed estates the guaranteed privilege of life-tenure, professional standards pressuring for guild interests, and the protective shield of Big Brother in the form of trustees, administrations, and the idea of the university.)[245]

These forces promote—indeed are intended to promote—distance from the rest of society, which is not so insulated from the ups and downs of markets and economic cycles and therefore is more sensitive to real-world conditions and possesses a need to assess what works best and what does not. An ethos of noblesse oblige and ready wealth transfer results, attitudes elevating idealistic or utopian thinking over realism and which tend to denigrate the world of trade and commerce—and profit-making in general—as holding few benefits beyond the jingle-jangle of consumerism.[246]

---

244 John Tierney, "Social Scientist Sees Bias Within," 2/7/2011, *N.Y Times*.

245 This may account for the emotional link between the liberal arts academy and the many ultra-rich who support government-control causes; like other economic aristocrats, neither has to worry much about productivity, growth, or the economy's ups and downs and are free to be free with other people's money.

246 Another factor is suggested by the observation that free markets

Thomas Sowell makes a similar point in describing Marxism and its adherents:

> Despite choosing a world stage on which to operate, Marx's vision was a very insular one. Much of Marx's conception of the capitalist and of the capitalist economy reflected the insularity of the urban intellectual. Marx repeatedly depicted and disdained the capitalist entrepreneur as an uncultured *parvenu*—someone lacking in bookish accomplishments, as if these were the universal litmus tests of contributions to society... The Marxist constituency has remained as narrow as the conception behind it. [Bright and articulate privileged young men without responsibility even for their own livelihoods, e.g., Marx, Engels, Lenin, Mao, Castro, Ho Chi Minh, and their lesser counterparts throughout the world.] But the crucial point is not privilege, as such, but the insulation from responsibility that that provides, particularly during youth. Intellectuals enjoy a similar insulation from the consequences of being wrong, in a way that no businessman, military leader, engineer or even athletic coach can. Intellectuals and the young have remained historically the groups most susceptible to Marxism.... [247]

---

operate in a spontaneous, unplanned (but not anarchic) fashion, what Friedrich Hayek called "the extended order of human interaction." F.A. Hayek, *The Fatal Conceit*, at 14 (U. Chicago Press 1988). For many, particularly those spending their lives as literary critics or scientists finding rational order in literature or nature, a planned approach to economic life is more congenial, regardless of the evidence of relative impoverishment such an approach ushers in. See *Literature and the Economics of Liberty: Spontaneous Order in Culture*, eds. Paul A. Cantor and Stephen Cox (Von Mises Institute 2010).

247 Thomas Sowell, *Marxism: Philosophy and Economics*, at 219-20 (William Morrow 1985).

As noted, Sowell calls the attitude that derives from this insularity "the vision of the anointed," in a book with title of that name.[248] This vision has been described as "a complicated thing. It is part ideology, part prejudice, part ignorance, part psychological projection and part (perhaps its biggest part) wishful thinking." "The vision of the anointed is at its heart a refusal—a knowing, intentional refusal—to deal with reality on reality's terms, or even to conscientiously encounter realities that are challenge to that vision or unpleasant."[249]

Most holders of the vision are unaware of the irony. Preachers denounce on Sunday the profit-seeking that fills their coffers and that their congregants rely upon the rest of the week. Many professors enjoy life tenure, profit from

---

248 Thomas Sowell, *The Vision of the Anointed: Self-Congratulation as a Basis for Social Policy*, at 3-6 (Basic Books 1995). "The vision prevailing among the intellectual and political elite of our time…[needs no supporting evidence and dismisses discordant evidence as biased]…and offers a special state of grace for those who believe in it. Those who accept the vision are deemed not merely to be factually correct but morally on a higher plane. Put differently, those who disagree with the prevailing vision are seen as being not merely in error, but in sin… The vision of the anointed is not simply a vision of the world and its functioning in a causal sense, but is also a vision of themselves and their moral role in that world. *It is a vision of differential rectitude…* Problems exist because others are not as wise or virtuous as the anointed… This vision so permeates the media and academia, and has made such inroads into the religious community, that many grow to adulthood unaware that there is any other way of looking at things, or that *evidence* might be relevant to checking out the assumptions of so-called "thinking people." Many of these "thinking people" could more accurately be characterized as *articulate* people, as people whose verbal nimbleness can elude both evidence and logic. This can be a fatal talent, when it supplies the crucial insulation from reality behind many historic catastrophes."

249 Kevin D. Williamson, "Thomas Sowell: Peerless Nerd," *Commentary* (December 2011), at 47.

on-the-side consulting, and meanwhile denounce profit-seeking behavior in others.[250] This led the great economist Frank H. Knight to ask why "the learned elite in particular, as they express themselves in various ways, choose nonsense instead of sense."[251] And George Stigler added, only partially facetiously, that students should have an action against professors and colleges "for imparting instruction since demonstrated to be false."[252]

---

250 Lenin used to call such high-minded fellow travelers "useful idiots." They are useful only to those politicians, media, academics, and others who have grown dependent on support from people demanding their product. Jesus is thought to have said, "Ye shall seek the truth, and the truth shall set you free." But sometimes seeking the truth is harder than resting on ancient and comfortable, if error-based, views.
251 Frank Knight, "The Role of Principles in Economics and Politics," *American Economic Review* (March 1951).
252 George Stigler, "A Sketch of the History of Truth in Teaching," in *The Citizen and the State,* at 189-193. Since most economic regulatory schemes could not pass the test, an action against government for creating and perpetuating programs of no net value would be equally beneficial.

CHAPTER IX:
The Time is Now to Set Us on the Right Course

We have proceeded from an understanding of the nature and virtues of free markets to the uniform findings of economic analysis that intrusive regulation and control of business by government is a failed exercise, seemingly endlessly repeated. We have seen how those uniform empirical findings in multiple industries apply to the subset of cases referred to as single-payer national health care systems throughout the world—indeed, are predicted by them. We described England's recent admission of failure of its NHS. Lastly we found that these same findings apply with remarkable clarity to Canada's system, which is touted as a model for America.

What is obvious in the progression of all this is that to follow this consistent path of regulatory failure is to deny all that we know and that the economic approach has taught us over the numerous decades since the New Deal. Hard as it is for some to swallow, there is no getting around the basic truth that free markets support incentives that generally work better than government controls and regulation at providing what people really need.

A straightforward solution to the problem of uninsured coverage that reflects the best of free market understanding is to return insurance to its classic role as protection against the unpredictable—which means universal HSAs tied to high deductible coverage, including for government-funded programs such as Medicare and Medicaid, with vouchers for those whose income does not allow them to pay for premiums or deductibles. Existing mandates and controls are unnecessary, harmful, and should be eliminated.

Polls support the notion that people will approve this course and, indeed, welcome it. An example is the January 2010 Massachusetts vote for US Senate, where the relatively unknown Republican Scott Brown claimed the "permanent" Ted Kennedy/Democratic seat in the US Senate. According to a poll by the Washington Post and Harvard School for Public Health, ordinary people—Independent, Republican, and moderate Democrat, and 63 percent of them, no less—saw the country going "severely off track." Two-thirds of those voting for Brown said theirs was a protest "against the Democratic agenda" in Washington, including health care.[253]

This has particular significance since Massachusetts reflects a three-to-one registration advantage in favor of Democrats, and it is also the home of "RomneyCare," upon which the 2010 Act was largely modeled. These were voters with experience; studies show Massachusetts' employer-sponsored premium costs increased 21 to 46 percent faster than the national average since 2005 and are now the high-

---

253 See Saturday, January 23, 2010, *Washington Post*.

est in the nation.²⁵⁴ Individual premiums are even worse, climbing at an annual rate of 30 percent since 2006.²⁵⁵

Massachusetts is a poster child for the harms of the regulatory state. According to Jay Gonzales, Secretary for Administration and Finance – Massachusetts' top budget official under Governor Deval Patrick – MassHealth (RomneyCare), CommonwealthCare, and the Group Insurance Commission, the State's public health programs, altogether account for about 41 percent of the state budget, up from 22 percent in 1998 (before RomneyCare). He told a local paper that:

> "Health care at the rate it's been going, has been crushing everything else in state government."²⁵⁶

I. A Better Mousetrap; Let's Build a Patient-Centered System That Puts the Patient in the Driver's Seat Again

Enacting a universal coverage system based on creating free markets in insurance combined with HSA-based vouchers for those too poor to foot the bill is comparatively easy. A federal law does the trick, if it: 1) eliminates state and federal mandates, price/product controls, and restrictions on out-of-state sales, while allowing the continuation of state systems for overseeing insurer solvency, 2) provides tax incentives for non-employer-based insurance and promotes HSAs with high-deductible coverage, including eventually Medicare and Medicaid, 3) funds the needy with vouchers and enables

---

254 See "RomneyCare Revisited," 1/21/2010, *WSJ*.
255 Review and Outlook, "Back to the ObamaCare Future," 2/28/2010, *WSJ*.
256 David Riley, "Health Care Squeezing Massachusetts Budget", *MetroWest Daily News*, 2/07/2012.

states to provide exchanges for preexisting conditions, and 4) promotes information and an educated consumer.

These can all be accomplished by *one simple federal statute*. In a stroke of the federal pen, federal and state mandates and price/product controls are removed, state insurance departments are allowed to continue to monitor carrier solvency, tax incentives can be shifted to favor high-deductible plans in HSAs, interstate bans on insurance can be lifted, vouchers scaled to income or average treatment costs can be created, and arrangements for preexisting conditions can be set up.

2. Our Own Cost Factor: Will Health Care Vouchers Bust the Budget?

The total cost/benefit of vouchers and the other elements set out here have not yet been analyzed, but the ten-year cost of a combination of somewhat similar proposals comes in at about $300 to 350 billion.[257] This is a small fraction of the projected cost of the 2010 Act and does not even include universal HSAs—the greatest cost-reduction driver—by which the individual is empowered with resources and choice and incentivized to achieve the best service available at the lowest cost. This driver of savings is difficult to price, but its benefits are obvious.

Additional cost savings come from the cessation of federal payments to providers for uninsured treatment:

---

[257] "In all, the Republican proposal would cost some $300-350 billion in its first real decade (about $60 billion for the provisions in the 2009 GOP bill, $150 billion more for community pools [for preexisting conditions], and $100 billion in decreased revenue, from tax credits [to support purchase of insurance]. That's about 15 percent as much as Obamacare's $2.3 trillion." Jeffrey H. Anderson, "The Replacement," 2/14/2011, *The Weekly Standard*.

CHAPTER IX: THE TIME IS NOW TO SET US ON THE RIGHT COURSE

Although such a [voucher] plan might not be cheap, it would not be nearly so expensive or complex as a single-payer system. The money for it could be taken, in part, from Medicaid funds now used to pay doctors and hospitals for care already provided to the uninsured, with such "uncompensated-care" programs gradually transformed into a voucher system for purchasing private coverage.[258]

Eliminating mandates, which providing vouchers allows, further reduces costs at the stroke of the federal pen.[259]

Even beyond these roads to cost reduction, perhaps the most important factor in the equation is the opportunity cost—how much better off or worse you would be under the alternative regime. Think of Germany. Would you rather have lived the fifty years up to 1991 in East Germany, luxuriating in the equality of impoverishment, or in West Germany? No amount of propaganda extolling equality salved the wounds of those trapped East Germans forced into rela-

---

258 Cohen and Levin, "Health Care in Three Acts," at 49. Compare John Cogan, Glenn Hubbard, and Daniel Kessler, "A Better Way to Reform," 2/24/2010, *WSJ* (estimate $100 billion savings from moving to high-deductible plans, damage caps, and interstate insurance sales). See also Goodman, Musgrave, and Herrick, *Lives at Risk*, at 230; Herzlinger, *Who Killed Health Care*, at 254.

259 Additional savings are there for the having. At over 50 percent of the American health dollar, "[t]he pricing of medical care in this country is either directly or indirectly dictated by Medicare; and Medicare uses an administrative formula which calculates 'appropriate' prices based upon imperfect estimates and fudge factors... No matter which formulas and variables are used at any given moment, the information derived will generally be inaccurate." Robert Swerlick, "Our Soviet Health System," 6/5/2007, *WSJ*. Eliminating these government distortions of health pricing will allow private providers flexibility to respond to the new era of competition. HSA-voucher based payments by individuals provides the incentive structure to drive lower costs, foster competition, and free Medicare to pay market prices.

tive impoverishment for their lifetimes. Similarly, for single-payer wait lines and deteriorating service, the opportunity costs in human terms are immeasurable.

3. Representative Ryan's "Roadmap" Alternative

It is not as though Congress lacked alternatives to the 2010 Act. It had in its hopper a set of proposals that provides a solid and principled foundation to create meaningful cost-effective reform. U.S. Representative Paul Ryan (R-Wisconsin) has set out ideas called "Roadmap for America's Future" (see www.americanroadmap.org). This proposes refundable tax credits—which seem the functional equivalent of vouchers—of up to $2,300 per person ($5,700 for families) available at the beginning of each tax year regardless whether taxes will be due, which lower-income folks can apply to the purchase of insurance. He also recognizes the need to go beyond employer-based, low- or no-deductible plans by removing their tax exemption, to allow out-of-state sales of insurance, and to retain health savings accounts tied to high-deductible plans.

Representative Ryan's health reform roadmap incorporates most of the things true reform requires and forms the basis for a repeal of the 2010 Act's mandates, cross-subsidies, and controls. Other important reforms (limits on non-economic tort damages, for example) have been suggested elsewhere.[260]

---

[260] See, for example, Dr. David Gratzer, *Code Blue* (1999); David Gratzer, *The Cure: How Capitalism Can Save American Health Care* (Encounter Books 2006); Regina Herzlinger, *Who Killed Health Care?: America's $2 Trillion Medical Problem—and the Consumer-Driven Cure* (McGraw-Hill 2007); Sally C. Pipes, *Miracle Cure: How to Solve America's Health Care Crisis and Why Canada Isn't the Answer*, (Pacific Research Institute & Fraser Institute 2004).

What the roadmap needs is centering the program on HSAs for all, which centers incentives in individuals, and eliminating federal and state mandates entirely. HSAs create cost-consciousness and the basis for competition to be effective. Creating vouchers makes unnecessary the vast ganglia of mandates designed to partially fill the shoes that vouchers fill completely, and it provides opportunities for enormous cost benefits to the American people.

Some private companies have taken the initiative. Take the example of Whole Foods. That company pays for 100 percent of each employee's premiums for high-deductible insurance and provides up to $1,800 per year in additional health care dollars through deposits into employees' "personal wellness accounts." As the CEO/founder explains: "Our [employees] therefore spend their own health-care dollars until the annual deductible is covered (about $2,500) and the insurance plan kicks in. This creates incentives to spend the first $2,500 more carefully. Our plan's costs are much lower than typical health insurance, while providing a very high degree of worker satisfaction."[261]

4. Conclusion: The New Progressive Approach

The conclusion is inescapable that the extensive governmental controls and interference with the market that the 2010 Act enacted are exactly the wrong approach. Grand designs based on government regulation of our health care promise much, but extensive experience in this road to equality shows it to be a false and dangerous path, which solves little at great cost. It sacrifices the patient/consumer on the altar of anti-market belief. It sacrifices the worker

---

261 John Mackey, "The Whole Foods Alternative to ObamaCare," 8/11/2009, *WSJ*.

on the altar of slow growth in jobs. It replaces the engine of incentives with the dead hand of regulation. It is fighting human nature, not working with it.

The process of enactment—secretiveness, wholesale log-rolling, use of arcane legislative ploys—marked the 2010 Act as the effort of a tenuous political elite to disregard the popular will and overplay their perceived mandate. The radical expansion of government it entails was done in secret because those in power did not trust the people and believed they knew best. Milton Friedman once observed that the greatest harms come from:

> ...men of good intentions and good will who wish to reform us. Impatient with the slowness of persuasion and example to achieve the great social changes they envision, they are anxious to use the power of the state to achieve their ends and confident of their own ability to do so. Yet if they gained the power, they would fail to achieve their immediate aims and, in addition, would produce a collective state from which they would recoil in horror...[262]

This nicely describes *The Bumbling Colossus*.

Meddling with Markets Proves to be No Free Lunch After All

Indeed, many people recoiled in horror at the 2008 to 2010 political enactments. Not just in health care, but also in the origins of the financial crisis, politicians imbued with the old progressive agenda and looking to the next election thought they could get a political free lunch by enlisting private markets to their ends. They did this by regulating what the market participants could or could not consider

---

[262] Milton Friedman, *Capitalism and Freedom*, at 201.

in their assessment of risk. In the financial area, this was by affordable housing goals implemented through HUD, which degraded traditional underwriting standards and created a world of risky derivatives based on unsound mortgages that brought the country to its knees. In health care, this has been through the WW II tax ruling exempting employer-supplied health benefits from employee incomes while allowing the company to deduct the expense, abetted later by mandates and controls forcing insurers (and thereby people seeking insurance) to include in coverage a wide range of unwanted risks.

In both cases, the unanticipated consequence of this pursuit of the Regulatory Illusion was to grossly distort the relevant markets and skew incentives in ways inflicting far greater harm on all than the benefit sought to be conferred upon the needy group that was the target of the intervention.

The tragedy is, the politicians could have achieved their goals by a forthright program of subsidy targeted to the population in need. But this would have entailed a transparent, accountable approach where the taxpayer/consumer could have assessed the costs and benefits, an outcome apparently not to the taste of the usual political mind. The free lunch fallacy is a powerful drug.

Each new generation imbibes this anew. The voices of television, newspapers, blogs, and electronic buzz overwhelm the ordinary citizen trying to sort out the best way ahead. Confusion reigns throughout the media, pulpit, lecture hall, and populace because, on the one hand, advocates of economic freedom are vulnerable to attacks on the rapacious rich while advocates of government control dress up their schemes in populist clothes appealing to the well-meaning, the needy and downtrodden, often promising a greater equality appealing to our ears.

Old progressive thought comes dressed in high moral sentence. Unmentioned and swept aside in the crusades are the downsides – the loss of investment, decline in capital stock, degrading of services, and ever-expanding costs to taxpayers and consumers that are the practical, inevitable result of the regulatory schemes enacted to achieve the professed high-minded goals.

As the euro-zone sovereign debt crisis that began in 2010 reminds, over-promising of the benefits government can bring ushers in an inevitable, if often prolonged, financial tsunami. Those most hurt by this are the very persons initially intended to be benefited—those lower down the income scale. It is a cruel irony when policies enacted to help the needy turn out to be their worst enemy, but that is the lesson of the story told here: the Bumbling Colossus.

The New Progressives

The old progressive agenda undermines and mocks the progressive impulse, destroying the integrity of the effort. What is needed is to marry the beneficent impulse with the knowledge most worth having to make that impulse more than just a dead-end political tool that ushers in waste and destruction.

We can avoid the Regulatory State and its illusions by refusing the promise of free lunch. Instead, political courage to address openly the shortfalls believed in need of correction brings such matters into public view where costs can be honestly reckoned and benefits honestly weighed and assessed. The struggle between the hope for security and the itch for risk bringing reward can be fought out in the political marketplace.

CHAPTER IX: THE TIME IS NOW TO SET US ON THE RIGHT COURSE

This new progressive approach relies upon the powers of free markets unimpeded by government regulation to achieve the bulk of what is needed for progress, supplemented by targeted, scaled subsidies or benefits where the need to include non-market participants in the benefits of markets is compelling. The regulatory Third Way is avoided based upon sound evidence that it fails to achieve the objectives its proponents seek for it. The socialist nightmare – government ownership that ushers in only decay and decline – is avoided entirely.

Keeping the progressive goals of benefit to those who need it, with growth of the great engine of progress found in markets, freedom, and competition, forms the basis for the new progressive thinking. This is the road to real benefit and social health.

For health care, put incentives for cost control and quality service in the right place at the foundation of the system—the individual or family. Provide for the needy with vouchers. Slash the bureaucracies. Liberate the economy from its yoke of mandates and controls, and the American people and their politicians from continuing frustration with ever-increasing health care costs and lowering quality of service.

It's a win-win for America.

APPENDIX A:
Summary of Required Changes for Health Care on the Right Footing

To recap, sensible market-reinforcing reform must do at least the following:

1) ***Promote High-Deductible Coverage for All Through HSAs.*** The fix for our present tax-distorted employer-based insurance regime is to create incentives for people to move from low- to high-deductible insurance covering only non-routine, major matters (ensuring cost-consciousness) in health savings accounts, which will allow real competition to revive and drive down premiums. The goal is to vastly reduce the role of soup-to-nuts coverage, which present tax-favoritism of employer-created plans encourage. Contributions to HSAs should be generous and fully tax-deductible, both by the individual and by his or her employer, if any. Those preferring to pay more to keep soup-to-nuts coverage may do so but without tax subsidy. This change is critical to cost control.

2) *Equalize Tax Treatment Regardless of Employment Status.* Although simply taxing employer-based coverage like any other form of income is the most direct, it is also politically difficult given the huge popular investment in the status quo. Therefore, the best way to achieve the goal of moving people to high-deductible coverage is to give everyone a tax break for paying premiums and contributing to HSAs, not just employees. Employers should get a deduction for contributing to the HSA as does the individual. This unlinks insurance from employment, encourages contributions to HSAs, and directly solves the non-portability problem, so all people are covered all the time regardless of whether or not they have a job or wish to change jobs. Payroll taxes would be adjusted to equalize treatment.

3) *Provide Federally Funded Vouchers Scaled to Income.* To create universality for those unable to fund their HSAs from their own sources, the federal government must fund the HSAs for lower-income persons by vouchers. Since the amounts in an HSA may only be used for health expenses, the voucher is redeemable only to an actual health good or service provider. The amount of the vouchers allocated into each person's HSA should be scaled to ensure adequate coverage below the level of the high-deductible insurance procured as part of the HSA.

4) *Include Medicare, Medicaid, CHIP, and other government programs.* Since Medicare, Medicaid, and CHIP were structured to mimic the employer-based all-inclusive approach, these programs need to be restructured to provide HSAs so that the 50 percent of the health insurance universe that is government-supported doesn't continue to drive the way providers act. Then all citizens will

APPENDIX A: SUMMARY OF REQUIRED CHANGES FOR HEALTH CARE

have incentives to shop for services and products below the deductible, while truly unpredictable costs over the deductible will be covered. Health vouchers make up the difference for those unable to pay. Phase-in over time is critical for Medicare to avoid upsetting reliance. Persons over a certain age, say fifty-five, and a certain income/asset level should be allowed to continue at their option under existing conditions and requirements.

5) *Allow Interstate Sales of Health Insurance.* State restrictions on interstate sales of insurance should be eliminated. This opens up competition among carriers, expands their markets, and drives down prices. State responsibility for the monitoring of investments and insurer solvency should continue.

6) *Promote State Insurance Exchanges for Preexisting Conditions.* Insurance is for risks, not certainties. The social choice to cover preexisting conditions requires public taxpayer subsidy of this class of health problem, while allowing the private market to cover an individual's unrelated health risks. Vouchers supporting the additional costs of coverage for preexisting conditions will be required for those unable to meet the costs.

7) *Include a Provision to Protect Against Bankruptcy.* For those whose health needs surpass the maximums in their catastrophic coverage, a community health fund could be created, funded by taxes or small charges on all insureds. This would prevent the threat of personal bankruptcy from unforeseen extraordinary health needs. To avoid creating an incentive for people to buy less-than-reasonably-adequate coverage, however, such a benefit

should not be available unless the patient has purchased maximum available coverage.

8) ***Promote Information on Prices and Costs.*** Today, patients and doctors proceed largely ignorant of costs and prices for services. Can you imagine shopping for toothpaste or food and not knowing the price? Decades of government and third-party payment have resulted in concealed price/cost information. A law requiring open pricing for health goods and services is needed, at least initially, to help open up the market. Because there will be an enormous demand for information, private services will develop to fill the void created by the present system, which seems designed to keep the patient/consumer in the dark. Government should help promote, but not supplant, these private sources.

9) ***Tort Reform.*** Although the subject of discussion and critique for decades, efforts at lifting the burdens of medical malpractice laws throughout the numerous states have not achieved the desired end of substantially curtailing unwarranted suits and disproportional awards. The best solution is to limit pain and suffering damages to, for example, twice actual damages, and to prohibit punitive damages entirely. State medical boards should be provided with stiffer means to discipline and sanction, because leaving the problem of negligent and grossly negligent medical behavior to the courts and juries is unsatisfactory, producing rents and a net social cost. A public fund could also be created to compensate on a scale such as worker's compensation. The opportunity provided by a national health care reform such as is set out here to also include substantial tort reform is tempting. However, the power of the plain-

APPENDIX A: SUMMARY OF REQUIRED CHANGES FOR HEALTH CARE

tiffs' personal injury bar to undermine effective change is legendary. A substantial portion of the excess reward generated by the one-third or greater contingent fee recycles back into the political system as donations, to ensure the system stays intact. It would be a mistake to include tort reform in the national legislation proposed here if it called out the full force of the plaintiffs' personal injury bar in opposition, making impossible an already difficult political landscape. Since tort reform is desirable under any system of health care, it is not specially treated here.

Areas for Future Analysis and Development: The HSA/voucher/free market in insurance approach spelled out here raises certain additional issues that require further tying down. These include:

1) *the timing and scheduling* of HSA availability for Medicare and Medicaid

2) *how to calculate and scale* the amount of subsidy in the voucher program

3) *what rules to implement for standard and minimum coverage* to assure that all are protected

4) *how to structure the preexisting condition* exchange market

5) *how to require, publish, and disseminate pertinent information* on provider prices, costs, and quality.

Much work has already been done in various contexts on scaling income supplements for welfare and health, and these efforts can be readily drawn upon. The other issues require studies and analysis to get the amounts and timings right so all are protected.

APPENDIX B:
Are Banking and the Environment Special Cases Requiring Extensive Regulation?

1. Banking

The banking industry and the environment present two much-discussed instances where government regulation has received considerable academic interest and enactments, and they present the strongest case for certain types of governmental intervention. Banks and other depositary institutions are built on leverage, which in turn relies on public confidence and trust and are subject to runs and panics, which not only undermine their solvency, but cause them to call in loans and refuse further credit to otherwise healthy businesses in the wider economy. The Federal Reserve's creation as "lender of last resort" to forestall runs, prompted by the Panic of 1907 and the creation of federal deposit insurance, while providing benefits, inevitably somewhat distort incentives to sound banking.

The Federal Deposit Insurance Corporation (FDIC) protects depositors up to a certain limit per account so that if the bank fails, the depositor's money is secure, reimbursed by the federal government's fund into which all FDIC-insured banks pay. The problem is, this takes away from the picture one of the most important forces in the market: watch-guarding and superintending bank solvency. Moral hazard is created, because bankers are, in effect, allowed to "play" with free, protected money. If instead of the FDIC, banks and depositors could arrange for private insurance, and banks had to obtain ratings from private watchdog sources, an important policing mechanism would be reintroduced protecting against the very threat of insolvency for which the FDIC was instituted, but without the moral hazard. Bankers would have to pay close attention to the private watchdogs lest their rating turn down. Getting rid of the FDIC and allowing private deposit insurance and rating watchdogs would go far to reintroduce true accountability and responsibility into American banking.

The Federal Reserve's open market operations (buying and selling notes to member banks) expand and contract the money supply through the effects on reserve levels. The power to set discount rates also affects the level of lending and investment. This active management of the money supply is a systemic interference that affects all depositary institutions throughout the economy and indirectly affects the soundness of individual banks. The discretion afforded to the Federal Reserve in setting these rates and engaging in the desired level of open market operations inevitably provides a constant threat of miscue (leading Milton Friedman to recommend mandating a fixed rate of growth in the money supply to eliminate it). Examples of devastating miscues are the Fed's failure to provide adequate liquidity in 1933-1934 and too much liquidity in 2003-2006.

In both cases, financial and economic catastrophe followed, with millions hurt. The overlong low rates during

APPENDIX B: ARE BANKING AND THE ENVIRONMENT SPECIAL CASES

the 2003-2006 period under Chairman Greenspan, providing incentive for housing to boom, today is looked back upon and with 20-20 hindsight is allotted some degree of responsibility for the financial crisis that hit in 2008. It is too soon to gauge the impact of Chairman Bernanke's prolonged low interest rate regime initiated in 2008 and still ongoing in 2012. These recent examples of the problem of human error in playing with the levers of the money supply and interest rates should give pause to those confident in the miraculous powers of government's "wise men."

Also significant is the "too big to fail" problem. The growth of money center banks, the decline in state branch banking restrictions, and the rapid rise of derivatives have created broad interconnectedness among banks and counterparties. Once government began bailing out large banks with taxpayer funds, a moral hazard was created. It became possible for bankers to think, "Well, I can take outsized risks because if I lose, the feds will come in and save me and my bank with public monies." Smaller banks get moved in on and closed by the Fed, their assets suddenly sold off to others. But the big fellows become ever more able to luxuriate in the possibility of government rescue—even preserving equity values to some degree in the process, although usually the hit is substantial.

One of the selling features of Dodd-Frank was its supposed deterrence of public bailouts for financial entities. It does improve the mechanism for easing through bank insolvencies. But it grotesquely increases an already fulsome cross-thatching of regulation. Supercommittees of wise men are supposed to spot systemic fault lines and act with perspicacity and wisdom in advance of pending catastrophe.

This will not work. Human vision does not include knowing the future. The idea that government can see ahead of the financial industry's own line of sight is contradicted by every example of every regulatory regime in history. Even if regulators were paid twice, thrice what counterparts in private industry are paid, perfect vision would elude. The only way to create a risk-free future for the financial world is to tamp down financial innovation and creativity—to stop or deter innovation and growth. But then you have a laggard and declining financial sector, leading to decline and slowness in the general economy. Such is a shortsighted program for sure failure.

The only way to stop "too big to fail" is to let the market decide, not the government. Eliminate the FDIC, and reintroduce private deposit insurance. Eliminate supercommittees and regulatory clogging of the financial arteries. Let private rating entities with full access to bank records and operations inform depositors and investors, creditors and borrowers, just what they are dealing with. One could call this "free banking" to give it a name. The studies of the 1930s and before reveal that letting one bank fail does not lead to a contagion effect where all banks fail amid general panic unless the Fed fails in its principal function of providing liquidity when depositors seek en masse to call on their funds.

This failure by the Fed (in fact it raised the discount rate instead) is what happened in the Great Depression, causing far greater calamity than otherwise. J.P. Morgan's famous midnight horse-collar of NYC's bankers to stem the Panic of 1907 (one of the precipitating events for the creation of the Federal Reserve System in 1913) showed private liquidity in action. These and other episodes are described in Milton Friedman's work, which is still, a half century

APPENDIX B: ARE BANKING AND THE ENVIRONMENT SPECIAL CASES

later, the most elucidating on this, summarized in *Capitalism and Freedom* (1962).

Informed people can tell the difference between weak and solid. Our present system camouflages true pictures behind legions of government agents and programs, supposedly for the benefit of the stakeholders, who have to operate on faith in government, not awareness of true risk. Informing people who care because they have something at risk is what the market is best at, not government. All government can do is pretend to shield people from risks that hide behind the skirts until the time of reckoning arrives, when they leap out and bring the house down.

The year 2008 was a prime example of this phenomenon. The legislative and political response to this meltdown, discussed above, far from alleviating and helping, only hid the problems further and ensured their return in spades. As the SEC investigation confirmed, the leaders of Fannie and Freddie concealed their true abyss behind obscure accounting perversions, misled the public, and greatly increased the harms. Thus does government protect and provide.

So what to do? Reintroduce more market forces. Eliminate the FDIC, and substitute private deposit insurance. Keep the levers of the money supply at a steady and predictable increase year by year. Avoid having to depend on the off chance of a financial wizard or genius at the center of things in the Federal Reserve; after all, how many of these exist and can be depended upon to be located by the political authorities to succeed one another in the hot seat?

And above all, keep the politicians away from interfering with sound banking—the essential weighing of credit risk. The single most important cause of the housing boom and bust, the financial crisis, and the subsequent prolonged recession was the government's forcing and incentivizing banks to create affordable housing (AH) loans for ever-weaker credits and then relying on the private market to mix these all up and cover the risks over with complex derivatives. As Raghuram Rajan has shown in the work discussed at length above, more than anything else, this underlay and brought on the 2008 credit crisis and the seize-up in interbank lending.

2. Environment

Environmental issues were widely thought to involve what economists came to term externalities—effects on outsiders to transactions—and for a long time were deemed the proper subject of government intervention because these "welfare effects" were not otherwise accounted for. A.C. Pigou first analyzed these issues in the early twentieth century, and Paul Samuelson, William Baumol, and others following his lead created the intellectual justification for the wave of environmental laws established in the 1960s and 1970s. But R.H. Coase showed the deficiencies of this approach in his "The Problem of Social Cost" (*Journal of Law and Economics,* 1-44, 1960), for which he received the Nobel Prize in 1991. Coase explained that so-called externalities are just another factor of production—meaning the right to carry out an activity—which inevitably involves opportunity costs of all affected persons, and which need to be taken into account.

Focusing on externalities distracts from the real analysis needed to address the issue, which involves the level of transaction costs in the way of bargaining and the practical options all affected parties have to increase benefits and minimize harms by pursuing alternative arrangements. This requires a very individual analysis. The danger of generalized regulation in the environmental area is that the total value of production is lowered because of erroneous cost/benefit analysis, in addition to the deadweight of the cost of the regulatory apparatus and its rules. The Pigou-Samuelson tradition "tends to overestimate the advantages which come from government regulation" (R.H. Coase, "The Problem of Social Cost," in *The Firm, the Market and the Law*, at 95, U. Chicago Press, 1988). More efficient alternatives—including promoting bargaining, letting things lie, and using the common law—are ignored.

3. Health Care

Health care is unlike the financial industry because it is not subject to panics and runs, is not built on leverage, and is not vulnerable to shifts in the money supply. It is unlike the environment because there is no case that can be built based upon supposed externalities. It is archetypically characterized by individual decision and patient-doctor relations. The conditions suggesting government intervention and regulation do not exist.

The case that can be made—and as shown that is a partial one—is for realigning tax incentives by eliminating the deductibility of employer-provided health benefits (treating such as income to the employee) or otherwise equalizing the treatment of non-employer-provided and employer-provided benefits. The case that can be made also supports financing the poor through health savings accounts that preserve individual responsibility for health decisions and payments for one's own and one's family. There is not a case for regulation of the health care industry.

This fact requires the abandonment of the ObamaCare approach, which is premised on government regulation and control of virtually the entirety of the health care landscape, and ever-increasing sweeping of all Americans into government programs relieving them of all payment control and responsibility.

Substituting for this Bumbling Colossus a system of individual and family responsibility based upon tax-favored health savings accounts, supplemented for the truly needy by federal- or state-funded support, and eliminating virtually all of the regulatory ganglia will create a better health system for all.

APPENDIX C:
Selected Major Provisions of the 2010 Health Act and Affordable Care Act (and companion Health Care and Education Reconciliation Act) of 2010

The bill contains provisions that go into effect at different times, but the relevant ones went into effect on September 23, 2010 (six months after enactment), and the remainder, unless altered or repealed, will go into effect on the first day of each new year and in 2014.

Effective immediately:

- Drug companies supplying Medicaid patients get paid 23 percent less for most brand name drugs.
- Insurance companies are prohibited from offering policies with lifetime dollar limits on essential benefits, like hospital stays, regardless of premium reduction or benefit.

- Dependents will be permitted to remain on their parents' insurance plan until their twenty-sixth birthday; dependents include children who no longer live with their parents, are not a dependent on a parent's tax return, are no longer students, and are married.
- Insurers are prohibited from offering policies that exclude preexisting medical conditions (except in certain grandfathered individual health insurance plans) for children under the age of nineteen, regardless of premium reduction or benefit in reduced premium cost.
- Insurers are prohibited from offering new policies that charge copayments or deductibles for most preventive care and medical screenings.
- Insurers are limited in ability to offer policies with spending caps regardless of premium reduction or benefit; caps are prohibited entirely by 2014.
- Insurers must include within your pool and cannot refuse a renewal policy to someone who has loss experience under an existing policy.
- Insurers must disclose details of their administrative and executive expenditures.
- Insurers are forced to provide a specific formalized appeals process for coverage determination and claims on all new plans.
- Non-profit Blue Cross insurers are required to maintain a loss ratio of 85 percent or higher (payments for medical reasons) or lose their tax standing.
- A temporary high-risk pool is established for adults with preexisting conditions as a prelude to the universal mandate proscribing this as a factor in 2014.

APPENDIX C: SELECTED MAJOR PROVISIONS OF THE 2010 HEALTH ACT

Effective January 1, 2011:

- Insurers will be required to spend 85 percent of large-group and 80 percent of small-group and individual plan premiums (with certain adjustments) on health care (or to "improve health-care quality"), or pay the difference to policyholders.
- Federal agencies must set up agencies to study new delivery and service models.
- You cannot use your health savings account or similar account to pay for any over-the-counter drug purchased without a prescription, except for insulin.

Effective January 1, 2012:

- Employers must ascertain the "value" of the benefits they provide beginning in January 2012 for each employee's health insurance coverage and disclose this on the employees' annual Form W-2. (This requirement was originally to be effective January 1, 2011, but was postponed by IRS Notice 2010-69 on October 23, 2010.)
- Corporations and individuals making payments over six hundred dollars to all corporations and individuals must be reported starting January 1, 2011. There are a number of limited exceptions, for example: personal payments, payments for merchandise, telephone, freight, storage, payments of rent to real estate agents. Everything else requires a 1099.

Effective January 1, 2013:

- An additional tax of 0.5 percent begins on self-employment and wages of individuals above $200,000 annually (or of families above $250,000 annually).

Effective January 1, 2014:

- Insurers cannot offer, nor customers obtain, any policy that excludes anyone with a preexisting medical condition, regardless of premium or cost benefit.
- Insurers cannot offer, nor customers obtain, any policy with any annual spending cap, regardless of premium or cost benefit.
- Health savings accounts and similar accounts are marginalized by limiting the amount that can be contributed to them to $2,500 per year.
- No significant deductibles—a maximum is set of a $2000 annual deductible for a plan covering a single individual or $4000 annual deductible for any other plan, regardless of premium reduction and benefit.
- Individuals with income up to 133 percent of the poverty line can get Medicaid, including adults without dependent children.
- Large subsidies kick in through health insurance exchanges with subsidized premiums—large increases in subsidized health insurance are created by setting up health insurance exchanges and subsidizing premiums for individuals with income up to 400 percent of the poverty line, as well as single adults. This subsidy comes as an advanceable, refundable tax credit, so anyone can get it regardless of whether they have any income tax liability or

APPENDIX C: SELECTED MAJOR PROVISIONS OF THE 2010 HEALTH ACT

pay any income tax. This benefit extends up to those earning $90,000. Members of Congress and their staff can piggyback on this.

- Employer mandate and penalty kick in—a $2000 per employee tax penalty is imposed on employers with more than fifty employees who do not offer health insurance to their full-time workers.
- Individual mandate and penalty kick in—an annual penalty of ninety-five dollars, or up to 1 percent of income, whichever is greater, is imposed on individuals who do not buy insurance; this will rise to $695, or 2.5 percent of income, by 2016. This is an individual limit; families have a limit of $2,085. Exemptions to the fine in cases of financial hardship or religious beliefs are permitted in agency discretion.
- A state-created insurance option arises—employees who pay more than 9.5 percent of their income on health insurance premiums can purchase insurance policies from a state-controlled health insurance option. This undercuts private insurance.
- Large cutbacks are scheduled in Medicare Advantage payments and coverage, as well as large reductions in Medicare and Medicaid drug reimbursement rates and large cuts in other Medicare and Medicaid spending. The size of these scheduled cuts is enormous in order to make the bill cost-balanced, given the huge increase in entitlements.
- A new tax on drug companies based on the market share of the company; it is expected to cost the industry $2.5 billion annually. Most or all of this will be passed on to patients.

- Most medical devices are taxed 2.3 percent, collected at the time of sale. This will also be passed on to patients.
- A new tax will be enacted on health insurance companies based on their market share; the rate rises each year between 2014 and 2018 and thereafter increases at the rate of inflation. The tax is expected to cost the industry (and therefore patients to whom the cost is passed on) $14.3 billion annually.
- Individual income tax deductions for qualified medical expense start at 10 percent exclusion, up from 7.5 percent.
- Chain restaurants and food vendors with twenty or more locations must show calories for foods on menus, drive-through menus, and vending machines. Additional information, such as saturated fat, carbohydrates, and sodium content, must also be made available upon request.

Effective January 1, 2017:

- A state may apply to the secretary of Health and Human Services for a waiver of certain sections in the law, with respect to that state, such as the individual mandate, provided that the state develops a detailed alternative that "will provide coverage that is at least as comprehensive" and "at least as affordable" for "at least a comparable number of its residents" as the waived provisions. The decision of whether to grant this waiver is up to the secretary (who must annually report to Congress on the waiver process) after a public comment period.

APPENDIX C: SELECTED MAJOR PROVISIONS OF THE 2010 HEALTH ACT

By 2018:

- All existing health insurance plans must cover approved preventive care and checkups without copayment, regardless of premium impact and benefit.
- A new 40 percent tax on high-cost, so-called "Cadillac" group employer-sponsored plans is supposed to come into effect, ten years after passage of the bill.

Made in the USA
Lexington, KY
21 August 2012